FINANCIAL
STATEMENTS
DEMYSTIFIED

FINANCIAL STATEMENTS DEMYSTIFIED

Second Edition

David Hey-Cunningham

ALLEN & UNWIN

First published in 1993
Reprinted six times
Second edition published in 1998

Allen & Unwin
9 Atchison Street
St Leonards NSW 1590
Australia
Phone: (61 2) 8425 0100
Fax: (61 2) 9906 2218
E-mail: frontdesk@allen-unwin.com.au
Web: http://www.allen-unwin.com.au

National Library of Australia
Cataloguing-in-Publication entry:

Hey-Cunningham, David.
    Financial statements demystified.

    2nd ed.
    Bibliography.
    Includes index.
    ISBN 1 86448 481 0.

    1. Financial statements. I. Title.

657.3

Set in 10/12 pt Galliard by DOCUPRO, Sydney
Printed by Ligare Pty Ltd, Sydney

10 9 8 7 6 5 4 3 2

■ Foreword

The oldest saying in financial analysis is: 'Figures don't lie, but liars can figure'. But, as in every other aspect of life, the more you know about the subject, the less chance the liars have of succeeding. Given the importance of private sector finance in modern Australian life, I'm surprised that some elementary financial concepts aren't taught to students at secondary level. The day they are, David Hey-Cunningham's book *Financial Statements Demystified* could well serve as a text. He takes the reader simply and lucidly through the elements of financial statements, ratio analysis and theories and assumptions upon which accountancy is based.

Unfortunately, accountancy itself has been undergoing extensive redefinition in recent years. A host of new accounting standards have emerged and the shape of financial statements has been changing accordingly.

However the standards change and however the financial statements move, the reader trying to analyse them is best served in the long run by common sense. If investments are valued at well above market, if a profit is based on unrealised gains on property that may never be sold, if ordinary operating costs have been capitalised as assets rather than written off against the profit and loss account, the investor should keep his or her guard high. When looking at an asset that stands at some unlikely value in the balance sheet, the automatic question should always be: 'What could I actually sell this for?' If the asset is something intangible, such as future tax benefits or capitalised advertising expenditure, the answer may well be 'zero'.

There is a persistent belief that financial statements are mystical, and beyond the understanding of the normal human being. This is nonsense. Once one has a grip on the jargon and the underlying concepts, they are no more mystical than the racing form in the weekend newspapers. Failure to grasp their essentials may more properly be attributed to a lack of interest rather than any inherent mystique. Writers such as David Hey-Cunningham, in helping to dispel that mystique, can only be welcomed.

TREVOR SYKES
SYDNEY, 1997

■ Contents

■ List of figures

■ Preface

The second edition of this book continues to be both a text and a reference. You can read it from cover to cover to gain a solid understanding of financial statements, or you can read sections of the book using the contents pages and index to locate topics of particular interest.

The purpose is to provide those unfamiliar with accounting—or those who are accounting novices—with a practical understanding of financial statements. Learn what financial statements do and do not tell you. Find out how to calculate and interpret ratios.

The book explains financial statements from the user's point of view, which can be quite different from the preparer's. This approach provides useful insights for those already familiar with financial statements.

Company managements know how users assess their accounts and thus prepare statements that paint the best picture in the circumstances. The book covers the areas where such 'picture painting' occurs. This means that analysts and other interpreters of financial statements can use the book as a resource for understanding common manipulations.

Although Australian accounts, rules and regulations are described, my experience in conducting seminars overseas is that the issues discussed here apply internationally. This second edition comments on the New Zealand situation in some sections where there are significant differences from Australia. Therefore I have endeavoured to make the book useful in any country where a Western approach to preparation and presentation of financial statements is used.

Financial Statements Demystified:

■ Aims to be readable and intelligible. I want to tell you about what financial statements show and what they mean, based on many years of conducting seminars on this topic. I have used fictitious and real illustrations. You might find some parts require careful and reflective reading to gain thorough understanding.

■ Adopts the perspective of the user instead of the preparer—that is, 'What does it mean and how do I use it?' Most financial statements literature written by accountants is from the preparer's perspective—that is, 'How is the information gathered, prepared and presented?'

■ Explains the common items in financial statements in chapters on assets, liabilities, equity, profit and cash flow. The fictitious company Alba Manufacturing Limited (in chapter 4) demonstrates most of the common items. Other items are explained using listed company accounts.

■ Uses financial statements of companies rather than those of other forms of structure because they are public documents and there are extensive rules and regulations in force. The same issues apply to other legal structures such as partnerships and sole traders.

■ Refers to business enterprises, where a major motivation is profit. However, most of the issues apply to every enterprise. Even non-profit organisations must grow over time to survive. They need to make a surplus (profit).

■ Advocates that assets—the things we own—should be valued at realistic market values. Entities should use professional valuers for major items. Ownership is more than legal title.

■ Advocates that liabilities should be valued at the amount that is owed at balance date. Liabilities are more than legally payable claims at balance date. Liabilities include items that will become payable in the future because of events and transactions that have already occurred.

■ Advocates that profit is the difference between all sources of gains and of losses, all revenue and expenses. These can be generated by selling goods and services, holding assets that appreciate or depreciate and selling major assets of the business.

■ Proposes that accounting is an art rather than a science. Organisations present the picture they want to, within the constraints imposed by the framework of rules and regulations governing accounting and reporting processes. If you read any of the financial or business press you will see how much journalists comment on the manner in which items are accounted for and presented. The art form can be very refined.

■ Challenges some of the accounting standard rules as causing incorrect pictures to be painted. Special attention is paid to what is profit, how income tax expense is calculated and how long term assets are valued and changes in their value recognised.

I believe those involved in the preparation of accounts make the most of the rules to suit their own purposes. They are often very vocal in commenting on drafts of the rules and regulations. This means the rules and regulations favour the preparers and not the users. Obstacles are thrown up to hold back reforms advantageous to users. Consider this comment by Fridson (1991, p. ix) in the preface to his book *Financial Statements Analysis*:

The financial statements that analysts encounter in practice do not always resemble the straightforward examples selected by accounting professors for pedagogical purposes. Nonrecurring items abound, and accounting practices change from one year to the next, at times making it difficult even to determine whether a company's financial condition is improving or deteriorating. Frequently, as well, a firm's most recent financial report ceases to represent its current financial condition, as management announces a major acquisition or write-off between statement dates.

If this situation is true, why have users, for whom accounts are prepared, been less involved? David Lamant, a user of reports in the UK, explains (Shaw et al. 1990, p. 81):

> In the discussion of the questions which arise under the general heading of 'Financial Reporting' the views of users are often expected but infrequently obtained. There are in fact very few expert users, and virtually none of us are paid to think about accounting standards or to use our time and the resources of our offices in that field of activity.

I hope this book will encourage you as users to take a greater role, to think more carefully about the validity of your ratio calculation models, and to be prepared to question and adjust the figures as presented in the financial statements so as to make the ratios more meaningful.

I also hope this book will encourage preparers, especially directors from a non-accounting background, to ask more questions, to demand understandable explanations and to ensure their financial statements make sense.

The book can be divided into seven major areas:

Chapters 1 and 2 Background information on the three basic financial statements—balance sheet, profit and loss, and cash flows—what they are and the differences between them. I consider the legal structures available, types of industries and the vital importance of planning and budgeting. The challenges of establishing an enterprise are demonstrated through the stories of Rachel Newbeing, whose venture (like most new businesses) fails, and Sally Planter, who is successful. Chapter 2 introduces the basics of financial statements. Those with some knowledge may want to read quickly, scan or skip these chapters.

Chapter 3 The regulatory framework globally and in Australia through Corporations Law, accounting standards and accounting practices.

Chapter 4 The financial statements of Alba Manufacturing Limited, our fictitious but realistic company used to explain most financial statement items. Alba has the typical items of a company of this kind. You have an example of a set of accounts using the rules and regulations in force at 30 June 1997. These may change in the years to come, but the issues discussed in this book will remain valid. The chapter includes brief descriptions of the components of financial statements.

Chapters 5 to 9 Explanations, descriptions and comments on the items and contents of financial statements—balance sheet, profit and loss, cash flows and notes to the accounts.

Chapters 10 and 11 Description of typical ratios used to analyse financial statements. The formulae are given and Alba is used to show how to calculate the ratios. Alba's performance is assessed over a five year period. In practice, analysts vary their formulae and use additional ratios. Chapter 11 adapts analysis to micro and small businesses.

Chapter 12 Explanation of consolidation, recognising combinations of more than one company through the techniques of equity accounting and joint ventures accounting.

Chapter 13 My suggestions of different or additional information which should be included in the annual accounts. My view that we should account in a way that creates realistic, pragmatic and relevant financial statements.

Chapter 14 A non-exhaustive listing of warning signals that could show financial problems or stress.

In addition to this book, my company has developed two Excel models for analysing financial statements.

■ **Listed and larger companies** This model allows you to enter balance sheet, profit and loss statement, statement of cash flows, and supplementary information from the notes and Stock Market. It provides summary ratio and financial statement information over time, shows details of ratio calculations in accordance with formulae given in chapter 10, lists abnormal items and summarises segment performance.

■ **Micro (Mum and Dad) and small business analysis** This model allows you to enter the type of legal structure, profit and loss statement and balance sheet information. The model calculates historical cash flows and useful ratios in accordance with the commentary given in chapter 11. It handles the four common legal structures: sole trader, partnership, company, and trust. Profit and loss is formatted to highlight how owners derive income from their businesses. Several Australian financial institutions are using or considering using the model.

Both models allow entry of up to 10 years and instructions are provided on disk with the model and in writing. IBM and Macintosh versions are available.

For further information, including ordering, prices and methods of payment, contact David Hey-Cunningham & Associates Pty Limited, fax (61 2) 9552 3308, e-mail davidhc@netspace.net.au

DAVID HEY-CUNNINGHAM
SYDNEY, 1997

1 Running an enterprise

This chapter is designed as an introduction for those with little or no knowledge of accounting or financial statements. Primarily, financial statements present in dollar terms the stories of enterprises such as businesses, non-profit organisations and government utilities. In other words, the activities, events and transactions of the enterprise are summarised and presented using the dollar as the common descriptive term. You can describe it as a dollar language. Your challenge is to gain some degree of mastery of this dollar language and this book aims to help you achieve that. The frightening extent of business failures shows that too few have sufficient understanding.

This chapter focuses on business. However, the need for planning, budgeting and monitoring applies to all situations—business, non-profit and government. Business aims to generate profit. Non-profit and government aim to provide quality service efficiently. Some government enterprises generate profit. Thus I believe this chapter provides relevant information for non-profit and government.

From this chapter you will learn about:

- the reality of business failure through the story of Rachel Newbeing;
- some statistics and reasons for business failures;
- basic types of businesses;
- legal structures of businesses;
- planning for business success through the story of Sally Planter, including budgeting and cash flow forecasting;
- the cycle of monitoring performance.

Those with some knowledge may wish to scan or skip this chapter.

A FAILED BUSINESS ENTERPRISE

Rachel Newbeing was free. She had quit her well paying 9 to 5 job to start her own business. It was a dream she had cherished for years and now it was a reality. She borrowed $100 000 from the bank by taking a second mortgage on her house. It was costly—12.5 per cent interest, but she would make a fortune now she had her own fashion clothing shop. Well, the mark up on cost of the garments was between 250 and 400 per cent. She had an accountant, a friend of the family who had helped arrange the finance and had offered to help her manage her financial affairs. But he wanted to charge $3000 for this management advice and Rachel thought paying him for preparing the financial statements and tax return was enough. She needed her money for the business!

The first year appeared to go well. The financial statements her accountant produced six months after the end of her financial year showed she had made a small profit. She had to pay some tax. She asked the accountant to help her keep the tax as low as possible. He mentioned something about valuing the inventory, but she didn't quite understand what he was getting at.

Year 2 seemed okay. It was a small loss this time. She didn't have to pay any tax. That was good. She had reduced her wage to help make ends meet. Some of her creditors were asking her to pay their invoices more promptly. She was only two months overdue and everyone was paid in the end.

Two years, ten months and four days after starting her dream she was *bankrupt!* How could it be? She had worked seven days a week. The shop was open long hours. Sundays were devoted to keeping the records and working out what she needed to order. She had kept up to date with the fashion magazines. True, she had held several clearance sales to get rid of inventory that wouldn't sell—some had been sold below cost. Rachel did not see the clearance sales as warning signals of financial difficulty. She had not sought assistance on management issues. Now it was too late. She was shattered.

Rachel returned to the job market. She lost her home as the bank sold it to recover her debt. It took her five years to repay all her creditors from the wages she earned. 'Don't go into business for yourself', Rachel told her friends. 'It isn't worth the hassle.'

In Australia over 50 per cent of businesses fail within the first three years; 80 per cent fail within ten years. Analysis of the reasons shows that it is mainly due to poor management. Many people start off with a good idea, but they lack the management skills to make it work. There is a reluctance to seek expert help to supplement the lack of management skills. Rachel may have succeeded had she allowed her accountant to advise her, and used the small business advisory service provided by her state government.

Like many people in business, Rachel did not understand financial statements let alone how to interpret them.

REASONS FOR BUSINESS FAILURE

The research on small business failure in Australia is sobering reading and should have been read by Rachel before she started her business. Some highlights from research by Alan Williams (Reynolds et al. 1989, pp. 22–7) show that:

■ only one in six or seven small businesses fail due to bankruptcy, the rest voluntarily close because they are insolvent, unprofitable or in financial difficulty

■ over 30 000 small businesses fail each year—that is, approaching 100 a day

■ the rate of failure from commencement of business is:

Year 1	32%
Year 2	17%
Year 3	13%
Year 4	7%
Year 5	5%
Total dead within 5 years	74%

■ major reasons for failure in order (Reynolds et al. 1989, p. 27) are:
  – financial management and liquidity problems
  – management inexperience and incompetence
  – problems coping with inflation and other economic conditions external to the firm
  – poor or non-existent books and records
  – sales and marketing problems
  – staffing
  – difficulties with unions
  – failure to seek and use expert advice.

Many failures also occur from purchasing an existing business and paying too much. Some USA research showed that about 70 per cent of all mergers and acquisitions fail financially. This means that in seven out of ten business purchases or combinations the new owners are in a worse financial situation than the previous owners. To quote Ron Flavel, General Manager of the Small Business Corporation of South Australia (Flavel 1991, p. 36):

> In addition to management inexperience, the reason why so many businesses fail is due to debt funding of unjustifiable 'goodwill' payments. As soon as there is a downturn in business activity, the commitment to pay a return on, and possibly of, debt capital is enough to sink the business.
>   Australia is currently going through a business finance crisis due to:
> ■ the market valuation of publicly traded shares being way beyond returns being generated by the companies concerned. Valuations from 15 to 20 times earnings per share (EPS) are not uncommon;
> ■ loan funds being made available, and taken, at rates of interest exceeding the return being generated by these funds;
> ■ imprudent gearing of a business entity, which increases the risk of failure during a downturn;
> ■ excessive sums being paid for 'goodwill' on sale of a business.

The business financial crisis may change over time but Flavel's four points remain pertinent.

We will consider these very important matters further in chapter 5. What can we conclude from these stark facts but *caveat emptor*; buyer beware—both investors and lenders beware!

TYPES OF BUSINESS

Financial statements present a business in dollar terms. This is only one form of representation. It is convenient because it shows the financial well-being of the business. The business itself consists of people, products, services, customers, suppliers, capital resources and finance. It must be a living and vital organisation to function well. A business functions successfully when based on a good concept, managed well and adapted to changing circumstances.

A business is built on a product or service, e.g. the service station operator sells you petrol and services your car. Sometimes a business is what is called 'vertically integrated', e.g. a company like Comalco Aluminium, which mines bauxite, refines it into aluminium and manufactures a limited amount of aluminium products. Comalco sells bauxite, aluminium and manufactured product to customers. Sometimes a business is 'horizontal' in nature, e.g. it is a manufacturer only of various metal products. Some businesses are 'conglomerates'—they cover a wide range of activities not directly related to one another, e.g. its activities cover mining, fast foods, retailing and tour coach operations. Conglomerates are usually large listed companies or large privately held companies.

The major classifications of businesses are:

- *Primary production*: These businesses are farming and closely related activities such as dairy cooperatives.

- *Mining and oil*: This includes underground and open cut mining of metals, minerals and coal and extraction of oil and gas.

- *Manufacturing* is the making of a product and ranges from a backyard operation to a fully automated production line.

- *Wholesalers* are the 'middlemen'. They buy from the primary producer and manufacturer and sell to the retailer. They exist because of their ability to work with both parties, by finding the primary producer someone to sell their goods to and providing the retailer with one place to purchase a wide range of products.

- *Retailers* start with your corner store and range in size to the massive Coles Myer group. Retailers obtain their goods from manufacturers, wholesalers and primary producers. Large retailers like Woolworths often do their own wholesaling and arrange for the production of their own brand names.

■ *Service*: The service sector has grown enormously in the last twenty years. It is the provision of services such as TV repairs, photo-developing, medical and legal. The business can be a backyard operation or a huge tourist facility. In Australia tourism has become one of our major industries.

■ *Banking and finance* provides finance for customers (by borrowing from other customers who lodge deposits) and other financial services (e.g. investment advice, insurance).

■ *Information*: Historians tell us we have entered the information revolution. We have passed through the industrial revolution which gave us the ability to mass-produce goods. Now information is the important commodity. Consider the increasing use of microcomputers. Television, radio, newspapers, magazines, books and the Internet bombard us with information. Fortunes are made and lost in the information industry.

TYPICAL LEGAL STRUCTURES

The following information is very brief and is designed as an overview of typical legal structures. Each person establishing an enterprise should choose an appropriate legal structure for their situation. This choice is based on more than the criteria discussed here and requires expert knowledge. Accountants and lawyers can provide the necessary advice.

There are four main legal structures used for business:

■ sole trader;
■ partnership;
■ trust;
■ company.

Each has advantages and disadvantages covering legal liability, tax and transfer of ownership, to name but three. Most people start in business as a sole trader or partnership and progress to a company structure if the business grows and is successful. Trusts are used mainly for family tax and succession planning purposes.

Non-profit organisations are typically associations, companies, and trusts and are regulated under Acts of Parliament. Government organisations are typically the government statutory authorities and companies.

The following briefly describes the four business structures.

Sole trader

Sole traders set up business in their own name. It is quick and simple. They are taxed as an individual and are personally liable for all debts. They can be sued for everything they own. The business can bankrupt them as happened to Rachel Newbeing.

Partnership

A partnership is used where two or more people want to share in the business. The partnership agreement prescribes how profits are shared, what money is contributed to fund the business and how partners can retire or join. The agreement can be written or oral. A written agreement reviewed or prepared by a solicitor is advisable.

A partnership recognised as valid by the Australian Taxation Office enables the partners in the business to be assessed on their share of the profits. Many try to establish husband and wife partnerships to share the tax burden. The tax authorities declare many of these to be shams and apply the full amount of tax against the party who does the work which generates the income. The tax aspect can be the most important consequence for a husband and wife team setting up a business. So it should be done correctly. Professional advice is necessary.

A disadvantage of a partnership is that each of the partners is liable for the partnership debts. So if the partnership cannot pay its debts from within its business resources, the partners have to pay the debts out of their own resources. If a partner cannot meet his or her portion of the debt, then the other partners who have sufficient resources have to meet that portion in addition to their own portion. So, if you were in partnership with nine others and they could not pay the debts and you could, you would have to do so. Typically, those in partnerships are careful about who they will admit as partners!

Trust

A trust is a means of running a business for the benefit of people specified as beneficiaries. Family businesses are often run through trusts so that all the members of the family can be made beneficiaries, while not necessarily having a say in how the business is run.

In Australia one of the driving forces for trusts is the ability to spread income among a larger number of people. Tax rates increase as income levels rise. By spreading the income among your family you are likely to be taxed at a lower overall level. The government is aware of this and has laws that set high minimum tax rates for minors (children under eighteen years of age), in particular, to make a trust less attractive.

A trust is established by a legal document called a trust deed. Under the trust deed the person establishing the trust is known as the 'settlor'. The trust deed must also name one or more trustees.

Trustees can be individuals or companies. The trustees are responsible for administering the trust in accordance with the deed for the benefit of the beneficiaries. The trustees are legally liable for all the debts of the trust. They are entitled to use the available assets of the trust to meet those debts, but if there is a shortfall, they must meet the shortfall from their own resources.

Company

A company is a popular vehicle for running a business because it provides limited liability. The liability is limited to the amount of the uncalled share capital (i.e. issued shares which are not fully paid). The shareholders contribute funds to the company to obtain their shares when the company issues the shares. A company can issue partly paid shares and call for additional payments at later dates. Generally a shareholder is only required to pay up to the issue value of those shares.

This means, where the debts of a company exceed the assets and the available shareholders' equity, the creditors lose their money. Creditors are not pleased with this situation. In family companies major creditors or lenders frequently require the major shareholders to pledge their own assets as security.

There is a cost to this wonderful advantage of limited liability. Companies are governed by the Corporations Law. A company can only be formed with the permission of the Australian Securities Commission. Each year an annual return must be submitted providing specified information. Annual accounts must be prepared by all companies and many companies must be audited. There are other demanding record keeping requirements. A disadvantage of a company is its many administrative requirements.

Companies are taxed at a flat rate. Individuals are taxed on a sliding scale. In Australia the tax paid on the first $30 000 or so by a company is higher than that paid by an individual. Tax matters are an important consideration in choosing whether or not to use a company structure.

In the mid-1990s the Australian Government is simplifying the Corporations Law. At the time of publication of this second edition it is incomplete and under review. This book only covers matters regarded as useful for obtaining a general understanding. Those of you, such as directors, probably need more information. Your internal or external accountant, auditor, lawyer or bodies such as the Australian Institute of Company Directors can assist.

Under Corporations Law there are different types of companies that may be formed. Once formed, a company can change from one type to another by following the requirements of the legislation. There are two main kinds being *proprietary* and *public companies*.

Prior to enactment of the *First Corporate Simplification Act 1995* on 9 December 1995 there were two kinds of proprietary companies being exempt and non-exempt. Now there are small and large proprietary companies.

A *proprietary company* can have from one to 50 non-employee shareholders. This means it can have more than 50 shareholders provided the excess consist of people who were employees of the company or one of its subsidiaries at the time they became a shareholder. The company can only raise money from shareholders or employees or from normal borrowings such as from a bank. It cannot raise funds in a manner which would require a prospectus, e.g. offering debentures or shares to the public.

There is a test which distinguishes between whether a proprietary company is classed as small or large. The proprietary company is large if it meets any two or all three of the following conditions, otherwise it is a small proprietary company:

- consolidated gross operating revenue is greater than $10 million a year;
- consolidated gross assets are greater than $5 million at year end; and
- number of employees at year end is 50 or more in the group of companies.

You will notice the definition mentions 'consolidated' and 'controlled entities'. These are described in chapter 12 (Groups of companies). Basically it means if the company owns other companies, or entities such as trusts, the whole lot must be added together to determine the revenue, total assets and number of employees. Operating revenue is as defined within the accounting standard (see chapter 8) and consists primarily of sales, interest earned, dividends received and proceeds from disposal of assets. Employees are full time equivalent positions which means two or more part time employees might make up the equivalent of one full time employee.

Thus you see the simple definition and distinction between small and large is not so simple after all. There are other complications which can arise but are beyond the scope of this book. If you are running a proprietary company you should seek advice from your professional accountant or lawyer so you are clear on the status of your proprietary company and what kind of accounts you need to prepare, what records you need to keep and what has to be lodged with the Australian Securities Commission.

A *small proprietary company* generally:

- does not have to prepare financial statements (annual accounts) in accordance with Corporations Law or accounting standards;
- has to maintain proper financial records from which financial statements can be generated;
- is not required to hold an annual general meeting of shareholders;
- does not need to appoint an auditor;
- lodges an annual return once a year by 31 January without providing any financial data.

Financial statements must be prepared if requested by 5 per cent or more of the shareholders or the Australian Securities Commission (ASC). Those requesting can require the statements to be audited. Audited financial statements must be prepared if the company was controlled (e.g. if more than

50 per cent of the voting shares were held) by a foreign company for all or part of the year and that foreign company did not lodge its consolidated financial statements with the ASC.

A *large proprietary* company must appoint auditors and prepare and lodge audited financial statements with the ASC. The ASC can grant exemption under a class order. The Corporations Law grants an exemption for companies which—were exempt proprietary companies at 30 June 1994; continue to satisfy the definition of being 'exempt'; and have been audited prior to the ASC accounts lodgement deadline each year since 1993.

A *public company* is a company which is not a proprietary company. A public company has no limit on the number of shareholders. The company must appoint auditors and lodge annual audited accounts with the ASC.

A *listed company* is a public company which has been listed on the Australian Stock Exchange. Listing requirements are set by the Australian Stock Exchange. These rules are separate and additional to those of the Corporations Law.

PLANNING—KEY TO SUCCESS!

Rachel Newbeing's business crashed because she did not manage her business effectively. In fact she chose not to seek advice, believing it was not a sensible way to spend her money. How do you know if your business idea will be successful? How do you obtain finance to establish your business? How do you determine which form of financing is best? How much of your own money should you use to finance it? These are valid questions.

Competent business advisers recommend that you start with a plan. Put your ideas on paper. Competent business people plan the start of the business, plan the future of their business and have a fairly detailed annual plan.

This book is about reading and understanding financial statements and not a guide for establishing or planning a business. However, an understanding of the basics of the planning and monitoring of a business provides a useful framework for the reader. The financial statements show the results of the planning, or lack thereof. The financial statements measure, or should measure, the end result of a cycle (one year) of the planning process.

Statistics show that a business that plans its future is more likely to have a future. When the stock market is in a 'bear run' (i.e. when share prices are falling), investment analysts tend to recommend the better managed companies as they are likely to perform better than the others. These better managed companies plan to achieve in the environment in which they operate.

Many companies will have a five year plan, some may have ten (or more) year plans. Naturally ten years out into the future is hard to plan. You can look at possible alternative futures for your business, consider what is required to achieve those futures and opt for the one you consider best. The plan is then modified to fit the changing circumstances.

Let's meet Sally Planter, who decided to establish a nursery business. She had been managing her home for seven years while her three children were young. With the youngest in school, she decided to go into business.

For two years Sally worked on the planning. She borrowed books from the library on all aspects of the nursery business, visited nurseries in and around the city, attended a TAFE course and talked to her bank manager, local accountant and state government small business advisers.

Sally developed a master plan with the help of the bank manager, accountant and information obtained from the small business advisers. She decided to establish her nursery in a nearby suburb. Her business name, *Sally's Plantery*, was registered with the Australian Securities Commission.

Sally's business plan covered the first five years and included information on:

■ location;
■ competitors;
■ projected growth;
■ suppliers of plants (she would be growing some of her product in her own backyard);
■ potential customers from the surrounding suburbs;
■ marketing strategy;
■ business structure;
■ method of financing—her own money and borrowing from the bank using her home as security;
■ nursery plans, including equipment required;
■ staffing.

In addition to this, Sally prepared a detailed projected profit and loss for the first year of the business. She started with sales. It took a lot of effort to determine realistic sales figures. She was surprised how helpful other nursery owners were in providing information. Her accountant gave her financial information on nursery businesses.

From the projected sales Sally could work out the cost of buying and growing the plants—her cost of sales (COS). She had to allow for the following costs:

■ maintaining plants in the nursery;
■ lease of the premises;
■ wages for an assistant;
■ depreciation of the equipment ('it wears out you know' says Sally);
■ repairs ('shouldn't be too much at first because the shelving and equipment is new');
■ lease of the computerised cash register;
■ printing of stationery;
■ local press advertising and leaflets ('you even have to pay someone to distribute them').

Sally needed to generate cash to be able to pay her bills. 'At least I will have a cash business', she remarked to her accountant. 'I'm glad you've explained

---

SALLY'S PLANTERY
grand opening sale

All plants 25%–40% off marked prices

Bargains galore

We specialise in quality, attractive, interesting and, yes, the unusual plant—plants for your home and wonderful presents for those special people in your life.

∗ indoor and outdoor ∗ hardy and exotic ∗ wide range

SALLY'S PLANTERY
open 7 days
10 a.m. to 6 p.m.

144 Woodlands Road
Rolling Hills
telephone 9222 3399
plenty of parking

---

the importance of monitoring when the cash goes in and when it goes out. I may give some of the larger and regular customers credit.'

'Be careful about that, Sally. Make sure you set ground rules on the terms of credit. How long will you allow them to pay? Typical terms are 30, fourteen and seven days. Make sure you promptly chase those who don't pay within the credit terms. Many business people only pay when they are chased.'

'Hmmm. I'll allow fourteen days. I'll need to print invoices. I've noticed the terms of credit are stated on the invoices. Can you give me a sample invoice?' And so the conversation continued to discuss these matters.

Sally prepared a cash flow forecast with the help of her accountant. This predicted cash coming in, being the cash sales and receipts from the limited number of debtors. It showed cash going out, which was wages, payments to creditors and bank loan repayments. There was even some cash to pay Sally's wages.

Her creditors included the landlord, the suppliers of plants and new shelving, and others such as the printers of the leaflets. Sally had to negotiate with them what the credit terms would be. The landlord wanted payment at the beginning of the month. The plant suppliers wanted cash for the initial purchase and then gave her 30 days and discounts on volume purchases. The printer wanted cash. He was a small business person like Sally and watched his cash flow like a hawk.

Sally and the accountant prepared the cash flow forecast to cover the first twelve months of the business. They projected it month by month for the year and week by week for the first three months.

'The beginning of any cash flow forecast period is the most critical', explained the accountant. 'In large corporations they monitor by the day. A

Sally's Plantery
Profit and loss budget
Year ending 30 June 1999

Description	Year	Months		
		JULY	AUG	SEPT
Sales				
Sale of plants	163 000	14 000	12 500	11 500
Sale of garden products	27 900	2 500	2 200	2 300
Total sales	190 900	16 500	14 700	13 800
less: **Cost of sales (COS)**				
Cost of plants	73 350	6 300	5 625	5 175
Water	20 375			4 750
Manure and plant food	4 890	420	375	345
Cost of garden products sold	14 508	1 300	1 144	1 196
Total COS	113 123	8 020	7 144	11 466
Gross profit (sales – COS)	77 777	8 480	7 556	2 334
less: **Expenses**				
Shop lease	26 070	1 200	2 350	2 170
Assistant's wages & superannuation	11 350	1 000	800	900
Depreciation of equipment	6 000	500	500	500
Repairs	950			100
Cash register lease	660	55	55	55
Printing	1 300	500		200
Advertising	2 450	500		300
Interest	9 000	750	750	750
Advisers' fees	2 875	1 500	125	125
General expenses	1 550	100	100	100
Total expenses	62 205	6 105	4 680	5 200
Profit before Sally's wages	15 572	2 375	2 876	(2 866)
Sally's wages & superannuation	10 493		1 187	1 438
Operating profit before tax	5 079	2 375	1 689	(4 304)

week will be sufficient for you. I suggest we update your cash flow forecast each three months. As your business grows, we will have more information and so can prepare a more accurate forecast. We will know your sales pattern and the actual expenditure better. Similarly you should update your budget so that it better reflects reality.'

'I thought we would do it once a year. I didn't realise it was such a frequent procedure.'

Sally's Plantery
Profit and loss budget
Year ending 30 June 1999 *(cont)*

	OCT	NOV	DEC	JAN	FEB	MAR	APR	MAY	JUNE
Months									
	12 500	14 000	17 500	10 000	12 500	13 500	14 000	14 500	16 500
	2 200	2 500	3 000	1 500	2 000	2 500	2 300	2 200	2 700
	14 700	16 500	20 500	11 500	14 500	16 000	16 300	16 700	19 200
	5 625	6 300	7 875	4 500	5 625	6 075	6 300	6 525	7 425
			5 500			4 500			5 625
	375	420	525	300	375	405	420	435	495
	1 144	1 300	1 560	780	1 040	1 300	1 196	1 144	1 404
	7 144	8 020	15 460	5 580	7 040	12 280	7 916	8 104	14 949
	7 556	8 480	5 040	5 920	7 460	3 720	8 384	8 596	4 251
	2 080	2 170	2 350	2 750	1 850	2 150	2 300	2 330	2 370
	1 000	1 000	1 200	750	800	800	1 000	1 000	1 100
	500	500	500	500	500	500	500	500	500
	50	50	150	250	50	50	100	100	50
	55	55	55	55	55	55	55	55	55
		150			250			200	
	300	300	100		100	300	100	250	200
	750	750	750	750	750	750	750	750	750
	125	125	125	125	125	125	125	125	125
	150	150	200	100	100	100	150	150	150
	5 010	5 250	5 430	5 280	4 580	4 830	5 080	5 460	5 300
	2 546	3 230	(390)	640	2 880	(1 110)	3 304	3 136	(1 049)
		1 273	1 615		320	1 440		1 652	1 568
	2 546	1 957	(2 005)	640	2 560	(2 550)	3 304	1 484	(2 617)

'Many people do it once a year or not at all. They do not use it to help them run their businesses successfully. That's why they fail!'

'I notice that depreciation isn't shown in our cash flow forecast.'

'The actual cost of the equipment is paid out of your initial contribution to the business and the bank loan. You then repay the bank as required by the terms of the borrowing agreement. The equipment is an asset of your business which lasts for a number of years. It does wear out over time. We allow for this when

Sally's Plantery
Cash flow forecast
Year ending 30 June 1999

Description	Year	Months		
		JULY	AUG	SEPT
Cash at bank at beginning	75 000	75 000	745	3 453
add: Cash coming in				
Cash sales	173 700	15 500	14 000	12 500
Receipts from debtors	15 900		800	1 000
Total receipts	189 600	15 500	14 800	13 500
Total cash available	264 600	90 500	15 545	16 953
less: Payments				
Suppliers of plants	110 000	50 000	5 000	5 000
Suppliers of garden products	19 200	5 000	1 400	1 400
Shop lease	26 070	1 200	2 350	2 170
Assistant's wages & superannuation	11 350	1 000	800	900
Repairs	950			100
Cash register lease	660	55	55	55
Printing	1 300	500		200
Sally's wages & superannuation	10 493		1 187	1 438
Bank repayments	9 000			2 250
Other creditors	61 500	32 000	1 300	1 300
Total payments	250 523	89 755	12 092	14 813
Cash at bank at the end	14 077	745	3 453	2 140

calculating your profit by depreciating it. The depreciation is not an outlay of cash. It is an allowance for the fact that the asset has a limited life. Depreciation is a typical example of an item which is recorded in the profit calculation but not the cash flows statement because it is not a cash item.'

This section contains the budgeted (projected) profit and loss and cash flows statements for the first year of operation of Sally's Plantery. Her accountant helped her prepare them. They submitted them to the bank with the five year plan and Sally received a $60 000 interest-only loan repayable in three years time.

Sally's budgets show that she expected an operating profit before income tax of $5079. The profit is the measurement of the sales less all the costs of the sales and expenses of running the shop during the year. However she started the year with $75 000 in the bank and budgeted to finish with $14 077. The beginning amount consisted of the $60 000 borrowed from the bank at 15 per cent interest plus $15 000 of her own money.

This money had to cover two major cash outflows of purchase of equipment and plants. Fitting out the shop and painting represents most of

Sally's Plantery
Cash flow forecast
Year ending 30 June 1999 *(cont)*

			Months					
OCT	**NOV**	**DEC**	**JAN**	**FEB**	**MAR**	**APR**	**MAY**	**JUNE**
2 140	1 455	(1 243)	4 437	(1 168)	2 707	4 862	5 307	9 370
13 500	15 000	19 000	9 500	13 000	14 500	14 500	15 000	17 700
1 400	1 300	1 600	1 500	1 500	1 700	1 700	1 700	1 700
14 900	16 300	20 600	11 000	14 500	16 200	16 200	16 700	19 400
17 040	17 755	19 357	15 437	13 332	18 907	21 062	22 007	28 770
5 000	10 000	5 000	5 000	5 000	5 000	5 000	5 000	5 000
1 400	3 000	1 000	1 000	1 000	1 000	1 000	1 000	1 000
2 080	2 170	2 350	2 750	1 850	2 150	2 300	2 330	2 370
1 000	1 000	1 200	750	800	800	1 000	1 000	1 100
50	50	150	250	50	50	100	100	50
55	55	55	55	55	55	55	55	55
	150			250			200	
	1 273	1 615		320	1 440		1 652	1 568
		2 250			2 250			2 250
6 000	1 300	1 300	6 800	1 300	1 300	6 300	1 300	1 300
15 585	18 998	14 920	16 605	10 625	14 045	15 755	12 637	14 693
1 455	(1 243)	4 437	(1 168)	2 707	4 862	5 307	9 370	14 077

the $32 000 paid to other creditors in July. The equipment in the leased shop will last at least for the five year term of the lease (provided the business is profitable). So the shop equipment costs are allocated (depreciated) over their anticipated useful life.

Sally also had to stock the shop with plants and garden products. This was a big initial payment as the customers must see a good selection of plants. Restocking regularly is not expected to be as big an outlay. Sally also started growing plants in her backyard and there were start-up costs here. The plants would take a while to grow ready for sale.

MONITORING PERFORMANCE

Sally opened the nursery on schedule in July 1998. The initial response was great! People liked her nursery. Everything was falling into place in line with her plans. Now Sally started the monitoring process. She kept a record of all receipts and payments using the cash register. She kept a file of her dockets. At the end of each month she took this information to her accountant who processed it on his computer. The computer produced results showing:

- sales and costs for the month compared with budget;
- sales and costs for the year to date compared with budget year to date;
- a statement of the assets and liabilities of the nursery at the end of the month.

Sally would discuss these with her accountant. Sometimes she sold more than budget, but the profit was lower. By looking at the figures they could see which expenses were higher than expected. Sometimes profit would be higher with lower than budgeted sales. Always they could compare the actual against the budget and see what had happened. Once a quarter they revised the budget and cash flow. They reconsidered what was likely for the future. As time passed they had more historical information on which to base their predictions. The budgets could be determined more realistically.

Sally's business began to prosper. In a year she opened another nursery in another part of the city. She and her husband bought the vacant block next to their house. Sally grew more of her own plants. After two years she was employing four people on a full time basis. She was now drawing a reasonable salary and the business was making strong profits. She had financed the increased business through further borrowing from the bank and investing more of their family funds in the business.

Sally founded a successful business. She had a good idea, researched it and learned about the industry before she started. She used the financial resources available to develop her own plans and then monitor the business. She did not think she knew everything.

Figure 1.1 shows the cycle of planning and monitoring.

POINTS TO REMEMBER

✔ A business, non-profit or government enterprise consists of people, products, services, customers, clients, suppliers, capital resources and finance. They function well when based on a good concept, are well managed and adapt to a changing environment successfully.

✔ The rate of new business failures illustrates how essential the planning and monitoring of a business are. An owner requires management skills (or must pay others with these skills) as well as a good product or service. Planning and monitoring are essential for all organisations.

✔ An enterprise requires a positive cash flow to enable it to keep functioning and a profit to enable it to grow. Even non-profit organisations need a level of profit to provide long term stability.

Planning and monitoring cycle

Figure 1.1

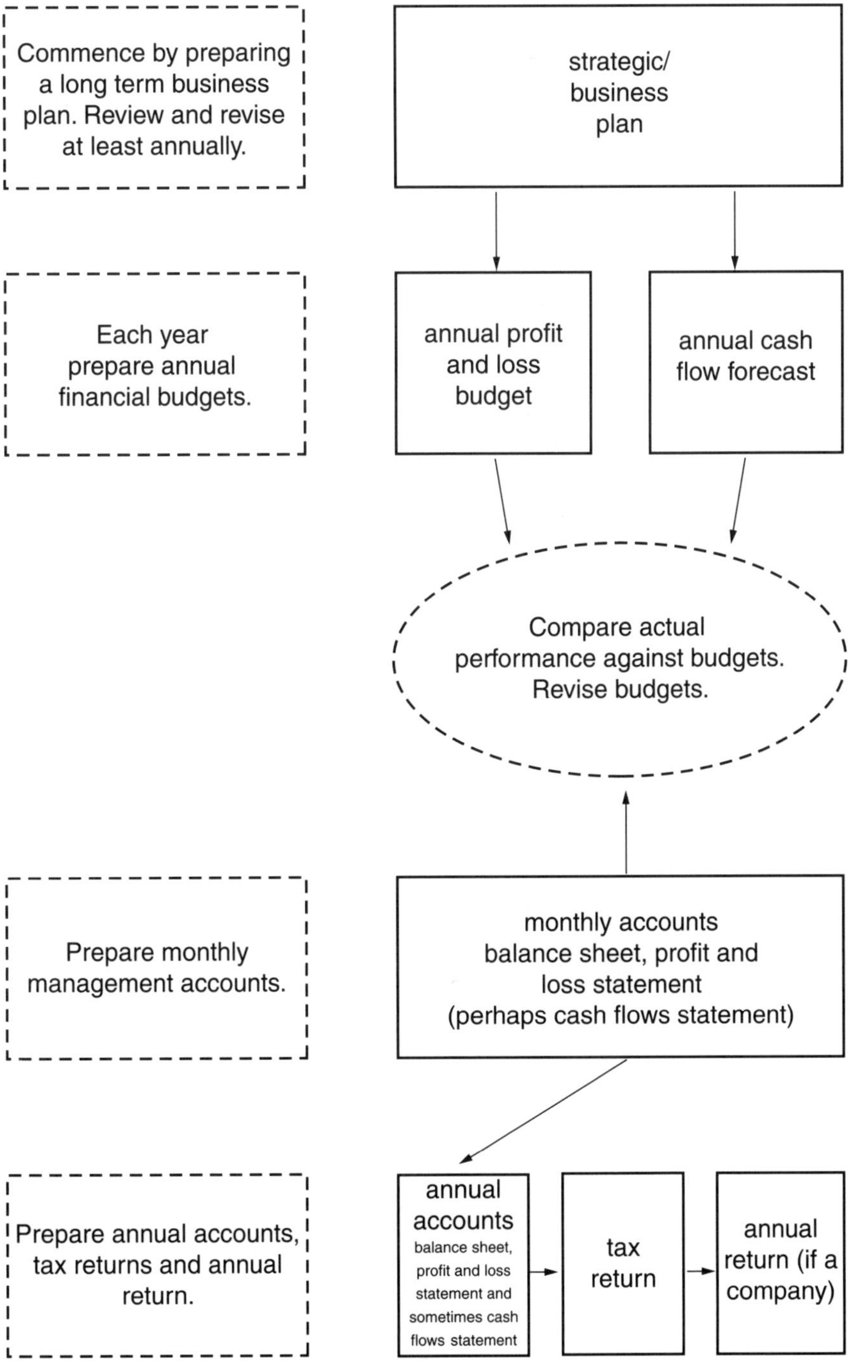

Commence by preparing a long term business plan. Review and revise at least annually.

strategic/ business plan

Each year prepare annual financial budgets.

annual profit and loss budget

annual cash flow forecast

Compare actual performance against budgets. Revise budgets.

Prepare monthly management accounts.

monthly accounts balance sheet, profit and loss statement (perhaps cash flows statement)

Prepare annual accounts, tax returns and annual return.

annual accounts balance sheet, profit and loss statement and sometimes cash flows statement

tax return

annual return (if a company)

✔ The main legal structures used for business are sole trader, partnership, trust and company. Factors to consider in choosing which structure include legal liability, income tax rates, administration requirements and future disposal of the business.

✔ Planning is essential. A business plan should consider market, competitors, means of production, projected growth, customer base, suppliers, financiers and staffing. Planning also requires detailed financial planning such as profit and cash flow projections.

✔ Profit and loss shows revenue and expenses incurred to generate that revenue. Revenue may be in cash or on credit terms. Expenses may be paid by cash or on credit and also through the wear and tear (depreciation) on assets previously acquired.

✔ Cash flow shows all receipts and payments of cash. Cash can be received from customers (paying for sales) and owners and lenders (providing finance). Cash is paid to suppliers, to staff, for property and equipment, and to repay borrowings. So cash flow concerns revenue and expenses and changes in equity (owners' interest), liabilities and assets.

✔ Performance should be monitored regularly, at least quarterly, preferably monthly. The monitoring includes actual revenue and expenses compared with budget and prior periods for the month and year to date, actual cash flow and review of assets and liabilities.

2 The basics of financial statements

Financial statements are a means of showing how a business or any organisation or individual is progressing in a manner which should help comparison of operation over the years and comparison with other enterprises. They are a means of communicating information in dollar terms.

This chapter describes the purpose of financial statements, introduces the balance sheet, profit and loss statement, cash flows statement and highlights the importance of assets generating profit and being prudently financed by borrowings and equity. Lastly, the three financial statements are summarised to provide an overview.

As with chapter 1, those of you with some accounting knowledge may wish to scan or skip this chapter.

Three financial statements are used to present the financial results, being the *balance sheet*, *profit and loss statement*, and *cash flows statement*. You were introduced to the last two being used for planning the future in the Sally's Plantery example in chapter 1.

The balance sheet is a snapshot of the assets, liabilities and owners' interest (equity) in the business at a point in time—being the date at which the balance sheet snapshot is taken—whereas the other two financial statements show the history (in summary form) of what has happened between the two balance sheet dates—typically twelve months for annual financial statements. The *profit and loss statement* is the revenue less expenses and shows how the owners' interest in the business has changed between the two balance sheet dates due to trading. The *cash flows statement* shows the cash in and cash out and shows how the cash has changed between the two balance sheet dates.

This is a simple statement about financial statements. You will find there are many layers of complexity. Remember accounting is a human system, not a natural system of nature. As such it is not absolute truth. Indeed it is a representation in dollars of what an organisation has done. Thus it is an analogy used to represent reality. No analogy is perfect. This book helps you learn the language of accounting and financial statements.

THE PURPOSE OF FINANCIAL STATEMENTS

The Australian 'Statement of Accounting Concepts', SAC2, *Objective of General Purpose Financial Reporting*, states in paragraph 26: '. . . the objective of general purpose financial reporting is to provide information to users that is useful for making and evaluating decisions about the allocation of scarce resources.'

The Statement lists users of financial reports as including those who provide resources, such as investors and lenders, those receiving goods and services, those reviewing the reports or with an oversight function such as government regulatory bodies, and management such as boards of directors and executives.

Investors and lenders, who are significant users, are interested in the financial position, profitability and cash flow of the entity (e.g. company, trust, partnership or sole trader). They are interested in the financial position to see what assets are available to cover liabilities and to generate gains for the owners. They are interested in profitability because a business needs to generate profit in order to cover interest, grow, add value for the owners and pay dividends. They are interested in cash flow because in the short and the long run an entity needs to generate cash in order to meet its expenses and repay liabilities.

Similarly a not-for-profit or government enterprise can be monitored using financial statements to assess performance against its objectives, e.g. providing services economically and efficiently, using assets fully and developing necessary infrastructure.

THE BALANCE SHEET

The monitoring of assets, liabilities and equity is an important aspect of managing an enterprise. These items are reported on the balance sheet.

At the most basic level a business must make profits and have sufficient cash to cover all payments. The business is financed through the owners' contribution and borrowings. These funds are used to acquire assets which are used in the business. In fact, the only valid business reason to own assets is to add value to business performance—usually by generating revenue. What this means is that total assets are funded by liabilities and owners' equity which can be expressed diagramatically as a *balance* situation as in figure 2.1.

This equation is expressed from the owners' perspective as $E = A - L$ (where E is equity, A is assets and L is liabilities). The assets are used to generate income—and, hopefully, profit—which covers the cost of interest, and the remaining profit is added to the owners' equity in the business. Management can choose to distribute all this to the owners (e.g. as dividend in a company structure), retain it all in the business to fund further business

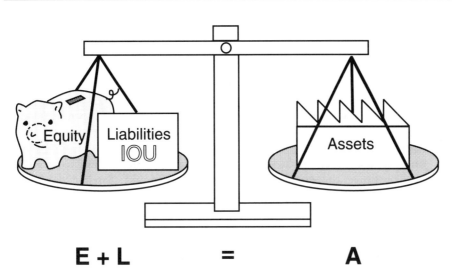

Figure 2.1

Balance sheet
equation

$$E + L \qquad = \qquad A$$

development, or have a combination of both. The third is the most frequently followed, and the most prudent.

Balance sheets for ongoing enterprises are produced at least once a year. The balance sheet is like a snapshot of the assets and liabilities existing at balance date. The net change over the year in assets and liabilities is reflected in the equity. Hopefully this is a gain. This gain is generally reported through the profit and loss statement.

PROFIT AND LOSS STATEMENT

The profit and loss statement is a summary of all the revenues generated and expenses incurred during the period covered by the statement. So, at the simplest level, profit is revenue less expenses. A detailed profit and loss statement is given and explained in chapter 4.

A typical format of a profit and loss statement used internally by a business is:

	Sales
less:	Cost of sales
gives:	Gross profit
less:	Selling expenses
	Administration expenses
add:	Other income such as interest earned
gives:	Operating profit/(loss) before tax
less:	Income tax expense
gives:	Operating profit/(loss) after tax

The profit is what remains of sales less all the expenses. The expenses are divided into three main categories:

■ cost of sales which represents all the expenses associated with buying in or manufacturing the goods or services sold—in a manufacturing enterprise the cost of sales may be 60–70 per cent of sales;

■ expenses which are all the other costs of running the business such as selling, storage of inventory and administration—in a manufacturing enterprise these may total about 20–30 per cent of sales;

■ income tax which is an impost from the government and is based on the profit of the enterprise—an enterprise should plan to legitimately limit this cost.

The profit after tax is available for dividends or to be retained in the business. The owners want some tangible reward for their investment which, in the case of shares, comes in the form of dividend. The rest of the profit is retained in the enterprise to help it grow, e.g. to finance new assets.

CASH FLOWS STATEMENT

A business needs cash flow to survive. A successful business generates strong cash flow which it can use to pay dividends, invest in new production capacity (such as plant), repay debt and purchase investments such as shares and investment properties.

The cash flows statement shows the cash coming in and the cash going out; that is, the cash receipts and cash payments. In annual financial statements it is a summary of the cash in and cash out for the year.

Internal cash flows statements are typically cash flow forecasts which show the cash in and cash out. The accounting standard cash flows statement provides a more useful format. All companies classified as reporting entities—see next chapter for an explanation of a reporting entity—must provide a cash flows statement as part of their annual accounts.

The format required by the cash flows standard shows cash in and cash out under three broad categories so that the net cash movement is shown for each category. A summary of the format is:

Cash flows from operating activities*
Cash flows from investing activities*
Cash flows from financing activities*
gives: Net cash movement for the year
add: Cash at the beginning of the year
gives: Cash at the end of the year

* Each shows cash in and cash out and is sub-totalled to give net cash movement under each category. The total of these three net cash movements gives the 'net cash movement for the year'.

ASSETS MUST GENERATE PROFIT

In the long run the rate of profit generated by the assets must be higher than the rate of interest paid on the interest-bearing liabilities. (The relationship between profit, the balance sheet and interest and dividends paid is shown in figure 2.2.)

Many of Australia's recent corporate collapses reflect the folly of not following this principle. Companies paid much more for the assets than warranted by the income they could generate from them—buying at inflated prices in boom times and forced to sell for low prices in recession times. Thus they never generated sufficient profit to cover the interest costs on borrowings incurred to finance the acquisition of these assets. When, on the collapse of a business, there are insufficient funds to repay the lenders and creditors, the owners get nothing!

In the short to medium term, borrowings may be required to build the asset (e.g. buildings, mines and ships) to a stage where it can generate income. During its 'development' phase the business incurs costs of building the asset, such as materials, labour and financing costs (e.g. interest). These costs are treated as part of the cost of the asset and not as expenses. On completion, the income generated over the time the asset will produce income must be greater than the cost of developing it and other costs incurred in operating it.

For example, a ship has to be sold at a price higher than the cost of making it plus any other costs such as launching and transporting it to the

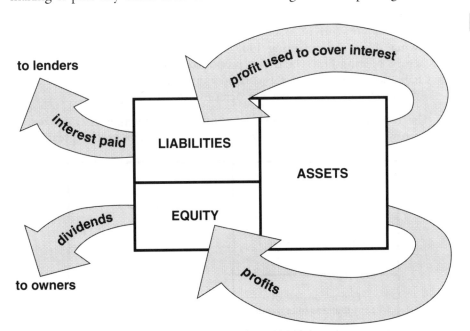

Figure 2.2

Generating profits

buyer. The cost of making the ship will include the materials used, labour and a proportion of the overhead costs of running the shipyard—this would include power, allowance for the wear and tear on equipment and local government charges on the property.

The fact that assets are generating profits which cover interest and add value to the owners' equity does not automatically guarantee that the business will be successful. Remember that Rachel Newbeing (in chapter 1) thought her business was profitable, but the cash flow was insufficient. So in addition to profitability, the structuring of assets and liabilities to assist cash flow needs is essential.

MAINTAINING SUSTAINABLE BALANCE

The long term financial viability of an entity is greatly assisted by borrowings which match assets. A business with mainly non-current assets (e.g. land and buildings) requires mainly long term borrowings (e.g. bank mortgage). The repayment of principal on the borrowing should match the period of cash generated by its use, by a future sale of the asset or by refinancing the borrowing.

Assets are classified as current when the asset is expected to be converted into another asset or cash, or used up within one year of the balance sheet date. Likewise, liabilities are classified as current when they are expected to be paid or extinguished in some other way within one year of the balance sheet date.

A recipe for collapse is to arrange short term borrowings to fund the acquisition of non-current assets. Ask a company liquidator! This is called 'borrowing short and investing long'. Figure 2.3 illustrates an apparently satisfactory relationship where the proportion of non-current liabilities to total liabilities approximates the corresponding asset proportions.

Two other important issues are demonstrated by figure 2.3:

■ The relationship between using equity and borrowings to fund assets. Borrowings incur interest; the greater the borrowings the greater the

Figure 2.3

Balancing the items

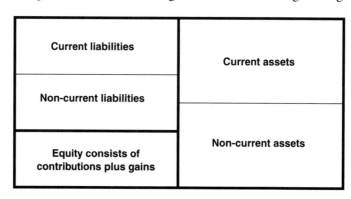

interest cost and the more adversely affected the business by increases in interest rates. Very heavy reliance on borrowings can drain all profits, resulting in losses which reduce equity. Thus a balance between liabilities and equity is needed. The proportion of liability to equity funding regarded as acceptable varies between industries and between countries. In Australia, a relationship for most businesses where interest-bearing borrowings are less than equity is considered prudent. The truly satisfactory situation is to borrow to the upper level where profits generated by assets are above the interest rate cost of liabilities and the total profit comfortably covers the interest expense. This important situation will be addressed further in chapter 10 on ratios.

■ What makes up equity? When a business begins, equity consists of the contribution made by the owners (which, in the case of companies, is funds contributed for shares). Once a business is operating, the gains made by the business also belong to the owners and are added to equity. Generally these gains are from the profits generated by trading. Other sources of gains can be through sale of a part of the business, sale of investment property, and revaluation of non-current assets. The difference in nature of the gain from revaluation of non-current assets compared with the other examples given is that the gain is unrealised—it has not been crystallised as a sale to a third party. However, providing the basis of revaluation is valid, the gain is very real, though simply an adjustment to asset values. Therefore equity consists of two types of items: contributions by owners and gains kept by the entity. There are two types of gains: realised gains (e.g. from trading) and unrealised gains. This will be discussed further in chapters 7 (Equity) and 8 (Profit and loss).

SUMMARY OF THE THREE FINANCIAL STATEMENTS

Accounting definitions and practices add to the complexity of understanding the three financial statements. Let's conclude this chapter with this overall summary and the lay definitions to keep financial statements in perspective.

The three financial statements can be summarised at the highest level as follows.

Balance sheet	*Profit and loss statement*	*Statement of cash flows*
Snapshot at a point in time, the balance sheet date	History of revenue less expenses over the period between balance sheet dates	History of cash in less cash out over the period between balance sheet dates
Formula $L + E = A$ or $\quad E = A - L$ where: $\quad$ A is assets $\quad$ L is liabilities $\quad$ E is equity	*Formula* $P = R - E$ where: $\quad$ R is revenue $\quad$ E is expenses	*Formula* Cash: In (Out)

Lay definitions of main financial statement elements

Balance Sheet
- *Assets* are things we own which we can sell. Market value (willing seller, willing buyer) is a useful value because there are only two things you can do with an asset: keep it or sell it.
- *Liabilities* are things we owe.
- *Equity* is the remainder of the assets less the liabilities and consists of two things: contributions made by the owners and gains (or losses) made by the business, kept by the business.

Profit and Loss
- *Revenue* is the income of the business which is recognised when it is earned.
- *Expenses* are the costs of the business which are recognised when they are incurred.
- *Profit* is the remainder of revenue less expenses. Thus how revenue and expenses are defined determines profit.
- Revenue and expenses are not the same as cash.

Cash Flows
- *Cash* is cash.
- The statement shows the *cash in* and the *cash out*.

- Beside preparing a fraudulent statement, the only means of manipulation is timing of receipts and payments. That is the arrangements of when the cash will come in and the cash will go out.

Later chapters include more complex definitions used by the accounting profession.

POINTS TO REMEMBER

✔ The purpose of financial statements is to provide information of use in making and evaluating decisions such as whether to invest or lend.

✔ The balance sheet equation is E + L = A or E = A − L where E is equity, L is liabilities and A is assets. The balance sheet shows the assets, liabilities and equity at a point of time, like a camera snapshot.

✔ Profit and loss is a summary of all the revenues and expenses. The main form of revenue is sales. The three main types of expense are cost of sales, expenses such as selling and administration and income tax. The remaining profit, if any, is divided between dividend paid to the investors and reinvestment in the business to finance further assets.

✔ Assets are acquired to produce profits. In the long run the rate of profits earned on assets should be greater than the rate of interest incurred on any borrowings used to fund these assets.

✔ The price paid for assets should be limited to an amount which allows the rate of profit earned on the asset to contribute to the entity—i.e. cover the cost of borrowings and leave some profit for the owners.

✔ The cash flows statement is a summary of all cash received and all cash paid. It shows all cash in and out and the net cash movement under the three broad categories of operating, investing and financing. The total of these three net movements gives the net cash movement for the year which is added to the cash at the beginning of the year to give the cash held at the end of the year.

✔ The enterprise must have a sound cash flow which requires appropriate matching of payments with receipts and repayment of liabilities with revenue generated or through the sale of assets.

✔ Assets should be funded by a mixture of liabilities and equity so that the interest burden and risk of interest rate increases can be managed with comfort from the profits of the enterprise.

✔ Equity in a business is increased by contributions (investment) by owners and by gains retained in the enterprise. These gains can be realised (e.g. profit from trading) and unrealised (e.g. gain from revaluing a property).

3 The rules

Accounting principles and legislated rules provide the framework in which financial statements are prepared. This framework varies from country to country. However, there is more in common than different. Accounting principles are more international, for instance, than laws.

This chapter provides background on the world scene and then deals specifically with the Australian system and, to some extent, the New Zealand system. Australia's and New Zealand's systems were inherited from and are still largely influenced by the United Kingdom. This situation generally applies to all countries which were once part of the British Empire. Thus, there are strong similarities in accounting standards and corporations laws across Asia–Pacific from Pakistan in the west to Fiji in the east. Other countries in the region are heavily influenced by the USA; some in the Pacific by France. The 'world background' section briefly comments on some of these influences.

A very common legal structure used throughout the world is the company or corporation. From this point on this book uses that structure unless otherwise stated. Examples quoted are all companies.

WORLD BACKGROUND

Accounting is a human concept used to present the story of organisations told in dollars. Accounting is a language which was first reported by Luca Pacioli (c. 1445 – c. 1517). Pacioli trained as an Italian Franciscan friar, tutored sons of a Venetian merchant and then taught in several universities. Pacioli learned the Venetian method of bookkeeping when tutoring in Venice. In his book *Summa de Arithmetica, Geometria, Proportioni et Proportionalitá* (Everything about Arithmetic, Geometry and Proportion) published in 1494, bookkeeping was just one of the subjects. In 1994 accountants from all over the world gathered in Rome for a conference celebrating 500 years since Pacioli brought bookkeeping to the world.

Today accounting has become a subject taught at universities and other tertiary institutions and is also taught at high school. Accounting is a complex subject with many theories and views of what it is. The dominant view is historical cost where assets and liabilities, revenue and expenses are recognised at the cost or amount at the date they were acquired or occurred. Thus, for instance, unless there is a choice or requirement to revalue assets, assets remain stated at the amount originally paid. Assets which wear out over time or are used up by the organisation are depreciated or expensed. However, assets which have increased in value might or might not be revalued.

Non-accountants I have taught about financial statements in Australasia and Asia since the mid-1980s suggest assets should be valued at market—willing seller, willing buyer. However non-accountants have little influence on accounting theory and financial statement presentation. Non-accountants are major users of the information produced by accountants. I believe the accounting profession should seek substantial input from informed non-accountants. I have come to respect the sense of the 'lay' view. Non-accountants usually take a simpler view than accountants.

I am concerned the accountancy profession is making accounting theory and principles used in deriving figures in financial statements more and more complex and, in some instances, less and less intelligible and useful.

■ A prominent example is tax-effect accounting which accountants in commerce can find hard to understand and often leave it to the auditors to work out. Tax-effect accounting is discussed in chapter 8.

■ In Australia we introduced a complex method of estimating non-current employee payables. The vast majority of business people would never estimate the liability in such a manner (see chapter 6).

■ Now Australia has changed the way it estimates residual value for depreciation calculation purposes. This could lead to increased depreciation expense and increase profits on disposal. This makes the depreciation effect on profit and loss more volatile (see chapter 5).

Today accountancy is recognised as a profession. Most countries have accounting bodies representing accountants which prepare or influence their national accounting standards and lobby governments on behalf of their constituents.

The International Accounting Standards Committee

The international body with growing influence is the International Accounting Standards Committee (IASC). The following is from the introduction to *International Accounting Standards 1995* (page 7) published by the IASC.

> The . . . IASC was formed in 1973 to work for the improvement and harmonisation of financial reporting, primarily through the development and publication of International Accounting Standards. IASC develops International Accounting Standards through an international due process that involves the worldwide

accountancy profession, the preparers and users of financial statements, and national standard setting bodies. IASC is now established as the only international due process for the development of International Accounting Standards.

The objectives of IASC are:

(a) to formulate and publish in the public interest standards to be observed in the presentation of financial statements and to promote their world-wide acceptance and observance;
(b) to work generally for the improvement and harmonisation of regulations, accounting standards and procedures relating to the presentation of financial statements.

The members of IASC are the professional accountancy bodies which are members of the International Federation of Accountants (IFAC). As at January 1995, there are 110 Member Bodies in 82 countries; these Member Bodies represent over one million accountants in industry and commerce, public practice, academic institutions, accounting firms and other organisations.

Strong international influences

As mentioned above, the United Kingdom has a strong international influence, through the historical British Empire, with the creation of similar laws concerning business organisation in many countries. Two other major influences are the USA and the European Union.

The United Kingdom and USA approaches concentrate on the owners' view making the profit and loss statement key; that is, what is the business generating for the owners? Alternatively, the European Union concentrates on the lenders' view making the balance sheet prominent; that is, what assets are available and what other indebtedness does the business have? The United Kingdom as part of the European Union has modified or added to its laws to accommodate European Union requirements.

The USA has the most accounting standards and, through the Securities Exchange Commission requirements and investment links with countries around the world, has a strong influence on national requirements of many countries.

When an overseas company wants to list its shares or some other listable financing method on the New York Stock Exchange, it has to re-format its accounts to comply with Securities Exchange Commission requirements. This often results in many differences. So you would probably find, at least in some years, substantial differences in the Australian and USA balance sheets and profit and loss statements for News Corporation or Westpac.

Japan has a distinct approach to accounting standards and in Germany tax law greatly affects what is included in the accounts. To obtain the tax benefit, the information has to be presented in the accounts as specified in the tax law.

These strong international influences affect the IASC. The IASC accounting standards can be a long time in gestation due to political influences.

Promulgated accounting standards might allow two, rather than one, methods of accounting for items, to accommodate political requirements.

National political and other influences

Political influences operate within each country's accounting standard setting processes. There are the laws governing the form and conduct of business, banking, the share market etc.

Another major influence can be income tax law requirements. Income tax is fundamentally only relevant in so far as determining income tax applicable to an organisation. Theoretically it should not influence any figures other than income tax ones. However, some countries' income tax laws do influence reported figures. For instance, revaluation of non-current assets, such as property, can be taxable in some countries. Thus revaluations will not occur in such countries to avoid the impost of income tax.

Thus informed readers need to have some understanding of the national influences on the financial statements they are examining in order to understand and interpret them in relation to other organisations of that country and across different countries.

THE AUSTRALIAN SCENE

In 1996 the Australian Accounting Standards Board (AASB) adopted a policy to harmonise Australian accounting standards with the international accounting standards. This is said to be not achievable in the short term. In the meantime the AASB aims to ensure that financial reports prepared in accordance with Australian accounting standards comply with the international standards and this is to be achieved by the end of 1998. This will mean changes to Australian accounting standards. This second edition has incorporated all changes issued by 30 June 1997 and which take effect for financial years ending on or after 30 June 1997.

Where the international accounting standards allow alternative methods of accounting and the Australian standards allow only one, the Australian approach will stand.

Australia will aim to issue exposure drafts and accounting standards at the time of and in line with the international ones. The Australian accounting profession will continue to be involved in the discussions of and formulation of international accounting standards through its role in the IASC.

Australia's link to the international scene is through the AASB, the Australian Accounting Research Foundation (AARF) and the accounting professional bodies of The Institute of Chartered Accountants in Australia (ICAA) and the Australian Society of Certified Practising Accountants (ASCPA).

Australia and New Zealand have also agreed to harmonise accounting standards and reporting requirements. This has led to increased cooperation in aiming to jointly issue draft and actual accounting standards. The New Zealand accounting professional body is the New Zealand Institute of Chartered Accountants (previously called the New Zealand Society of Accountants until October 1996).

FOUR SOURCES OF RULES FOR AUSTRALIAN COMPANIES

There are four major sources of rules which govern financial statements for corporations. These are:

- statutory laws of government;
- accounting standards;
- Stock Exchange listing requirements;
- precedents and recognised texts.

The increasing number of standards and other legally enforceable reporting requirements has narrowed the choices of accounting policies and improved the quality of policies. However, there is still scope for choice and the 'toughness' of some of the standards is limited. The preparer is still able to paint a picture on a fairly broad canvas within the framework of the rules. Accounting is more an art than a science!

LAWS OF GOVERNMENT

This section covers the laws governing companies. Certain kinds of companies and other legal structures are covered by specific legislation or by common law (law derived from applying results of court cases). There are laws covering banks, building societies, credit unions, life and general insurance companies, superannuation funds, cooperatives, trusts and partnerships. These laws affect what is included in their financial statements. The trend is to move more closely to the reporting format and requirements of company law.

Historical development since the 1960s

Up to the 1980s each Australian state and territory had its own versions of company law legislation. True, they were similar, but companies had to comply with laws which varied in each state or territory in which they did business. The laws we have today are still fundamentally similar to this period, but are administratively standardised. The laws of other Commonwealth countries such as Singapore and Malaysia are very similar to these earlier laws.

The Australian laws have been dramatically overhauled twice since 1980. In 1981 a cooperative national scheme was introduced whereby the federal government and state governments passed the same legislation. The major piece of legislation governing annual reporting requirements was the Companies Code and Schedule 7 of the Regulations. The body responsible for enforcement of the legislation was the National Companies and Securities Commission (NCSC). Each state corporate affairs commission looked after its own jurisdictions and cooperated with the NCSC.

The fully national scheme took effect from 1 January 1991. The legislation governing annual reports was then contained in the Corporations Law and Schedule 5 of the Regulations. The body responsible for enforcement is the Australian Securities Commission (ASC), which replaced the NCSC and the state corporate affairs commissions.

When the new Corporations Law took effect in 1991, the financial statements requirements did not change significantly; however, significant changes have since occurred. One important change with amendments effective from the beginning of 1992 was the compulsory compliance with accounting standards. Previously, the overriding requirement was to present a 'true and fair' view. If the directors believed the application of an accounting standard would not give a true and fair view, then it was not applied. Now the legislation takes the position that a true and fair view can only be obtained by applying the accounting standards.

A second important 1992 amendment dealt with accounting for a company which operates through a number of companies. These groups of companies are required to produce consolidated accounts. The amendments widened the kind of entities included in consolidated accounts. This had far-reaching implications. Consolidation is a very important area and is covered in chapter 12.

Under the effort to simplify Corporations Law the reporting of small companies was reduced significantly from December 1995. As discussed more fully in chapter 1, small companies are proprietary companies which satisfy any two of these three tests:

- consolidated annual gross operating revenue is less than $10 million;
- consolidated gross assets at balance sheet date are less than $5 million;
- the group has less than 50 employees.

A small proprietary company does not need to prepare statutory accounts for its shareholders or the ASC, nor hold an annual general meeting. A large proprietary company and public companies must prepare annual accounts.

From financial years ended on or after 30 June 1997 accounting standard AASB 1034, *Information to be Disclosed in Financial Reports* (issued December 1996), specifies all required disclosures not covered in other accounting standards.

Previously Schedule 5 of the Corporations Regulations specified all additional disclosures. Most Schedule 5 requirements were taken up in AASB 1034 or a relevant accounting standard such as AASB 1017, *Related Party Disclosures*. Some items were dropped.

A major shift of this change was the removal of the requirement to provide the balance sheet and profit and loss statement in a specified format. I believe this is a disadvantage for non-accountants because it adds another variable to the information. The accounting standard AASB 1034 provides, in an appendix, a sample format for the profit and loss statement and the balance sheet.

The profit and loss statement is very different from the usual disclosure in that its format includes:

	Sales revenue
less:	Cost of sales
gives:	Gross profit
less:	Selling, general and administrative expenses
add:	Other revenue
gives:	Operating profit before abnormal items

Previously 'cost of sales' and 'selling, general and administrative expenses' were not disclosed. The sample format is not part of the standard. Some organisations might be prepared to disclose these additional items, but I think most will not unless forced to by a change to AASB 1018, *Profit and Loss Accounts*. Alba Manufacturing Limited, the sample company in chapter 4, follows fairly closely AASB 1018 and previous Schedule 5 formats. (At the time of publication there is a proposal to amend disclosures in the inventory accounting standard to require disclosure of cost of goods sold.)

The balance sheet in the AASB 1034 appendix is very similar to Schedule 5. The same vertical format is used—being assets (current and non-current) less liabilities (current and non-current) gives net assets and finishes with equity which equals net assets. The main change is more items are named on the balance sheet instead of being described as 'other' with a note reference. In chapter 4, Alba's balance sheet has been structured the same way. It is very similar to the old Schedule 5 format. Thus, reading and understanding Alba's balance sheet will assist you with reading balance sheets prepared under the Schedule 5 format.

Key accounting requirements

Important matters covered by the Corporations Law and AASB 1034 concerning annual financial statements (which are demonstrated in the accounts of Alba Manufacturing in chapter 4) are:

■ preparation and content of the directors' report, statement by directors and auditors' report;
■ preparation of a profit and loss statement, balance sheet, cash flows statement and supporting notes which present a true and fair view of the situation of the company or economic entity;

- requirement to disclose certain classes of assets, liabilities and equity including totals of current, non-current and total assets; current, non-current and total liabilities, net assets and equity;
- specific details and additional information about items making up the profit and loss statement and balance sheet which are to be included in notes to the accounts;
- additional information on items that will be of interest to users, such as assets exceeding fair value contingent liabilities, commitments to future payments (such as lease payments), valuations of investments, borrowing costs included as part of the carrying amount of an asset.

Differential reporting

The Corporations Law follows a differential reporting approach where different types of companies, which must prepare accounts, disclose differing levels of information. Listed companies are required to disclose the most. Listed companies and certain others must prepare half-yearly accounts and provide continuous disclosure to the Stock Exchange. Companies which have borrowed from the public (e.g. through issuing public debentures) or are above a prescribed size are required to give greater disclosure.

In Australia accounting standards are given the force of law. This was introduced into the former Companies Code during the second half of the 1980s, through the establishment of the Accounting Standards Review Board to approve proposed accounting standards. This improved the level of compliance with accounting standards. Under the Corporations Law the Australian Accounting Standards Board (AASB) was established to develop and approve accounting standards.

An accounting standard issued in 1992 adds another dimension to financial statement reporting. Accounting standard AASB 1025, *Application of the Reporting Entity Concept and Other Amendments*, only requires entities which are classed as 'reporting entities' to prepare annual reports (called general purpose financial statements) which comply with accounting standards. A reporting entity is an entity (company) for which it is reasonable to expect that there are readers who depend on general purpose financial statements to help them make decisions such as whether or not to invest in or lend to the entity. (Under the Corporations Law most entities are companies.)

Listed companies are reporting entities while most small proprietary companies are not reporting entities. Thus most small companies do not have to apply accounting standards. In fact they generally do not have to prepare financial statements (see chapter 1).

The Corporations Law requires the preparation of true and fair accounts. The Corporations Law specifies that true and fair accounts can only be prepared by complying with applicable accounting standards. This requirement seems to conflict with permitted non-compliance for companies which are not reporting entities. The argument is that the only applicable accounting standard is AASB 1025, which then allows non-compliance with other accounting standards.

To sum up, companies required to comply with Corporations Law and apply accounting standards are those defined as reporting entities. A 'reporting entity' company only applies accounting standards if they are relevant and the items covered by the standard are material.

In my view the fact that an entity may not be required to disclose certain information does not mean it need not or should not have the information available internally. Good management is only possible with good financial information.

ACCOUNTING STANDARDS

Accounting standards set forth what are regarded as acceptable ways of determining and presenting financial information. In this book, the requirements of accounting standards are explained to the degree considered necessary for understanding financial statement items affected by the standards.

Around the world, accounting standards have mainly been prepared by the professional accounting bodies. In Australia this involves the Australian Accounting Research Foundation (AARF), established in 1966 and funded by the two professional accounting bodies, The Institute of Chartered Accountants in Australia (ICAA) and the Australian Society of Certified Practising Accountants (ASCPA). The Research Foundation submits proposed accounting standards to both bodies for their approval. After approval these become Australian Accounting Standards and they apply to all entities other than companies. Part of the responsibility of members of either body is to encourage compliance with these standards.

Accounting standards which apply to companies are those approved by the Australian Accounting Standards Board. These standards are based on those of the profession, which in turn usually adjusts its standards to agree with any alterations made by the Board. The AARF drafts the Board's standards as well. There is a strong linkage between the accounting profession and the Standards Board through the AARF, together with the fact that members of the Board are accountants.

At the beginning of 1995 the Urgent Issues Group (UIG) was established to provide guidance on financial reporting issues not specifically covered by accounting standards. The UIG selects issues for determination from those submitted to it. Guidance can only be published when consensus is achieved. These views are mandatory for members of the accounting bodies preparing or auditing general purpose financial reports.

A significant benefit of this group has been the resolution of some matters regarded as contentious. An example is the limiting of amortisation of goodwill to the use of the straight line method (see chapter 5). The existence of the group enables more timely consideration of matters which might not be included in accounting standards for years, if at all.

Procedure followed for creating standards

The AARF usually follows a procedure of issuing draft accounting standards for comment by interested parties. All submissions are considered when preparing a proposed standard for approval.

Accounting standards in Australia normally allow only one method of accounting for the matters covered, whereas the international accounting standards might allow two methods. Different methods will give different accounting results. The international standards reflect the results of compromise. Australian accounting standards aim to follow the international standards but may be more stringent or take a differing view on some matters.

The reality in Australia, as well as internationally, is that political considerations influence the standard setting process. Sometimes this results in an approved standard having less stringent requirements than the draft.

Another important influence has been that those involved in preparing the standards and commenting on them have been associated with preparers of financial statements. Users have been sparsely represented. In 1992 the Standards Board membership was increased by two user representatives, bringing the number of users to four out of eleven. Perhaps the greater influence of users will lead to increased demand for useful information and better specification of acceptable means of deriving that information. An example of the need is the failure to specify acceptable bases of revaluing non-current assets—discussed in chapter 5.

Conceptual framework

The conceptual framework of accounting was developed from the late 1980s onwards. Its purpose is to provide a general framework in which all accounting issues are decided. This means all future accounting standards should be consistent with the framework and existing standards should be revised to be consistent.

At 30 June 1997 there were four existing Statements of Accounting Concepts (SAC) covering: what type of entity should prepare financial reports; the purpose of the reports; the qualitative aspects of financial information; and definition and recognition of the elements of financial statements.

The qualitative characteristics required are that all relevant and material financial information should be included in general purpose reports and the information should be reliable and timely. The information presented should be able to be compared over time within the one entity and with other entities. The reports should also be understandable. Paragraphs 36 and 37 of SAC3 suggest that understandability can be complex:

> General purpose financial reports ought to be constructed having regard to the interests of users who are prepared to exercise diligence in reviewing those reports and who possess the proficiency necessary to comprehend the significance of contemporary accounting practices.
>
> Preparers should present information in the most understandable manner without sacrificing relevance or reliability. In meeting this objective, it may not always be possible to report complex transactions and events in simple or simplified terms. It should be borne in mind that professional advice can be obtained by the users of general purpose reports.

At best this shows it will not be easy to be an effective user. You have to be prepared to learn about financial statements so you can understand them. At worst this shows that preparers can justify complex ways of presenting information on the basis that simplicity is impossible. To parody Gilbert and Sullivan, 'a user's lot is not a happy one'.

At the beginning of the 1990s accounting concept statements became a critical and controversial issue in Australia. They were designed to be the base upon which all accounting standards and policies must be built, the hub of the accounting wheel. However, there were some strong objections, particularly concerning parts of SAC4, *Definition and Recognition of the Elements of Financial Statements.*

SAC4 contains definitions of assets, liabilities, equity, revenue, expenses, profit and loss which are used as a starting point in the chapters on these topics. SAC4 was intended to be mandatory from the beginning of 1994. Instead, due to widespread dissatisfaction, it was made non-mandatory and is used for guidance. It was revised and reissued in March 1995. The definitions in SAC4 are used in the following chapters to introduce items.

The International Accounting Standards Committee, the standard setters in the USA, Canada, the UK and New Zealand, have issued or are issuing concept statements. So Australia is part of this new direction in framing accounting practices. SAC4 is largely consistent with similar overseas concept statements.

Accounting policies

Annual financial statements must include a note to the accounts explaining all significant accounting policies. This note immediately follows the main statements (profit and loss, balance sheet and cash flow).

The standard covering companies is AASB 1001 *Accounting Policies*. This standard was reissued in September 1995. Paragraph 6.1 requires the accounting policy note to:

(a) state that the financial report is a *general purpose financial report* which has been prepared in accordance with *Accounting Standards*;

(b) identify the accounting policies adopted in preparing and presenting the financial report where alternative accounting policies are permitted in an Accounting Standard, or an accounting policy has been adopted in the absence of a requirement specified in an Accounting Standard; and

(c) identify the fact and reasons for not applying the *going concern* or *accrual accounting bases*, where the financial report has been prepared otherwise than in accordance with the going concern or accrual accounting bases.

Item (b) reduced the accounting policies needing to be disclosed. Prior to the amendment of the accounting standard, all significant accounting policies had to be disclosed. Now, only where an accounting standard allows a choice or there is no accounting standard, is disclosure required. This means it is assumed those reading financial statements will know the requirement of accounting standards where only one policy is permitted. How realistic do you think this is?

Companies can choose to disclose more. Gowings Bros Limited is one such company which maintained the same level of accounting policy information in their 1996 annual accounts.

Item (c) would usually only apply to companies in liquidation or voluntary administration. However, if the company is experiencing difficulty paying its debts as and when they fall due, the directors must consider if the assumption of 'going concern' can be validly applied.

Accounting standard AASB 1001 covers companies and AAS6 *Accounting Policies: Determination, Application and Disclosure*, covers other entities. The accounting concept statements, particularly SAC4, provide the guiding principles on which accounting policies must be formed. These two standards present principles for setting policies which may differ from the concepts. These principles reflect the traditional accounting thinking with which accountants are familiar.

The general principles of accounting policies are worth considering because they provide insight into traditional thinking (which continues to influence). The five requirements are:

Concerning the selection and application of accounting policies

■ *Relevant* financial information must be supplied to assist users in making decisions. It might be relevant because of its nature and/or magnitude (AASB 1001, paragraphs 4.1.2 and 4.1.3).

■ *Reliability*—information faithfully conveys to users the transactions and events that have occurred and is free from bias and undue error (ibid. paragraphs 4.1.5 to 4.1.7).

■ *Substance* or reality of transactions should override the legal form (ibid. paragraph 4.1.9).

Concerning disclosure of accounting policies

■ To facilitate *comparability* of accounting information over time, accounting policies should be applied on a consistent basis. If, due to changed circumstances, it is more appropriate to change the policy, then information on the change should be provided. Accounting policies must be changed to comply with requirements of new AASB accounting standards (ibid. paragraphs 5.1.1 and 5.1.2).

■ Information should be *understandable* without compromising the other principles. 'It is assumed that users possess the proficiency necessary to comprehend the significance of contemporary financial reporting.' (ibid. paragraphs 5.1.4.)

Some of these—materiality, substance over form and changes in accounting policy—are worthy of further consideration.

Materiality

Materiality is an important concept. Accounting standard AASB 1031 *Materiality* was introduced in September 1995. In paragraph 5.1 materiality is defined as:

> . . . in relation to information, that information which if omitted, misstated or not disclosed has the potential to adversely affect decisions about the allocation of scarce resources made by users of the financial report or the discharge of accountability by the management or governing body of the entity . . .

This concept of materiality is applied throughout financial statement preparation and disclosure. It allows for the likelihood that there will be errors and irregularities within the financial statements. (After all, people make mistakes.) However, there should not be deliberate error or irregularity, especially of a material nature. It is the responsibility of management and auditors to detect all errors and irregularities which would cause a material misstatement (due to inclusion or omission) in the financial statements.

Therefore when you read audited financial statements you should be able to rely on them being materially correct. The vast majority are, but occasionally they aren't because of oversight or deliberate misrepresentation.

Substance over form

This is the most important accounting principle as its requirement is that the reality should be presented. Matters may have to be structured in certain ways to meet legal requirements, but the legal form does not show the reality of the situation.

A typical example of this is consolidation which presents financial information for the amalgamation of a number of different entities, typically companies. The legal entity is each individual entity. The consolidated group has no legal substance. The creditors can only claim against the entity to which they lent or supplied items, except to the extent that guarantees from other entities have been arranged. However, the economic reality is the whole group. The structure and legal forms are simply used as a means of creating and operating the whole. So the substance is to present financial statements for the group.

In recent years, a great deal of attention has been given to 'creative accounting'. Creative accounting is the calculation and presentation of financial information in a manner which makes the entity look financially healthier than it really is (extensive picture painting within the regulatory framework). Most commentators would think creative accounting extends the art of accounting too far.

I suggest most, if not all, creative accounting involves structuring a situation (or financial transaction) with a legal form which is so strong that it hides the true situation—that is it puts form over substance (the opposite of the accounting policy principle). A typical area of creative accounting is 'off-balance sheet' items. A major 'off-balance sheet' item is borrowings which are structured so as not to be considered borrowings for legal purposes. Leases are an example and are discussed in chapter 6.

Therefore you, the user, face a major difficulty because the legal form can be so effective there is little or no disclosure in the accounts to alert you to the existence of a situation or transaction of importance in understanding the true financial position of the entity.

Changes in accounting policies

All changes in accounting policies must be disclosed showing:

- the nature of the change;
- the reason for the change (unfortunately, sometimes this is simply that the directors decided to—which seems less than the standard intended);
- the financial effect of the change if it is material in the year of the change.

Look for changes in accounting policy. These can have dramatic effects on reported profits. These changes frequently produce higher profits or reduce the nastiness of poor results.

Until the 1991/92 recession some listed companies reported record profits for up to twenty succeeding years. If you took the trouble to look closely at the accounts you usually discovered that in one or more years it was a change in accounting policy that enabled the group to report another record profit. So, in truth, such groups did not have unbroken records.

Accounting standard AASB 1001 requires changes in accounting policies to be reported in an accounting policy note. This was not always the case. In other countries the requirements might not be as strong. When reading the other notes watch for information on changes in accounting policy.

An example of a change in accounting policy follows:

	1990 $000	1989 $000
Operating profit before abnormals (as reported)	111 410	121 812
1990 includes amortisation of brand names in the operating profit which did not exist in prior years	2 357	—
So comparative on same basis as 1989 would be	113 767	121 812

The company's accounting policy note on intangibles disclosed the change in accounting policy as:

> Amortisation of brand names commenced on 1 July 1989 and the financial effect of the change has been to increase the amortisation charge by $2.357 million for the year. An adjustment of $4.288 million [see below] has been made to retained profits at the beginning of the year.

The beginning of the accounting policy note included a sentence which said 'The accounting policies adopted are consistent with those of the previous year except where stated'. This begs the question—'What are the changes?'

This accounting policy change reduced the current year reported profit compared with the prior year. The 1990 profit was already lower than 1989. So this change made it look worse.

In the USA the previous year's profit would be adjusted to the revised accounting policy. In the USA we would see a lower 1989 figure reflecting the amortisation relevant to 1989. The adjustment of $4.288 million against retained profits at the beginning of the 1990 financial year is for amortisation relevant to 1989 and prior years. We cannot tell how much can be allocated to 1989 but it may be similar to 1990.

Basic assumptions

Accounting standard AASB 1001 assumes that 'accrual' and 'going concern' principles have been applied unless the accounting policy note states otherwise.

The 'accrual basis' or 'accrual accounting' is where revenue is recognised *as earned* rather than when cash is received, and expenses are recognised *as incurred* rather than when paid. This distinction is particularly important as some of the revenue and expenses might be recognised in the profit and loss statement in a different financial year from that when they are recorded in the cash flow statement. The principle is discussed with examples in chapter 1 as part of the discussion of cash flow compared with profit.

Another related principle is 'matching'. Matching means deducting expenses from the *relevant* revenue and allocating revenue and expenses to the periods in which they are earned or incurred.

The 'going concern basis' is that the accounts have been prepared on the assumption that the company will remain in business. This means the company will be able to buy and sell its product or service and purchase and sell major items such as plant and equipment in the normal course of events. There is no pressure to dispose of goods or assets. The company has adequate cash or credit facilities available to pay its debts as and when they fall due. Where the company is unable to pay its debts as and when they fall due, then 'going concern' cannot be applied. The value of assets and the ability to trade has to be reassessed on the basis of forced sale. This means realising assets at a significant discount on their normal market price.

LISTING REQUIREMENTS

Around the world, market economies have stock exchanges which regulate trading in shares. These exchanges set listing requirements over and above the laws of the regulatory authorities. In Australia listed companies must comply with disclosure requirements of the Australian Stock Exchange. Probably the most useful disclosures are corporate governance and share-holder information. The Stock Exchange released a sample note on corporate governance but requires each listed company to write their own specific information. Some of the requirements overlap with statutory requirements such as disclosure about directors' shareholdings.

These requirements only apply to companies with shares listed on the Stock Exchange.

PRECEDENTS AND RECOGNISED TEXTS

When statutory and accounting standards requirements do not address an accounting issue, accountants consider precedents (i.e. what other companies have done), and refer to well respected texts. These are texts which are used in courses by reputable tertiary institutions.

Less reference is required to these other sources as more accounting standards are issued. This is a helpful trend because precedents followed have at times been questionable. There were occasions when a company would find another company who had accounted for a matter the way they wanted. The accounting policy may not have been the most valid from a philosophical view, but was the most useful from a 'picture painting' view.

POINTS TO REMEMBER

✔ Accounting theory and rules can be complex. Financial statements assume a level of knowledge about accounting principles and standards.

✔ There is increasing commitment to consistent accounting standards throughout the world. The International Accounting Standards Commit-tee (IASC) issues international accounting standards. The Australian Accounting Standards Board, in 1996, announced it intends to harmonise Australian standards with the international standards. Australia is one of more than 80 countries who have accounting bodies affiliated with the IASC. However, due to various national interests, real harmonisation is many, many years away.

✔ The rules consist of a combination of government laws and regulations under the Corporations Law; accounting standards (which for Australian companies have the force of law); Stock Exchange requirements for listed companies; and, finally, reputable texts and precedents.

✔ In Australia the Corporations Law and AASB 1034, *Information to be Disclosed in Financial Reports* (prior to 30 June 1997 Schedule 5 existed instead of AASB 1034) specify much of the content and suggest a format of the balance sheet and profit and loss statement. They must include a directors' report, statement by directors, auditors' report, profit and loss statement, balance sheet, cash flows statement and notes.

✔ Accounting standards specify acceptable means of accounting for matters and information to be reported. The increasing number of standards has reduced the options of entities for alternative accounting policies.

✔ Australian accounting standards are developed by the Accounting Research Foundation, vetted by the two professional accounting bodies and, for companies, approved by the Accounting Standards Board.

✔ The accounting policy note provides the user with some of the significant accounting policies used to prepare the accounts. This information assists the reader when comparing accounts with another entity, as allowance can be made for differing policies when assessing performance. However the reader is presumed to know accounting policies required by accounting standards. These policies do not have to be disclosed.

✔ Accounting policies adopted should be relevant, reliable and reflect substance over form; they should be applied on a consistent basis and information should be understandable (to a person with proficiency).

✔ The reader should always be alert for changes in accounting policy as these affect the assessment of performance and are frequently favourable to the company's reported results.

In September 1997, the federal Treasurer, Peter Costello, announced plans for a major overhaul of accounting rules to align them with international accounting standards. The plan includes a new accounting standards body funded by government as well as the accounting profession. This proposal is part of the government's endeavours to provide a state-of-the-art, efficient, low-cost business climate to facilitate Australian company growth and encourage foreign companies to use Australia as a regional base.

The existing Australian Accounting Standards Board already has in place a program of harmonisation with international standards. Will the new approach better enable this task? Or, is this a sign of increased politicisation of accounting?

4 Alba Manufacturing Limited

To enable us to look at the elements of financial statements, I have created a fictitious company, Alba Manufacturing Limited. This chapter presents background information on the company, its annual report for the year ended 30 June 1997, a brief description of each section of the financial statements, and a detailed profit and loss statement (which is not publicly available).

COMPANY HISTORY

Alba Manufacturing Limited manufactures and sells light production machinery, and spare parts for those machines.

Alba was formed in 1978 by Mr Arnold Blair. For many years he had wanted to run his own business. He had gained a broad depth of experience in the manufacturing sector, initially in research using his science qualifications, and later in management positions. Arnold was confident that he could successfully develop his own manufacturing business. Now, at the end of 1997, his company's history records the success. Arnold is now enjoying a well-deserved comfortable retirement. His involvement with the company continues as chairman of the board.

Barry Montrey first met Arnold at Stacy Ballbearings. Arnold was general manager and Barry joined as marketing director. They enjoyed a good working relationship and found their skills complemented each other—Arnold with production, research and general management, and Barry with sales and marketing. So, it was logical that soon after Arnold started Alba, he invited Barry to join him to head up the marketing effort. Now Barry has ascended to the post of chief executive.

Arnold began Alba by investing a substantial portion of his family inheritance and borrowing from the bank. For many years they operated out of rented premises. In 1983 they bought their first property. With continuing expansion, the property outlived its usefulness. So in December 1995 it was sold and larger premises, which allowed for considerable expansion, were acquired. The directors believed this new property would serve their requirements for at least ten years. By 30 June 1997, the property had increased in value substantially. Barry believed this vindicated his recommendation to the board to go into further debt and buy property.

Prudently, Barry had arranged for variable interest rates on the borrowings. The easing in interest rates over the last two years had substantially reduced the level of interest from that originally budgeted.

In the long run, a company depends on good relationships with its customers. Alba's corporate philosophy is to provide quality product promptly. The high standard of quality is evidenced by the low level of warranty experience. The company ensures that major stock lines are always available by carefully planning production. Customers will accept waiting for minor stock items, but will soon take their business elsewhere if they cannot get usual stock lines when wanted.

Another advantage of the high quality of the product is that customers are willing to pay the prices set, even when the few competitors lower their prices. This situation enables the company to maintain its margins and so ensure continuing profits.

Barry is very keen to increase revenue over time at least in line with inflation. As he says, 'if you are not growing, you'll soon be dead'. On the other hand, control of expenses is also important. So Barry makes sure his managers monitor the level of expenditure. He likes to see the increase in expenditure limited to or below the increase in revenue. There are exceptions to this rule to allow for development of future business opportunities. Barry is seriously considering either exporting, using their increased capacity potential available in the larger property, or licensing companies in other countries to produce their product.

The growth of the company has required investment of new funds from time to time. This has been achieved through additional borrowings and issuing of new shares. The last issue of shares was 100 000 issued at a price of $2.00 each in October 1995. This was done to help finance the new property because the proceeds on sale of the old property and the level of borrowings available were regarded as insufficient at the time. The issuing of new shares over time has resulted in the company moving from having a small group of shareholders to a larger group, including a couple of their major customers.

Today the company is a public company—though not listed on the Stock Exchange. This means the company is required to produce a significant amount of information in its financial statements.

(Small proprietary companies and other forms of business structure (unless they are reporting entities) are not required to produce this level of information publicly. However, within their own organisation, they should have this information, and more, available. Thus the principles and information provided here generally apply to all entities which generate and spend dollars.)

ALBA MANUFACTURING'S ANNUAL REPORT

Annual reports consist of:

■ The directors' report, which provides a general outline of the business for the year and some disclosure about the interest of directors. (You will find that *listed* companies expand upon this using glossy photographs and commenting about what has happened during the year.) It is interesting to consider how useful the information is—is it general and vague or is it specific and focused? It is also worthwhile considering how consistent it is with the accounts.

■ The auditors' report, which is an expression of their opinion on the accounts. They are required to express an opinion based on their audit work. When they disagree with the accounts as presented, they give a 'qualified' opinion—that is, they explain the situations and reasons which they believe cause the accounts not to be true and fair or limit their truth and fairness. So, users of financial statements are particularly interested in qualified opinions and the nature of the qualifications. (Auditors are successfully sued when the court establishes that the auditors were negligent in the conduct of their work in reaching the opinion expressed and that the plaintiff suffered a financial loss due to their negligence.)

■ A statement by directors in which they are required to state that the balance sheet and profit and loss are true and fair. They also assert the company is able to pay its debts as and when they fall due. (Companies which own other companies or entities must produce consolidated accounts, which are explained later in chapter 12. In consolidated accounts, the directors are required to state the group's balance sheet and profit and loss are true and fair, but not comment on the group's ability to pay its debts as and when they fall due.) Please note that the directors are the ones responsible for producing true and fair accounts.

■ The profit and loss account (statement), which is a summary of the profit earned or loss for the year and how it relates to retained profits carried forward year by year in the balance sheet as part of shareholders' equity. Additional information about revenue, some of the expense items and income tax is provided in the supporting notes to the accounts. The appropriate notes are referenced from the statement.

■ The balance sheet, which provides a summary of the assets, liabilities and shareholders' equity. As stated in chapter 2, the assets and liabilities are grouped under current and non-current. Current assets are those assets which will be used up or converted to cash or another form of asset within twelve months of the balance sheet date. Similarly for liabilities, current liabilities are those liabilities which will be paid or removed in some valid manner within twelve months of the balance sheet date. Substantial additional information about the balance sheet items is provided in the referred notes to the accounts.

■ The cash flows statement shows where the cash came from and how it was used during the year. It shows the cash flows coming in and going out under three categories: operating, mostly from the day to day trading of the company; investing, cash used in developing productive capacity or other kinds of investments or cash gained from selling major non-current assets; financing, cash raised from new borrowings and share issues and cash used in repaying borrowings and paying dividends. The net cash flow under each of these categories is added to give the net change in cash for the year. The cash at the beginning of the year is added to the net cash flow to give the cash at the end of the year (which agrees with items of cash in the balance sheet).

■ The notes to the accounts, which, as stated above, provide additional information on the profit and loss statement, balance sheet and cash flows statement. These notes also provide further information such as significant accounting policies, a note on lease commitments, and information on items which may become liabilities in the future.

Throughout the world, where there is a reasonable level of government regulation and an established professional accounting body, the accounts will reflect similar information to those of Alba Manufacturing.

Alba's 1997 accounts provide a good deal of information about the balance sheet, but limited detail about the profit and loss (see end of chapter for Alba's detailed profit and loss). There is also valuable information on the movement in cash flow.

I suggest you read Alba's accounts to gain an appreciation of the content and structure of financial statements and then read the following chapters for explanations on the items in the accounts.

In preparing these fictitious public company accounts I have tried to make some of the commentary more meaningful than might typically be the case. This has been done particularly for financial instruments where I believe disclosures required by accounting standards do not help the reader identify real risks. Wording used in other areas such as the inventory accounting policy might seem to not really explain matters. This is designed to reflect what accounts can be typically like. It reflects the accounting standard setters' view that a reader will have some proficiency.

The accounting policy disclosures in note 1 of the accounts have been limited to only those required by the accounting standard AASB 1001 *Accounting Policies* as explained under that title in chapter 3. Accounting firms might still recommend disclosure of all significant accounting policies to help the accounts 'stand alone'. It's a case of reducing the volume of information versus the usefulness of more disclosure.

All the items in the three financial statements and notes are explained in chapters 5 to 9.

FUTURE EFFECT OF REVISED DIRECTORS' REPORT AND STATEMENT

At the time of producing this second edition the Second Corporate Law Simplification Bill was still to be passed by the Australian Parliament. It was expected to become law sometime during 1997 but is now subject to a broader review. If, and when, it is made law it would modify the directors' report and statement as shown for Alba.

The directors' report 'must give members the information they need in order to be able to understand the overall position of' the entity (section 300(3) of the exposure draft, June 1995).

Alba's review of operations would be expanded to give more information and analysis including some financial information covering the total and key business segments. Alba has only one key business segment. Information would have to be given on any key strategic initiatives, major commitments and sources of funding those commitments, unusual or infrequent events or transactions, likely developments, trends and events which have or are likely to have a significant effect. The last two items can be omitted to the extent the disclosure of information 'is likely to result in unreasonable prejudice' (section 300(5)). Such omission must be mentioned in the report.

These requirements would replace principal activities, profit, significant changes in the state of affairs, subsequent events and likely developments. Alba does not disclose likely events as allowed under existing legislation, on the basis of prejudicing its situation.

Other information in Alba's directors' report is still required but can be included in the accounts rather than the directors' report. This information is the directors' names, directors' meetings, dividends, interests in the shares of the company, indemnification of officers, and directors' benefits plus options granted to directors (already required but not applicable to Alba).

The statement by directors remains very similar. The true and fair view statement is expanded to cover the profit and loss statement, balance sheet, statement of cash flows and notes. This includes consolidated statements where applicable. The statement must also state compliance with accounting standards. Further, 'any other information or explanation necessary to give a true and fair view' is required (section 297(1)(i)). As shown in Alba, early adoption of accounting standards and commentary on solvency is still required.

COMPANY ACCOUNTS

ALBA MANUFACTURING LIMITED DIRECTORS' REPORT

Your directors submit their report for the year ended 30 June 1997 made in accordance with a resolution of the directors.

1. **Directors**

   The names of the directors in office at the date of this report are:

A L Blair, BSc, MSc (Chairman)	A L Blair has served as non-executive chairman since his retirement as chief executive in 1989. Mr Blair established Alba Manufacturing in the late 1970s, bringing experience gained from employment in research and management in the manufacturing sector.
B A Montrey (Chief Executive)	B A Montrey has been a director and served in management capacities since Alba Manufacturing commenced business. Mr Montrey has extensive experience in marketing and general management.
I M Loyer, LLB	I M Loyer is a practising solicitor and acts as a non-executive director of the company and several other unrelated companies.

2. **Directors' meetings**

   The number of meetings of the company's directors held during the year was 10. There are no committees of directors. All directors were in office throughout the financial year and remain in office at the date of this Directors' Report. There were no other directors in office during this period. Attendance by directors of the 10 possible meetings was:

A L Blair	10
B A Montrey	10
I M Loyer	8

3. **Principal activity**

   The principal activity of the company in the course of the financial year was the manufacture and sale of light industrial machinery and spare parts.

4. **Profit**

   The net amount of the profit of the company for the financial year after income tax was $211 704.

5. **Dividends**

   The following dividends have been paid by the company or recommended by the directors since the commencement of the financial year—

(a) Final dividend of 7.5 cents a share fully franked out of the profits of the year ended 30 June 1996 and which was included in the accounts at that date and shown in the previous directors' report, paid on 15 November 1996	$30 000
(b) Out of profits for the year ended 30 June 1997:	
(i) an interim dividend of 7.5 cents a share fully franked paid on 15 March 1997	$30 000
(ii) a final dividend declared by the directors of 7.5 cents a share fully franked payable on 15 November 1997	$30 000

6. **Review of operations**

   The company continued to trade profitably in line with planned activities. Demand for products remained strong even in the current adverse economic conditions. While sales of new machinery declined slightly, sales of spare parts more than offset this decline giving an overall pleasing increase in sales for the year.

7. Significant changes in the state of affairs

There were no significant changes in the state of affairs of the company during the financial year.

8. Subsequent events

No matter or circumstance has arisen since the end of the financial year that has significantly affected or may significantly affect the operations of the company, the results of those operations or the state of affairs of the company in financial years subsequent to the financial year.

9. Likely developments

In the opinion of directors the inclusion of any information referring to likely developments in the operations of the company and the expected results of those operations in subsequent years would prejudice the interests of the company. That information has therefore not been included in this report.

10. Interests in the shares of the company

As at the date of this report the interests of the directors in the shares of the company were:

	$1 ordinary shares
A L Blair	50 000
B A Montrey	15 000
I M Loyer	1 000

11. Indemnification of directors and officers

As allowed by the Corporations Law the company's Articles of Association provide for an indemnity of every officer against any liability incurred in his or her capacity as an officer of the company to another person unless the liability arises out of conduct involving a lack of good faith by the officer. It does not allow an indemnity against the company or a body corporate related to the company. The Articles also provide for an indemnity for legal costs incurred by officers defending proceedings in which judgement is given in their favour, they are acquitted or the Court grants them relief. The company has obtained insurance cover for these liabilities in respect of its directors and executive. Under the contract, the terms and premium cannot be disclosed.

12. Directors' benefits

Since the end of the previous financial year no director of the company has received or become entitled to receive a benefit (other than a benefit included in the aggregate amount of emoluments received or due and receivable by directors shown in the accounts or the fixed salary of a full time employee of the company) by reason of a contract made by the company or a related corporation with the director or with a firm of which he or she is a member, or with a company in which he or she has substantial financial interest except any benefit that may accrue by reason of professional fees paid in the ordinary course of business to the company's firm of solicitors of which Ms Loyer is a partner.

On behalf of the Board

A L Blair
Director

B A Montrey
Director
Sydney, 15 October 1997

AUDITORS' REPORT TO THE MEMBERS OF ALBA MANUFACTURING LIMITED

Scope

We have audited the financial statements of Alba Manufacturing Limited for the financial year ended 30 June 1997, being the profit and loss statement, balance sheet, statement of cash flows, notes and statement by directors. The company's directors are responsible for the financial statements. We have conducted an independent audit of these financial statements in order to express an opinion on them to the members of the company.

Our audit has been conducted in accordance with Australian Auditing Standards to provide reasonable assurance whether the financial statements are free of material misstatement. Our procedures included examination, on a test basis, of evidence supporting the amounts and other disclosures in the financial statements, and the evaluation of accounting policies and significant accounting estimates. These procedures have been undertaken to form an opinion whether, in all material respects, the financial statements are presented fairly in accordance with Accounting Standards and other mandatory professional reporting requirements (Urgent Issues Group Consensus Views) and statutory requirements, so as to present a view which is consistent with our understanding of the company's financial position, the results of its operations and its cash flows.

The audit opinion expressed in this report has been formed on the above basis.

Audit Opinion

In our opinion the financial statements of Alba Manufacturing Limited are properly drawn up
  (a) so as to give a true and fair view of:
      (i) the company's state of affairs as at 30 June 1997 and its
          profit and cash flows for the financial year ended on that date; and
      (ii) the other matters required by Division 4, 4A and 4B of Part 3.6 of the Corporations
           Law to be dealt with in the financial statements;
  (b) in accordance with the provisions of the Corporations Law; and
  (c) in accordance with applicable Accounting Standards and other mandatory professional
      reporting requirements.

C & A Accountants
Chartered Accountants

A U Ditor, Partner
Sydney, 15 October 1997

STATEMENT BY DIRECTORS

In accordance with a resolution of the directors of Alba Manufacturing Limited, we state that:
In the opinion of the directors:

(a) the profit and loss statement is drawn up so as to give a true and fair view of the profit of the company for the financial year ended 30 June 1997;

(b) the balance sheet is drawn up so as to give a true and fair view of the state of affairs of the company as at 30 June 1997; and

(c) at the date of this statement there are reasonable grounds to believe that the company will be able to pay its debts as and when they fall due.

Accounting standard AASB 1033 *Presentation and Disclosure of Financial Instruments* has been applied early in these financial statements. The directors made an election in writing to do this. This election is in accordance with subsection 285(3) of the Corporations Law. The standard must be applied for years commencing on or after 31 December 1997.

On behalf of the Board
A L Blair
Director

B A Montrey
Director
Sydney, 15 October 1997

ALBA MANUFACTURING LIMITED
PROFIT AND LOSS STATEMENT
YEAR ENDED 30 JUNE 1997

	Note	1997 $	1996 $
Operating revenue	2	3 462 880	3 617 431
Operating profit before abnormal items	3	302 502	287 645
Abnormal items	4	26 814	157 881
Operating profit after abnormal items and before income tax		329 316	445 526
Income tax attributable to operating profit before abnormal items	5	(117 612)	(114 805)
Income tax attributable to abnormal items	5	—	9 663
Income tax attributable to operating profit		(117 612)	(105 142)
Operating profit after income tax		211 704	340 384
Retained profits at the beginning of the financial year		296 645	195 983
Total available for appropriation		508 349	536 367
Interim dividend paid		30 000	25 000
Final dividend declared		30 000	30 000
Transfers to reserves	16	26 814	184 722
		86 814	239 722
Retained profits at the end of the financial year		421 535	296 645

The attached notes should be read in conjunction with this profit and loss statement.

ALBA MANUFACTURING LIMITED
BALANCE SHEET
AS AT 30 JUNE 1997

	Note	1997 $	1996 $
Current assets			
Cash	6	225 632	158 731
Receivables	7	433 905	389 850
Inventories	8	508 723	454 245
Prepayments		6 984	6 475
Total current assets		1 175 244	1 009 301
Non-current assets			
Loan to a director	29	50 000	50 000
Investments	9	121 104	63 904
Property, plant & equipment	10	988 256	900 425
Future income tax benefits		73 250	62 580
Total non-current assets		1 232 610	1 076 909
Total assets		2 407 854	2 086 210
Current liabilities			
Accounts payable	11	382 156	354 028
Borrowings	12	93 453	98 327
Provisions	13	211 116	188 492
Total current liabilities		686 725	640 847
Non-current liabilities			
Borrowings	14	322 542	322 241
Provision—long service leave		59 194	46 945
Total non-current liabilities		381 736	369 186
Total liabilities		1 068 461	1 010 033
Net assets		1 339 393	1 076 177
Shareholders' equity			
Share capital	15	400 000	400 000
Reserves	16	517 858	379 532
Retained profits		421 535	296 645
Total shareholders' equity		1 339 393	1 076 177

The attached notes should be read in conjunction with this balance sheet.

ALBA MANUFACTURING LIMITED
STATEMENT OF CASH FLOWS
YEAR ENDED 30 JUNE 1997

	Note	1997 $	1996 $
Cash flows from operating activities			
Receipts from customers		3 851 939	3 543 784
Payments to suppliers and employees		(3 460 389)	(3 092 683)
Dividends received		5 168	3 684
Interest received		12 671	8 581
Interest and other costs of finance paid		(36 457)	(39 228)
Income tax paid		(112 984)	(86 948)
Net cash provided by operating activities	19	259 948	337 190
Cash flows from investing activities			
Money placed on short term deposit		(70 000)	(80 000)
Proceeds from sale of investments		32 751	—
Payment for investments		(63 137)	—
Proceeds from sale of property		—	484 560
Proceeds from sale of plant and equipment		12 786	6 847
Payment for property, plant and equipment	17	(46 847)	(777 915)
Net cash used by investing activities		(134 447)	(366 508)
Cash flows from financing activities			
Proceeds from issue of shares		—	200 000
Proceeds from borrowings		—	150 000
Repayment of borrowings		(5 600)	(70 000)
Finance lease payments		(49 522)	(44 973)
Dividends paid		(60 000)	(50 000)
Net cash (used by) or provided in financing activities		(115 122)	185 027
Net increase/(decrease) in cash held		10 379	155 709
Cash at the beginning of the financial year		28 745	(126 964)
Total cash at the end of the financial year		39 124	28 745
Reconciliation of cash			
Cash	6	75 632	78 731
Bills of exchange receivable	7	13 874	6 824
Bank overdraft	12	(50 382)	(56 810)
		39 124	28 745

The attached notes should be read in conjunction with this statement of cash flows.

ALBA MANUFACTURING LIMITED
NOTES TO AND FORMING PART OF THE FINANCIAL STATEMENTS

1. Summary of significant accounting policies

(a) Accounting principles

This general purpose financial report has been prepared in accordance with Accounting Standards and UIG Consensus Views. The accounting policies are consistent with those of the previous year.

(b) Foreign currencies

Purchases or sales of goods and services in foreign currencies are recorded in Australian dollars at the time of purchase or sale at the exchange rate prevailing on that day.

Amounts payable or receivable in foreign currency at the end of the financial year are converted to Australian dollars at exchange rates prevailing on that date.

All unrealised and realised exchange gains or losses relating to monetary items are brought to account in the period in which they arise.

To the extent that a transaction is hedged, the exchange gains and losses arising up to the date of purchase or sale together with related costs, premiums and discounts are included in the cost of the purchase or sale.

(c) Derivative financial instruments

When considered appropriate foreign currency forward exchange contracts are used to reduce currency exchange fluctuation risks on importing and exporting product. There is no speculative trading in forward exchange contracts. No other derivative financial instruments have been used or transactions conducted during or since the end of the financial year.

(d) Non-current assets

The carrying value of land and buildings is reviewed regularly and at least every three years. Land and buildings are included in the accounts at either cost or valuation. The details of the valuation are included in note 10.

There would be a capital gains tax liability in relation to the revalued property if it was sold at the stated book value. This amount has not been included in the financial results as the intention is to hold the property. The amount of capital gains tax is disclosed as a contingent liability in note 21.

In determining the recoverable amount of non-current assets, the expected cash flows have not been discounted.

(e) Depreciation

Depreciation on buildings, plant and equipment is calculated on a straight line basis at rates anticipated to allocate their cost or valuation less estimated residual value at the end of the useful lives of the assets, against revenue over their estimated useful lives.

Major depreciation periods are:

Freehold buildings	— 40 years
Plant and equipment	— 5 to 10 years
Leased plant and equipment	— 3 to 10 years

Additions are depreciated from the first whole month in the year of acquisition and disposals are depreciated to the last whole month in the year of disposal.

(f) Investments

Bank deposits included in current assets and all non-current investments are included at cost. Interest revenue is recognised when due on the basis of the actual amount due. Dividend revenue is recognised when received. Purchases and sales of investments are recognised on the trade date.

Investments are written down to their estimated net fair value when this amount is less than the carrying amount unless the company believes it will recover the carrying amount. Net fair value is the amount for which the investment could be exchanged between knowledgeable, willing parties in an arm's length transaction and after deducting costs expected to be incurred were the asset to be exchanged. The fair value of investments is described in note 9.

(g) Accounts receivable

Trade accounts receivable is the estimated amount which will be collected in the normal course of business. This is regarded as approximating their net fair value. Bills of exchange are shown at their face value being the amount due to be received on maturity. All bills are arranged for a maximum period of 90 days.

The loan to a director is valued at the principal outstanding. This is the anticipated amount which will be recovered.

(h) Valuation of inventories

Inventories are valued at the lower of cost and net realisable value.

Costs incurred in bringing each product to its present location and condition are accounted for as follows:

Raw materials—purchase cost on a first-in, first-out basis.

Finished goods and work in progress—cost of direct material, direct labour and a proportion of variable and fixed manufacturing overheads based on normal operating capacity.

(i) Borrowings

Borrowings are initially recorded at the principal outstanding. The liability is reduced by repayments of principal. The liability is not revalued to reflect net fair value (see notes 12 and 14). Interest expense is recognised as it falls due and payable.

(j) Employee benefits

An accounting standard requires the estimation of non-current employee benefits such as long service leave to be measured at the present value of expected future payments to be made in respect of services provided by employees up to balance sheet date. In assessing expected future payments the company, as allowed by the accounting standard, has used a 'short-hand' measurement technique. The non-current long service leave liability has been estimated using the remuneration rates current at balance sheet date for all employees with five or more years service. The directors believe this method provides an estimate of the liability not materially different from that using the present value basis of measurement.

(k) Cash

The items included as cash in the preparation of the cash flows statement are cash at bank and on hand, bills of exchange receivable which can readily be discounted for cash and bank overdraft which is used as part of the daily cash management of the company.

	1997 **$**	**1996** **$**
2. Operating revenue		
Sales revenue	3 399 504	3 113 819
Other revenue:		
Dividends—other corporations	5 168	3 684
Interest—other corporations	12 671	8 581
Proceeds on sale of non-current assets		
– investments	32 751	—
– property	—	484 500
– plant and equipment	12 786	6 847
	3 462 880	3 617 431
3. Operating profit before tax		
Operating profit before income tax is arrived at after:		
Charging against profits:		
Depreciation		
Buildings	7 423	3 714
Plant and equipment	27 222	27 461
Plant and equipment under lease	51 328	46 869
Bad debts—trade debtors	4 982	6 874
Provided for doubtful debts—trade debtors	2 500	(2 000)
Provided for diminution in value of inventories	500	—
Interest—other corporations	36 457	39 228
Finance charges—lease liability	28 402	28 382
Loss on sale of plant and equipment	2 906	4 099
Rental—operating leases	9 445	8 879
Foreign currency translation (gains)/losses	(924)	2 748
Provided for warranty	1 000	500
Provided for employee entitlements	18 575	16 847
Crediting the following item:		
Profit from sale of plant and equipment	(2 563)	(1 125)
4. Abnormal items		
Profit on sale of investments (no tax effect)	26 814	—
Profit on sale of property (no tax effect)	—	184 722
Write-off of obsolete inventory	—	(26 841)
(income tax applicable)	—	9 663
Abnormal items before income tax	26 814	157 881
Abnormal items net of income tax	26 814	167 544

	1997 $	1996 $
5. Income tax		
The prima facie tax on operating profit differs from the income tax provided in the accounts and is calculated as follows:		
Prima facie tax on operating profit at 36%	118 554	160 390
Tax effect of permanent differences:		
Rebateable dividends	(1 860)	(1 326)
Non-deductible items	13 108	11 544
Abnormal items	(9 653)	(66 500)
Under/(over) provision of previous year	(2 537)	1 034
Income tax attributable to operating profit and total income tax provided	117 612	105 142
Income tax provided comprises:		
Provision attributable to current year	128 282	116 555
Provision attributable to future years		
Future income tax benefits	(10 670)	(11 413)
	117 612	105 142
6. Cash		
Cash at bank and on hand	75 632	78 731
Bank short term deposits	150 000	80 000
	225 632	158 731

The bank short term deposits are deposited for 90 days and rolled over on maturity unless required for daily cash needs. Interest rate earned during the year 4.2% to 5.9% (1996—5.2% to 6.5%).

7. Receivables (current)		
Trade debtors	424 695	387 329
Provision for doubtful debts	(12 500)	(10 000)
	412 195	377 329
Bills of exchange	13 874	6 824
Other debtors	7 836	5 697
	433 905	389 850

The company incurs credit risk with its trade debtors. The company manages this risk through following its credit policy which has been authorised by the Board of Directors. Payments received from and credit limits of all debtors are regularly monitored. There is no concentration of debtors which would expose the company to additional risk.

	1997 $	1996 $
8. Inventories		
Raw materials	231 138	208 080
Provision for diminution in value	(2 500)	(2 000)
	228 638	206 080
Work in progress	30 468	25 528
Finished goods	249 617	222 637
Total inventory at lower of cost and net realisable value	508 723	454 245
9. Investments (non-current)		
Investments at cost comprise:		
Shares – listed on a prescribed stock exchange	62 465	36 947
– unlisted	12 574	12 574
	75 039	49 521
Debentures – listed on a prescribed stock exchange	2 874	2 874
Fixed interest securities		
– listed on a prescribed stock exchange	35 576	3 894
Interest in unit trusts		
– listed on a prescribed stock exchange	4 741	4 741
– unlisted units	2 874	2 874
	7 615	7 615
Total book value of investments	121 104	63 904
Aggregate net fair values of investments listed on a prescribed stock exchange at balance date comprise:		
Shares	75 874	62 874
Debentures	2 674	2 574
Fixed interest securities	38 040	3 538
Unit trusts	3 874	3 295
	120 462	72 281

Aggregate net fair values of unlisted investments have been determined based on a directors' valuation of the underlying assets and liabilities shown in the latest audited accounts for each of the investments. An assessment was made of market value of any major non-current assets.

	1997 $	1996 $
Shares—unlisted	13 962	13 687
Unit trust—unlisted	3 046	2 735
	17 008	16 422
Total net fair value of investments	137 470	88 703

	1997 $	1996 $

10. Property, plant and equipment

Freehold land:

At cost	—	368 471
At directors' valuation 1997	440 000	—
	440 000	368 471

Buildings on freehold land:

At cost	—	297 154
At directors' valuation 1997	326 000	—
	326 000	297 154
Provision for depreciation of buildings—at cost	—	3 714

Written down value of buildings on freehold land:

At cost	—	293 440
At directors' valuation 1997	326 000	—
	326 000	293 440

Plant and equipment:

At cost	218 834	187 281
Provision for depreciation	88 961	68 024
	129 873	119 257

Plant and equipment under lease:

At cost	203 371	196 744
Provision for depreciation	110 988	77 487
	92 383	119 257

Total property, plant and equipment:

Cost	422 205	1 049 650
Directors' valuation 1997	766 000	—
	1 188 205	1 049 650
Provision for depreciation	199 949	149 225
	988 256	900 425

The directors revalued land and buildings as at 30 June 1997. The revaluation was based on market value not exceeding an independent valuation. The directors review the values of land and buildings regularly and determine a current valuation at least every three years. The asset values of these revaluations are taken up in the financial statements if determined in a Board resolution.

11. Accounts payable (current)

Trade creditors	284 874	259 341
Accrued expenses	93 461	87 815
Other creditors	3 821	6 872
	382 156	354 028

		1997 $	1996 $
12. Borrowings (current)			
Unsecured			
Other loans		5 600	5 600
Secured			
Bank overdraft		50 382	56 810
Lease liability	note 20	37 471	35 917
		87 853	92 727
		93 453	98 327

The bank overdraft is secured by a floating charge over the assets of the company. Interest rate is variable. Average interest rate during the year 7.8% (1996—8.5%). The lease liability is secured over the assets leased.

	1997 $	1996 $
13. Provisions (current)		
Dividends	30 000	30 000
Income tax	110 819	95 521
Warranty	12 000	11 000
Annual leave	51 493	46 332
Long service leave	6 804	5 639
	211 116	188 492

		1997 $	1996 $
14. Borrowings (non-current)			
Unsecured			
Other loans		16 800	22 400
Secured			
Bank loans		150 000	150 000
Lease liability	note 20	135 742	129 841
Other loans		20 000	20 000
		305 742	299 841
		322 542	322 241

The bank loans are secured by a first mortgage over the land and buildings. The interest rate is reviewed annually at 31 December in line with prevailing market interest rates. The effective interest rate at 30 June 1997 is 9.95% (1996—10.45%).

Other loans are secured by a second mortgage over the land and buildings. The lease liability is secured over the assets leased. These borrowings and the unsecured loans are at fixed interest rates to date of maturity. Market interest rates have declined since these borrowings arose. Thus the market value of the borrowing has increased and net fair value exceeds the book value.

The carrying value and the net fair values of these borrowings at balance sheet date are:

	1997		1996	
	Carrying Amount $	Net Fair Value $	Carrying Amount $	Net Fair Value $
Other unsecured loan	22 400	23 217	28 000	29 112
Other secured loan	20 000	22 367	20 000	22 791
Lease liabilities	173 213	178 835	165 758	171 396

	1997 $	1996 $
15. Share capital		
Issued and paid up:		
400 000 ordinary shares of $1 each fully paid	400 000	400 000
16. Reserves		
Reserves comprise:		
Capital —		
Share premium	100 000	100 000
Asset realisation	306 346	279 532
Asset revaluation	111 512	—
	517 858	379 532
Movements in reserves:		
Share premium		
Balance at beginning of year	100 000	—
Premium on issue of shares	—	100 000
Balance at end of year	100 000	100 000
Asset realisation		
Balance at beginning of year	279 532	25 236
Transfer from profit and loss	26 814	184 722
Transfer from asset revaluation	—	69 574
Balance at end of year	306 346	279 532
Asset revaluation		
Balance at beginning of year	—	69 574
Surplus on revaluation of —		
Land	71 529	—
Buildings	39 983	—
Transfer to asset realisation	—	(69 574)
Balance at end of year	111 512	—

	1997 $	1996 $

17. Non-cash financing and investing activities

During the financial year the company acquired plant and equipment with an aggregate value of $28 574 (1996—$23 684) by means of finance leases. These acquisitions are not reflected in the statement of cash flows.

18. Financing facilities

The company has an overdraft facility in place to 31 March 1999, and able to be extended upon agreement with the bank. The limit of the facility at the end of the financial year is $200 000 (1996—$200 000).

19. Reconciliation of operating profit after income tax to net cash provided by operating activities

	1997 $	1996 $
Operating profit after income tax	211 704	340 384
Depreciation provided	85 973	78 044
Finance lease charges	28 402	28 382
Provision for doubtful debts	2 500	(2 000)
Provision for inventory obsolescence	500	—
Provision for employee entitlements	18 575	16 847
Provision for warranty	1 000	500
Loss on sale of plant and equipment	343	2 974
(Gain) on sale of property	—	(184 722)
(Gain) on sale of investments	(26 814)	—
Increase in income tax payable	15 298	29 607
(Decrease) in deferred taxes	(10 670)	(11 413)
Changes in assets and liabilities		
(Increase) in trade debtors	(37 366)	(51 368)
(Increase) in other debtors	(2 139)	(1 203)
(Increase)/decrease in inventories	(54 978)	60 391
(Increase)/decrease in prepaid expenses	(509)	2 638
Increase in trade creditors	31 180	26 447
Increase/(decrease) in other creditors	(3 051)	1 682
Net cash provided by operating activities	259 948	337 190

	1997 $	1996 $

20. Expenditure commitments

Capital expenditure commitments

Estimated capital expenditure contracted for purchase of plant and equipment at balance date but not provided for, payable not later than one year after the end of the financial year

	26 347	15 968

Lease expenditure commitments

Operating leases:

Not later than one year	11 158	10 639
Later than one year and not later than two years	10 228	9 183
Later than two years and not later than five years	15 429	13 852
Aggregate lease expenditure contracted for at balance date but not provided for	36 815	33 674

Finance leases:

Not later than one year	75 226	69 715
Later than one year and not later than two years	73 652	66 438
Later than two years and not later than five years	119 341	117 969
Total minimum lease payments	268 219	254 122
Future finance charges	(95 006)	(88 364)
Lease liability	173 213	165 758

Current liability	note 12	37 471	35 917
Non-current liability	note 14	135 742	129 841
		173 213	165 758

21. Contingent liabilities

Guarantees given to other parties in the ordinary course of business	24 000	17 500

Capital gains tax would be payable if the revalued property was sold at balance date. No provision has been made for this liability because disposal of the property is not anticipated.

	37 597	—

	1997 $	1996 $

22. Superannuation

The company contributes to a defined benefits plan, the Alba Superannuation Fund. The company contributes in accordance with the Superannuation Guarantee Charge legislation at the rate of 6% of defined wages, at rates in terms of the trust deed and at rates contained in certain employee contracts. Participating employees contribute a minimum of 5% of salary.

Company contribution to the Fund	58 487	54 969

An actuarial review of the Fund is performed every three years. The last review occurred at 30 June 1996. The accrued benefits for the Fund year ended 30 June 1996 is the actuarial estimate and the amount for the Fund year ended 30 June 1997 reflects additional accrued benefits since the date of the actuarial review.

Accrued benefits	734 389	692 038
Net market value of the plan assets	692 003	638 311
Shortfall	42 386	53 727
Vested benefits	389 615	337 625

The company has not recognised a liability for the shortfall between the accrued benefits and the net market value of the plan assets. The company has undertaken to make additional contributions during the three years to the next actuarial review for the Fund year ended 30 June 1999. The level of these contributions is designed to reduce the shortfall by at least 50%. The company will review the situation again at 30 June 1999 to determine whether an additional contribution is still required.

23. Employee entitlements

Total aggregate employee entitlement/liability consists of:

Accrued wages and salaries (part of accrued expenses in note 11)	11 046	10 529
Provision for employee entitlements		
Current—note 12	58 297	51 971
Non-current—balance sheet	59 194	46 945
	128 537	109 445

24. Remuneration of directors

Amounts received or due and receivable by directors of the company includes salary, bonus, superannuation and other benefits	112 500	107 500

The number of directors of the company whose remuneration falls within the following bands is

$0 – $9 999	2	2
$50 000 – $59 999	1	1

	1997 $	1996 $
25. Auditors' remuneration		
Amounts received or due and receivable by auditors for:		
Auditing the accounts	15 000	14 000
Other services	3 687	3 294
	18 687	17 294

(The auditors did not receive any other benefits)

26. Franking account

The franking account at financial year end after allowing for income tax to be paid and dividends to be distributed is franked as follows:

	1997	1996
Franked at 39%	—	3 491
Franked at 33%	177 460	177 460
Franked at 36%	188 328	116 555
	365 788	297 506

27. Derivative financial instruments

The carrying value of foreign currency forward exchange contracts at balance sheet date was nil.

	1997	1996
Forward exchange contracts—net fair value at balance date	13 089	12 147

The notional principal or contract amounts of foreign currency forward exchange contracts outstanding at financial year end were as follows:

	1997	1996
Purchase commitments	23 605	21 477
Sale commitments	31 379	19 674

All foreign currency forward exchange contracts are conducted with reputable trading banks. The company does not expect any loss on these contracts due to the credit worthiness of the trading banks which are expected to perform their obligations.

28. Segment information

The company manufactures and sells light industrial machinery and spare parts within Australia.

29. Related party transactions

(a) The directors of Alba Manufacturing Limited during the financial year were:

A L Blair

B A Montrey

I M Loyer

(b) The following related party transactions occurred during the financial year:

(i) The company paid professional fees of $3013 to the law firm in which Ms Loyer is a partner.

(ii) Aggregate amounts of directors' remuneration are shown in note 24.

(iii) Aggregate amount of a loan to a director is shown on the balance sheet.

DETAILED PROFIT AND LOSS STATEMENT

The following *detailed* profit and loss statement would not be provided to the public. I have provided it here so you can see an example of what a detailed profit and loss may look like within an entity's own records. There is no specific form that must be followed, however most businesses would use formats similar to the one used here. A summary of the typical main categories of a detailed profit and loss statement for Alba is as follows.

ALBA MANUFACTURING LIMITED
TRADING AND PROFIT AND LOSS SUMMARY

		$
	Sales	3 399 504
less:	Cost of sales	2 124 601
gives:	Gross profit	1 274 903
plus:	Other income	17 839
gives:	Gross profit and other income	1 292 742
less:	Expenses	
	Warehousing	—
	Distribution	—
	Selling	498 378
	Administration	491 862
	Finance	—
	Total of expenses	990 240
gives:	Operating profit before income tax	302 502

The detailed profit and loss is generally split in two parts:

■ The manufacturing and trading statement which shows the revenues less the cost of sales to give gross profit. The cost of sales for those manufacturing goods consists of the cost of acquiring raw materials and manufacture whereas for those wholesaling or retailing goods it consists of the cost of acquiring goods. Those selling services can also use this concept.

■ The detailed profit and loss statement which starts with the gross profit and deducts other types of expenses, such as selling and administration, and recognises other income. The result of this sum is the operating profit before tax.

The cost of sales consists of the cost of materials, direct labour and manufacturing overheads. The manufacturing overheads are the costs associated with producing the goods or services. For Alba this would consist of all the costs (other than materials and direct labour) associated with the production process.

The other major types of expenses such as selling and administration are further overhead costs that Alba incurs. They are grouped under categories that describe the activity of the business: selling expenses are those associated with marketing and selling the products; and administration covers the other expenses which cannot be grouped under the other specific types of expenses.

Alba has not separately allocated expenses under warehousing, distribution and finance. Management has decided this segregation is not necessary for helping them monitor their expenses. So management has included warehousing and distribution expenses with their selling expenses, and finance expenses (interest costs and finance lease charges) with administration expenses. As stated above, there are no fixed formatting requirements.

When you read the following detailed profit statement you will see the same expenses often occur under each classification. An example is wages which is shown as direct labour within cost of goods sold, and wages within each of selling and administration. The company has people working in the factory, as sales people and in administration—for example, the accountant and receptionist. This means the total wages paid by Alba is the sum of the wages figures shown in each classification.

The classification of expenses by the function performed within the business enables management to monitor costs of running that function. Management is then able to take appropriate action to control the expenditure within a function.

A statement by the auditors similar to the following usually accompanies the detailed profit statement for companies whose accounts are required to be audited. The auditors do this to ensure that the company, and any others who see the statements, are aware that these statements are not audited.

Alba's manufacturing and trading statement and detailed profit and loss statement appear on the following pages.

COMPILATION REPORT TO THE MEMBERS OF ALBA MANUFACTURING LIMITED

On the basis of information provided by the directors of Alba Manufacturing Limited, we have compiled in accordance with APS 9 'Statement of Compilation of Financial Reports' the Manufacturing and Trading Statement and the Detailed Profit and Loss Statement for the financial year ended 30 June 1997.

The directors are solely responsible for the information contained in the Trading Statement and the Detailed Profit and Loss Statement.

Our procedures use accounting expertise to collect, classify and summarise the financial information, which the directors provided, into the two financial reports. Our procedures do not include verification or validation procedures. No audit or review has been performed and accordingly no assurance is expressed.

To the extent permitted by law, we do not accept liability for any loss or damage which any person, other than the directors or members of the company, may suffer arising from any negligence on our part. No person should rely on the two reports without having an audit or review conducted.

The Manufacturing and Trading Statement and the Detailed Profit and Loss Statement for the financial year ended 30 June 1997 were prepared exclusively for the benefit of the members of the company. We do not accept responsibility to any other person for the contents of these reports.

C & A Accountants
Chartered Accountants

A U Ditor, Partner
Sydney, 15 October 1997

ALBA MANUFACTURING LIMITED
MANUFACTURING AND TRADING STATEMENT
YEAR ENDED 30 JUNE 1997

	1997 $	1996 $
Gross sales	3 894 287	3 580 943
Sales tax	(494 783)	(467 124)
Sales	3 399 504	3 113 819
less: Cost of goods sold		
Material cost		
Stock on hand at beginning of the year	454 245	523 925
Purchases	1 413 699	1 157 524
Customs and duty charges	10 873	9 573
Customs clearing charges	1 435	1 529
Freight inwards	3 573	3 384
	1 883 825	1 695 935
less: Stock on hand at end of the year	508 723	454 245
Total material cost	1 375 102	1 241 690
Direct labour	395 956	367 282
Manufacturing overheads (see page 73)	353 543	330 181
Total cost of goods sold	2 124 601	1 939 153
Gross profit	1 274 903	1 174 666

	1997 $	1996 $
Manufacturing overhead expenses		
Annual leave provided	5 871	4 292
Cleaning	5 824	5 718
Depreciation	22 386	20 510
Depreciation—leased assets	13 948	12 847
Diminution in value of inventories	500	—
Finance charges—lease liabilities	11 284	11 731
General	2 840	2 973
Insurance	28 473	25 178
Light and power	36 741	33 844
Land tax	2 741	2 584
Long service leave provided	1 698	1 711
Loss on sale of fixed assets	2 854	3 576
Profit on sale of fixed assets	(1 251)	(382)
Packing materials	26 687	22 821
Payroll tax	28 743	26 996
Rates	3 805	3 681
Realised exchange (gains)/losses	(924)	2 748
Rent—operating leases	2 641	2 554
Repairs and maintenance	28 874	25 372
Staff expenses	13 974	8 276
Superannuation	31 743	29 996
Supervisory salaries	83 091	82 655
Warranty provided	1 000	500
Total manufacturing overheads	353 543	330 181

ALBA MANUFACTURING LIMITED
DETAILED PROFIT AND LOSS STATEMENT
YEAR ENDED 30 JUNE 1997

	1997 $	1996 $
Gross profit	1 274 903	1 174 666
Interest received—other corporations	12 671	8 581
Dividends received—other corporations	5 168	3 684
Total of gross profit and other income	1 292 742	1 186 931
Selling expenses		
Annual leave provided	2 941	2 793
Advertising	56 142	46 815
Commissions	184 962	162 874
Depreciation	3 385	3 281
Depreciation—leased assets	10 854	9 364
Entertainment	28 743	25 385
Finance charges—lease liabilities	4 283	4 067
Freight and cartage	48 235	46 174
General expenses	938	2 841
Insurance	4 922	4 527
Land tax	587	554
Long service leave provided	1 745	1 598
Loss on sale of fixed assets	—	523
Profit on sale of fixed assets	(465)	(85)
Motor vehicle expenses	13 847	11 936
Motor vehicle leasing—depreciation	8 274	7 894
Payroll tax	5 009	4 736
Rates	1 055	864
Rent—operating leases	2 847	2 697
Repairs and maintenance	3 957	2 066
Salaries	83 471	78 935
Superannuation	7 008	6 736
Travelling	25 638	22 847
Total selling expenses	498 378	449 422

Unaudited—Refer to the Compilation Report

	1997 $	1996 $
Administration expenses		
Annual leave provided	2 635	3 842
Auditing fees	15 000	14 000
Auditors' fees for other services	3 687	3 294
Bank charges	2 974	3 841
Bad debts	4 982	6 874
Computer expenses	18 752	17 296
Directors' fees—full time (excluding salaries)	2 500	2 500
Directors' fees—other	10 000	10 000
Depreciation	8 874	7 384
Depreciation—leased assets	10 829	9 939
Doubtful debts	2 500	(2 000)
Entertainment	7 671	6 684
Finance charges—lease liabilities	12 835	12 584
Fringe benefits tax	3 684	3 527
General expenses	3 842	3 628
Insurance	6 742	7 265
Interest paid—other corporations	36 457	39 228
Land tax	687	594
Long service leave provided	3 685	2 611
Loss on sale of fixed assets	52	—
Profit on sale of fixed assets	(847)	(658)
Motor vehicle expenses	4 865	4 477
Motor vehicle leasing—depreciation	7 423	6 825
Payroll tax	11 006	10 040
Postage	16 487	13 338
Printing and stationery	20 633	18 742
Rates	2 563	2 274
Rent—operating leases	3 957	3 628
Repairs and maintenance	4 722	3 685
Salaries and wages	183 425	167 338
Subscriptions and donations	3 685	3 247
Superannuation	19 736	18 238
Telephone	39 847	36 214
Travelling	15 972	9 385
Total administration expenses	491 862	449 864
Total of selling and administration expenses	990 240	899 286
Operating profit before income tax	302 502	287 645

Unaudited—Refer to the Compilation Report

POINTS TO REMEMBER

✔ In Australia, large proprietary and all public company annual reports consist of a directors' report, auditors' report, statement by directors, profit and loss account, balance sheet, cash flows statement and notes to the accounts. Similar information is published in many other countries. Enterprises which are not required to provide public annual reports should have similar information available, at least internally.

✔ The directors' report includes information on the directors, profit earned, dividends, review of operations, significant changes in the state of affairs, events subsequent to financial year end and likely developments.

✔ The auditors' report provides the auditors' opinion on the truth and fairness of the financial statements. Any qualified opinions (i.e. where the auditors express some exception or concern about the accounts) should be carefully considered.

✔ The statement by directors gives the directors' opinion on the company's and group's accounts and on the company's ability to pay its debts as and when they fall due.

✔ The profit and loss statement (account) shows the operating profit and income tax expense; extraordinary items and income tax expense; adds the year's total profit to retained profit at the beginning of the year; and shows other movements (such as dividends) to give the profit retained in the company (and group) at the end of the year. Referenced notes provide additional details.

✔ The balance sheet summarises the shareholders' equity, assets and liabilities. Assets and liabilities are classified as current or non-current based on change or usage within (current) or after (non-current) twelve months of the balance sheet date. A significant amount of information is contained in referenced notes.

✔ The cash flows statement shows the cash inflows and outflows grouped under three broad categories of operating, investing and financing. The net cash inflow or outflow is added to the cash at the beginning of the year to give the cash at the end of the year. Additional information on cash flows and related financing issues is included in the notes.

✔ Besides information on the profit and loss statement, balance sheet and cash flows statement, the notes to the accounts provide information on matters such as significant accounting policies, contingent liabilities and future commitments.

✔ The detailed profit and loss is not required to be published but must be produced internally. The format is not prescribed but generally groups revenue as sales and other income; and expenses as cost of sales, warehousing, distribution, selling, administration and finance.

5   Assets

In this chapter you will learn about the typical assets you find in company reports—what they are and how they are valued. You will also discover that they are not always owned in a strict legal sense and that they cannot always be sold, yet they are regarded as assets. Most of the assets are included in Alba's accounts. Alba does not have any intangible assets but they are included in this discussion because intangibles are important and fairly common.

WHAT ARE ASSETS?

The Statement of Accounting Concepts SAC4, *Definition and Recognition of the Elements of Financial Statements*, defines and requires recognition of assets as follows:

> 'Assets' are future economic benefits controlled by the entity as a result of past transactions or other past events (paragraph 14).

> An asset should be recognised in the statement of financial position when and only when:
> (a) it is probable that the future economic benefits embodied in the asset will eventuate; and
> (b) the asset possesses a cost or other value that can be measured reliably (paragraph 38).

Control of an asset is defined (paragraph 14) as 'the capacity of the entity to benefit from the asset in the pursuit of the entity's objectives and to deny or regulate the access of others to that benefit'. The word 'probable' is defined as being more likely rather than less likely.

At the most fundamental level assets are items owned which can be sold to another party. The SAC4 definition covers items controlled as well as owned. 'Controlled' can be viewed as using the items as though they are your own.

Assets are used in the business to generate cash and make the goods and services for sale. For example, manufacturing plants manufacture goods, fax machines communicate with customers and computers produce information. Inventory are the goods you hope to sell. When you sell on credit you get another asset called debtors. You want your debtors to pay so that you have cash to use in the business.

VALUATION OF ASSETS

A reason you might produce a personal balance sheet is to obtain a loan. Those of you who have filled in a loan application will remember that you have to list your assets and your liabilities. The value you are asked to use for the assets is market value. Why? Because the lender wants to know what you are worth financially. Market value is the value a willing seller and willing buyer would agree on in a situation where neither party is under undue pressure to sell or buy.

Well, don't we as users want to know what the company is worth? Isn't market value the most useful value? The answers are 'yes', but this is not what you get. Assets are generally valued at cost except to the extent that they are revalued. Financial statements are prepared on the historical cost principle. This principle is reasonable if the purpose of financial statements is limited to measuring stewardship (i.e. the value of assets is maintained), and if the value of money and items remains fairly constant. However, today, these are irrelevant. Market value shows the value the company can obtain with its external world in a willing buyer, willing seller situation. As users of financial statements we want assets stated at market value. So, when reading financial statements we will be interested in how close the assets, especially significant assets, are to market value.

Several measures of performance are affected by the values assigned to the assets. For example the return on assets (i.e. the profit as a percentage of assets). The total value of assets is the aggregation of the individual assets. Under historical cost accounting the value of major non-current assets is often well below their current value except to the extent they have been revalued. This means the calculated profitability on assets will be overstated because the denominator (i.e. the total assets) are understated, giving a higher calculated profitability. How can you properly compare profit performance between two companies if one has revalued assets and the other has not?

Another potentially important implication of valuing assets at market value is how to account for those that have no market value—that is do you include them at some other value or exclude them? Consideration of this issue (other than what is covered in this chapter) is beyond the scope of this book.

There are two possible difficulties with assets being valued at cost or some basis of valuation other than market valuation. First, the assets may be understated because market values have risen significantly. Second, the market values may have fallen below the recorded value (e.g. because of a property crash or new technology). Perhaps the potential overstatement of asset value is less desirable because the real situation is worse than shown.

Financial statements preparation rules require:

■ current assets to be valued at realisable value when this is less than the existing recorded value;

■ non-current assets not to be valued above their recoverable amount (AASB 1010, *Accounting for Revaluation of Non-Current Assets*).

Valuation of non-current assets

Accounting standard AASB 1010, *Accounting for Revaluation of Non-Current Assets*, allows a good deal of scope for picture painting because it does not cover all the issues involved in valuing non-current assets. This section considers what the standard requires and the implications of what it does not cover.

All assets are initially recorded at cost. In Australia, non-current assets can be revalued to independent or directors' valuation. The value of non-current assets cannot exceed their recoverable amount.

The accounting standard specifies how to account for revaluations of assets and the gain or loss on disposal. The standard does not specify what are acceptable means of valuing assets, or suggest how frequently assets should be valued. Unfortunately, though required when assets are reported at directors' or independent valuation, the basis of valuation is not always meaningfully disclosed, that is it is disclosed as directors' or independent valuation but without disclosing on what premise the valuation was conducted.

Paragraph 6.2 of AASB 1034, *Information to be Disclosed in Financial Reports*, requires companies which must produce annual financial statements to provide a directors' or independent valuation of land and buildings every three years. The company can either use the valuation as the basis of valuation of the assets in the balance sheet or simply report the information in the notes to the accounts and leave the balance sheet value untouched. At least for these types of companies, a recent valuation of land and buildings is reported.

Readers tend to assume an independent valuation means market value —but it could mean economic usage, replacement cost or some other basis agreed with the valuer. Valuers have expressed concern about this lack of specification of acceptable means of valuation in the legislation. The *Sydney Morning Herald* of 17 November 1990 reported on this situation, including some comments of Mr Chris Breach, director of valuations, Jones Lang Wootton:

> The Companies Code (now replaced by Corporations Law) should be amended to stipulate valuations be independent, he said.

In Australia there are no commonly accepted standards and how properties are valued depends on the instructions of those asking for the valuation—the owner, manager or a lender . . .

In the past, a developer could ask for a valuation which assumed an unfinished project was completed and fully tenanted.

In valuing a shopping centre or office building, it had been common for the valuer to only be given a list of tenants and what was supposed to be a typical lease, and individual discounted deals were never revealed, he said. Banks that had been burnt by such valuations were now learning from the experience but in the past they had only looked at the final valuation figure without considering the assumptions on which it was based, he said.

Most clients were honest but valuers would now have to conduct far more stringent due diligence investigations and inspect every lease, he said.

In Australia our lack of specification probably increases the risk of overvaluing assets. From 30 June 1992 onwards the limitation on the ability to potentially overvalue non-current assets is that they cannot be valued greater than the recoverable amount.

In 1996 valuers introduced new standards and guidelines specifying acceptable approaches to property valuations. The *Sydney Morning Herald* of 10 February 1996 reported comments from Mr Bob Connolly, a Wagga Wagga valuer who pioneered many of the reforms while he was on various valuation industry boards. Gone are the days when valuers can accept instructions which direct them to arrive at a specified value.

A standard for general purpose finance reporting for assets will complement the comprehensive valuation report that should be done for commercial properties worth more than $1 million.

'Importantly these standards will flow through to all institutional and corporations property valuations and will reflect current property values in company documents including financial reports and prospectuses,' Mr Connolly says.

'We are taking time on the standards because we also want to conform to the standards of the related professional bodies, such as accountants and lawyers, and statutory authorities including, State and Federal Government bodies.'

Until 1996 is a long time for a response to concerns about how valuations were conducted in the 1980s. These concerns were being raised in the financial press in the early 1990s.

The New Zealand approach

The New Zealand SSAP–28, *Accounting for Fixed Assets*, limits the basis of valuation to net current value for existing use prepared in accordance with the New Zealand Institute of Valuers *Asset Valuation Standards* (paragraphs 4.15 and 4.16). Net current value is defined as 'the price for which an asset might reasonably be expected to be sold at the operative date, less the costs of disposal that could reasonably be anticipated' (paragraph 3.7).

Annual revaluations are encouraged. Valuations should be performed by independent valuers or, if done internally, by people with appropriate qualifications with the basis of valuation reviewed by a qualified independent valuer. This standard was operative from late 1991. However, many New Zealand listed companies choose not to revalue, leaving property at cost with commentary in the notes on market value.

The New Zealand SSAP–17, *Accounting for Investment Properties and Properties Intended for Sale*, requires investment properties to be recorded at 'their net current value' (paragraph 5.4), prepared in accordance with New Zealand Institute of Valuers *Asset Valuation Standards* (paragraph 4.13). They should be valued annually by a qualified independent valuer with experience of the type of property within the local area and the property should not be depreciated. This standard applied from 31 March 1989.

New Zealand had a much faster and more specific response·than Australia. Revaluations are limited to independent market valuations for existing use. This approach is in accord with most participants at seminars I have conducted. I would like to see Australia follow the New Zealand lead.

Accounting for revaluations of non-current assets

Aspects of the Australian accounting standard and related issues explained below are:

■ accounting for revaluations;
■ revaluing classes of assets;
■ capital gains tax;
■ recoverable amount;
■ disclosures required.

Accounting for revaluations

Revaluations are accounted for in a different manner from devaluations following the doctrine of conservatism. Gains on revaluation are not recognised as part of profit but are simply added directly to an asset revaluation reserve as shown in Alba's note 16. Devaluations are recognised as an expense in the calculation of profit and loss. The exception to both of these rules is where the revaluation reverses a previous devaluation (then is part of profit) or the devaluation reverses a previous revaluation (then is deducted from revaluation reserve). This is further explained under Revaluation of non-current assets in chapter 8.

The revaluation gains added directly to asset revaluation reserves can never be reported as part of profit. When combined with the accounting for profit on disposal of non-current assets (see Profit and loss on disposal later in this chapter), the implications are serious. Consider this fictitious but very possible situation. Three companies buy adjacent identical pieces of land on 1 March 1995, each paying the same price of $200 000. Conservative Ltd does not revalue assets, Pragmatist Ltd revalues when the mood takes directors and Relevant Ltd revalues to independent market value each year. Each sells their land on 30 September 1998 for $350 000. The profits reported and cumulative effect over the years are:

Date	Description	Conservative Ltd $	Pragmatist Ltd $	Relevant Ltd $
1/3/95	Land at date of purchase	200 000	200 000	200 000
30/6/95	Balance sheet value	200 000	200 000	200 000
	Revaluation gain			50 000
30/6/96	Balance sheet value	200 000	200 000	250 000
	Revaluation gain		75 000	40 000
30/6/97	Balance sheet value	200 000	275 000	290 000
	Revaluation gain			35 000
30/6/98	Balance sheet value	200 000	275 000	325 000
	Selling price	350 000	350 000	350 000
30/9/98	Reported profit on sale	150 000	75 000	25 000
	Revaluation Reserve balance	—	75 000	125 000

Each profit on sale is reported in accordance with the accounting standard, which means each is 'true and fair' in accordance with Australian requirements to follow accounting standards. Which do you think is the real profit?

Let's think about the asset revaluation reserves of Pragmatist and Relevant. If no other properties held at 30/9/98 had been revalued and all revaluation gains recorded on former properties sold had been transferred to the asset realisation reserve, then the balance of their asset revaluation reserves would be as shown above. For both companies this amount when added to the reported profit totals $150 000, but the asset revaluation is never reported as profit!

In summary the reporting is:

■ gains on revaluation added direct to asset revaluation reserve;
■ calculated profit on disposal included in profit and loss;
■ the balance in the revaluation reserve relating to the property disposed of may, if the directors want to, be transferred to an asset realisation reserve (but can never be included in the calculation of profit);
■ the gains on revaluation recorded in prior years may not be within the amount of the asset revaluation reserve at the time of sale because the reserve has been used for dividend (e.g. the issue of bonus shares).

You may wonder what the tax situation is. Capital gains tax rules would apply in the same manner to each company. The tax law ignores the accounting treatment. Capital gains tax would be the selling price less the original cost indexed upwards at the published indexing rate.

Can you see the scope for creating a desired profit on disposal by revaluing? A few listed companies do revalue prior to disposal and report a zero profit or loss on disposal.

These effects are greater when depreciable assets are revalued upwards. The revaluation gain is the difference between the revalued amount and the written down value (WDV). Depreciation starts again based on the revalued amount. This creates additional depreciation expense and means reported depreciation expense over the life of the asset will exceed the original cost, maybe even considerably. The revaluation gain has been added direct to the asset revaluation reserve. So here is a method of reducing reported profit—that is, by revaluing depreciable assets additional depreciation expense is created which reduces reported profit and the revaluation gain is never reported as profit. Directors can only revalue up to the limit of the recoverable amount.

The scope of picture painting would be reduced by treating revaluation gains as part of profit. When treated as part of profit the results for each of Conservative, Pragmatist and Relevant would all show the same profit over the four years. However, they would report different amounts of the profit in each year.

Perhaps the risk is that the gains are never really consummated by a sale of the asset which realises the valuation amount. The problem here is not the treating of an unrealised gain as profit, but the substance of the valuation. The addressing of acceptable bases of valuation will limit the risk. Valuation is discussed below.

Revaluing classes of assets

The accounting standard requires an entire class to be revalued for the entity or the group. Alternatively a systematic cyclical approach is allowed when the class of asset is substantial. This still allows freedom to choose to revalue one class and not other classes or choose to revalue each class in a different way or in different years. So land could be at independent valuation, buildings at directors' valuation and plant and equipment left at cost. This is like adding two apples, three oranges and one pear—the total is six pieces of fruit. How meaningful is it?

Before 30 June 1992 the revaluation did not have to be made for the class of assets for the *group*. The standard allowed each class of assets within each company to be treated independently, so when you read earlier sets of consolidated group accounts you may see a class of assets such as land at directors' and/or independent valuation for a number of different years. This situation continued after 30 June 1992 until the class of assets was revalued again.

After a class of assets has been revalued, there can be additions made to that class, e.g. when additional amounts are spent on a revalued building or a new building is purchased. These additions are shown at cost and will remain shown at cost until the class of assets is revalued again. This means that under the revised standard a class of assets can show one of two kinds of valuation—independent or directors' (with date shown) and cost for the items acquired since the valuation.

Capital gains tax

Where capital gains tax applies, a company will not realise the full value on disposal. It will hopefully receive the valuation but will have to pay capital gains tax. The amount of capital gains tax is usually taken into account in one of two ways. One approach is to show the valuation net of capital gains tax. Another approach is to show the gross valuation and disclose the fact that capital gains tax would apply (if the property was sold), preferably by disclosing the amount.

Alba's note 1(d) discloses that capital gains tax would be payable if the property was sold but does not disclose the amount. The amount is disclosed as a contingent liability in note 21.

Recoverable amount

The accounting standard requires that assets be carried at a value no greater than the recoverable amount. Recoverable amount is defined (paragraph 12.1 of AASB 1010) as 'in relation to an asset, the net amount that is expected to be recovered through the cash inflows and outflows arising from its continued use and subsequent disposal'.

This requires the predicting of anticipated cash flows relating to that asset into the future. Cash inflows are the revenues expected to be generated. Cash outflows are the costs of operating and maintaining the asset in working order. The predicted inflows and outflows are added together and the net amount becomes the recoverable amount. When the recoverable amount is less than the book value, the asset must be devalued to the recoverable amount.

This approach applied as described does not allow for the time value of money. Cash to be received in the future is worth less in today's dollars because of inflation and potential to earn interest if the cash is available now. So a better way to estimate recoverable amount is to discount the future cash flows to obtain a present value in today's dollars. A discount rate has to be selected. This adds yet another estimation.

The standard prefers the discounting of future cash flows, but does not require it. However, disclosure is required of whether or not discounting has been used in determining recoverable amount. The implication for users is that directors may choose not to discount, and so obtain a higher recoverable amount and so minimise or save having to reduce the book value of the assets.

But, what is the relevant value for users? It is market value. Market value may or may not relate to recoverable amount. As stated earlier, market value is the estimated price the asset would be sold for between a willing seller and a willing buyer. My view is that market value is the best 'recoverable amount' value.

Paragraph 5.1 of the standard only allows the devaluation of an asset when the 'carrying amount is greater than its recoverable amount'. Does this mean that assets cannot be written down to market value where market value is less than book value but recoverable amount is greater than book value? If so, it is an unfortunate rule because it may provide users with inappropriate, irrelevant and unrealistic information. Hopefully many directors will interpret market value as a substitute for 'recoverable amount'.

Disclosures required

Paragraph 9 of the standard requires disclosure of:

- the financial year in which a revaluation was made or the dates of a progressive revaluation period;
- the basis of the revaluation (often only limited information provided);
- the approach to determining which assets are revalued each year during the allowed three years of a progressive revaluation;
- whether amounts have been determined in accordance with an independent valuation (directors' valuations are often based on independent ones);
- in the year when an independent valuation is first used, the name and qualifications of the valuer;
- information on any policy of regular revaluation of any class of assets;
- accounting policy adopted regarding capital gains tax;
- for each class of depreciating assets clearly state which are at cost, directors' or independent valuation (including date of directors' or independent valuation); the accumulated provision for depreciation; and the net amount.

How are non-current assets valued?

The purpose of this section is to describe in broad terms how valuers determine market values for assets such as property and intangibles like brand or trade names. Basically it revolves around estimating future revenues and expenses arising from an asset and discounting the net profits back into today's dollars using a selected interest rate.

Properties

First, let's consider a commercial property such as a city office block where the value is the estimated 'normal' net profit multiplied by a capitalisation rate (see below). This is a variation of the general principle. Net profit is the rent revenue less the expenses.

Annual rental is the result of the amount of available floor space multiplied by the rate per square metre. Upper floors and ground floor shops tend to attract higher rent. The valuer has to predict future rent rate increases.

The rent increases projected in 1988 were higher than those projected in the early 1990s when Australian cities had a great deal of vacant space. The valuer must allow for the vacancy rate of the building because unoccupied space reduces available rent and so future revenue. The higher the vacancy factor, the lower the value of the property.

Next the future expenses must be predicted. These include items like local government and state government charges, repairs and maintenance of the building and its equipment, and utilities such as water and electricity not able to be recharged to the tenant. Interest incurred on financing the purchase of the property is not included as this is a cost of the way an owner structures the acquisition—that is, the balance between owner's contribution and debt financing.

The value is calculated on a 'normal' annual profit which is determined by taking the annual revenue and deducting expenses. This typical year's result is converted to a property value by dividing by a capitalisation rate. The lower the capitalisation rate the higher the property value, meaning there is a perceived higher inherent value and security of value. The lower the capitalisation rate the more exposed a purchaser is to losses if the valuer's assumptions prove incorrect.

When the property market is healthy, the capitalisation rate for a prime location city building may be around 6.5 per cent. If the 'normal' net income of the property was assessed as $15 million, the value of the property is about $230 million (15 000 000/6.5% which is [15 000 000 × 100]/6.5). However, if the market was not as healthy a higher capitalisation rate might be 8 per cent, which gives a value of almost $190 million (15 000 000/8.0% which is [15 000 000 × 100]/8.0). Thus slight variations in the capitalisation rate give wide variations in value.

Consider what these capitalisation rates mean. They relate to the rate of return on the investment prior to interest costs and income tax. A capitalisation rate of 6.5 per cent means it will take more than 15 years before the profits recover the cost of purchase (i.e. 100/6.5) whereas at 8.0 per cent it is reduced to 12.5 years.

Why do property investors accept such low yields? The assumption is that rents can be increased at time of rent reviews and so the real rate of return is increased. This works in property boom times but not during slumps. So investors did not fare well during the early 1990s when they had bought properties at the height of the boom in 1987/88. These investors offered tenants inducements to stay or free fit-outs to obtain new tenants. They went into liquidation or waited a long time to really make money.

The recoverable amount over time may exceed the price paid for the property. The current market value may be substantially less than the price paid for the property. I would prefer to see the property included at the current market price because it is a realistic value reflecting the current situation.

The introduction of standards and guidelines for property valuations was discussed earlier.

Intangibles

The same principles apply to other non-current assets. Consider the intangible asset of a newspaper masthead. The masthead (the name of the newspaper) has value when the name means sales—that is, if the name is changed there are likely to be fewer sales.

The value is calculated by estimating the sales above the level that *any* newspaper would attract in that market. The revenue of those additional sales is projected into future years. The revenue arises from the selling price of the newspaper plus the advertising revenue. A good masthead newspaper is more attractive to advertisers because of its larger readership and prestige.

There are expenses associated with these extra sales, such as the cost of printing and distributing. These expenses are deducted to give the net cash flows attributed to the additional sales generated by the good name of the newspaper.

The estimated net cash flows of the future years are discounted back into today's dollars using a discount rate. The higher the interest rate the lower the calculated value. The effect of the interest rate is similar to the capitalisation rate for properties. The base discount rate is based on a risk-free interest rate such as federal government bonds. The rate is increased to allow for factors such as the risk of the investment. Discount rates used are not disclosed.

The price paid for the privatisation of the Fairfax group in 1987 included intangible asset values calculated at a very favourable economic time shortly before the Australian share price collapse. It also preceded the recession of the early 1990s which reduced the advertising revenues of the newspapers. So the Fairfax group was placed into receivership and sold to new owners. Those who privatised it lost hundreds of millions of dollars. Those who purchased it out of liquidation have made hundreds of millions of dollars. The same pattern occurred with the three commercial television networks.

Considerations for users of financial statements

The two illustrations above show there are many assumptions required, e.g. future revenues, expenses, interest and capitalisation rates. Generally values calculated at the top of an economic cycle will be far higher than those at a lower point. Perhaps this reflects our Western world preoccupation with short term returns and performance measurement. A longer term view might result in some allowance for the effect of the economic cycle.

A further complicating factor is how those valuing the assets are remunerated. If this is based on the value of the asset (which it often is), there is at the very least a subtle pressure to produce high valuations. Consider also that the values are usually commissioned by the current owners in whose interest it is to have as high a value as possible.

When we look at the values from potential purchasers' point of view, if they pay the full valuation amount they must make a better rate of return than the rate reflected in the valuation in order to make any real profit on the asset. The discount rate used may not sufficiently allow for risks arising from owning the assets. They will also have to finance the purchase. This is assuming that all the estimates are reasonable. The potential purchaser needs to allow an element of risk when buying and so should evaluate the asset using a higher interest rate. Should we be so bold as to say only a foolish purchaser pays the full valuation amount?

CASH

	1997 $	1996 $
Total cash as shown on Alba's balance sheet	225 632	158 731

First read Alba's accounts note 6.

Cash is the money in the bank accounts and petty cash held on the premises. Banks and retailers also have cash in the till. We expect cash to be worth the amount it is stated at, but the management must check that the cash is collectable. Some banks have failed and a company or other entity with cash in a failed or suspect financial institution must evaluate the recoverability and allow for likely loss. This is usually rare.

How do management know they have recorded the right amount? They can check their records against the bank statements. There will be differences such as unpresented cheques which have been sent to suppliers but not yet deposited by the suppliers. In this case the entity's records are correct. Another difference can be the month's bank charges which are not known until the bank statement is received. The entity's records are adjusted because the bank statement provides new information that should be included in the entity's records. The principle of checking internal records against available external records is one of the best means of internal control.

Many entities also have cash on deposit with banks, financial institutions and, sometimes, with major corporations. These deposits are usually cash that is surplus to day to day needs, or a deliberate investment decision because the interest rate is a good rate of return compared with other forms of investment. Effective management of cash includes maximising interest earned as well as minimising interest paid. Large organisations monitor their cash needs on a daily basis and will make deposits and withdrawals against money on deposit each day.

Alba has cash on deposit of $150 000. You may find cash on deposit disclosed on the balance sheet or under cash, current receivables or current assets—other. If cash has been placed on deposit for more than twelve months (which is unusual), then it would be a non-current asset. You need to read the supporting notes to the accounts to find this information. Remember the balance sheet is a summary statement; to be fully informed you must read the notes.

RECEIVABLES

	1997 $	1996 $
Balance sheet: current receivables	433 905	389 850
Non-current receivables: loan to a director	50 000	50 000

First, read Alba's accounts notes 7 and 1(g).

Current receivables consists of all the items owing to the entity due to be paid within twelve months of the balance sheet date. Most exist because something has been sold on credit terms rather than cash. The largest item is usually trade debtors.

Trade debtors

Trade debtors represent money owing by customers. The amounts are due to be paid within the credit terms of the entity. However, some debtors pay slowly and, worse still, some never pay. Organisations should have credit control checking to minimise the risk of selling to a customer which fails to pay its debt.

An entity must keep records for each debtor, monitoring sales and payments. Total debtors is the aggregate of the amounts owing by debtors at a given date. Most organisations monitor their debtors over a monthly cycle:

	Opening balance
add:	Credit sales
less:	Cash receipts
less:	Credits, e.g. returns of inventory, overpricing
gives:	Closing balance

Most entities' trade debtors are current, however trade debtors can also be non-current. Have you borrowed from a financial institution, such as a bank, to buy a car or a home? You repay the loan over a period much greater than a year. You are one of the financial institution's trade debtors. So most of its trade debtors are likely to be non-current. Other organisations may also sell to some customers on terms longer than one year. Those selling to farmers may be willing to tie the payment to the receipt of money on the sale of the harvested crop.

Alba does not have any non-current trade debtors.

Provision for doubtful debts

The entire amount owing from all debtors is unlikely to be received. There probably will be some debts that will become bad debts. Trade debtors are required to be shown at the amount that will be collected. Management does this by writing off (removing) all known bad debts during the year and creating a provision for doubtful debts, which is shown as a deduction from trade debtors in note 7 of Alba's accounts.

Typically the provision for doubtful debts is only seen as a deduction from trade debtors. However, management must consider all debtors and create a provision for the amount considered doubtful against any of these debtors. This applies to non-current as well as current debtors.

In New Zealand accounts, the provision for doubtful debts does not have to be, and thus is usually not, disclosed.

Bills of exchange

These are promissory notes Alba has received from some of its debtors as payment of debt. At the end of the period of the bill of exchange (usually 90 days), the issuer of the bill has to pay the debt to Alba. Perhaps Alba will allow another promissory note to be issued, but continual reissuing may indicate an inability to pay (honour) the bill and, thus, a bad debt situation.

Bills of exchange can often be discounted with a bank. The bank pays cash for the bill, but not the full face value of the bill. An amount is deducted as interest. The banks have a rate of interest they charge. When the discounted bill is due for payment, the bank collects the face value of the bill from the original issuer. If this party cannot pay, the bank generally has recourse, in turn, to each of the parties who accepted and then passed on the bill.

If Alba has any bills out on discount at balance sheet date, then there is a potential liability—that is, if the issuer does not pay the bank when the amount is due, then Alba becomes liable for repayment of the money to the bank. In the accounts there is no such liability, which indicates no issuer has forfeited on their repayment. Any discounted bills at balance sheet date would be included in the contingent liability note 21. Alba should show the face value of all outstanding discounted bills receivable at balance sheet date. The fact that the note does not disclose this means there are no discounted bills at balance sheet date.

Other debtors

These are amounts owing to Alba within twelve months of the balance sheet date but they have arisen for reasons other than trade debtors and bills receivable. Typical items can be deposits paid as surety to providers of electricity and gas services, amounts owing as a result of sale of old equipment on credit, and refund due on a cancelled insurance policy.

Loans to directors

Amounts owing by or to directors must be separately disclosed. The balance sheet shows this company has a small loan of $50 000 owing by a director. It is due for payment more than twelve months after the balance sheet date and so is included as non-current. Many proprietary companies have loans to directors. There can also be tax consequences with the Taxation Office viewing the loan as a remuneration to the directors. These are often not repaid until retirement. Sometimes they are even forgiven by the company over a period of time.

The nature of the terms and conditions are disclosed in the year of the loan. This is not a new loan and so this disclosure is not required. The Corporations Law requires companies other than proprietary companies to have shareholder approval for the granting of a loan. Because of the abuse of loans to directors, the approval processes required have been tightened considerably since the early 1980s.

Accounting standard AASB 1017, *Related Party Disclosures*, gives the disclosures required for directors and other people or entities classed as related to the reporting entity. The standard is wide ranging with its definitions, to try to catch any related party. So 'loans to directors' includes directors' spouses and other close relatives and their (or their spouses') relatives' companies.

Why has a standard with such convoluted definitions been created? The late 1980s saw many high-flying entrepreneurs who took more than a reasonable amount from their listed public groups. Often little was disclosed, as they used means that were not classed as related parties to extract the money. So the definition of related party has been incredibly tightened. The danger still exists that the unscrupulous will disguise the related party transaction to such a degree that fellow directors and auditors will be hard pressed to find it.

Loans

Companies, other than financial institutions, quite frequently may lend to third parties beside directors. It is not a major business activity. Perhaps some relationship exists such as an important customer needing some financing.

The loan is classified as current or non-current based on repayment terms. If the loan is secured, it should be described as a secured loan. These loans are generally only a modest amount compared with most assets on the balance sheet. A reader should be concerned if these loans are a major amount and the entity is not in the business of lending money.

Alba does not have any loan assets other than directors' loans.

INVENTORIES

	1997 $	1996 $
Total inventory at lower of cost and net realisable value	508 723	454 245

Read Alba's accounts notes 8 and 1(h).

For a retailer, wholesaler or manufacturer inventory is the core of its business. The successful management of inventory means the success of the company. You should only buy or make inventory which you can sell. Predicting the market for your products and the right product mix is a very difficult and demanding task.

The financial results are governed by the inventory included in the balance sheet. As shown in chapter 1, the basic formula for calculating profit is:

	Sales
less:	Cost of sales ------>
gives:	Gross profit
less:	Selling expenses
	Administration expenses
add:	Other income such as interest earned
gives:	Operating profit/(loss) before tax
less:	Income tax expense
gives:	Operating profit/(loss) after tax

Cost of sales is calculated as:

Opening inventory
add: Purchases (plus factory labour and manufacturing overheads for a manufacturer)
less: Closing inventory
gives: Cost of sales

Thus the higher the closing inventory, the lower the cost of sales and the higher gross profit and operating profit. From the readers of financial statements viewpoint we want to be satisfied the inventory exists, is owned and is appropriately valued. Valuation is especially important for damaged, old and obsolete inventory.

The following sections cover retailers and wholesalers as well as manufacturers.

Accounting standard AASB 1019, *Measurement and Presentation of Inventories in the Context of the Historical Cost System*, specifies the acceptable approaches to inventory, which are covered in this section.

Classification

The three main classifications for inventory are raw materials, work in progress and finished goods. Wholesalers and retailers generally only hold finished goods.

Work in progress is all the inventory in various stages of production—that is, the raw materials have begun the production process, but the finished goods are not yet completed. (An example is the manufacture of a chest of drawers—some might only have the frame made; some might have the frame plus incomplete drawers; some might have the frame and drawers but not yet varnished; some might be varnished but the drawer handles not yet attached.)

In some balance sheets you may see other classifications such as 'in transit'. An example is goods onboard ship—the inventory became the property of the purchaser when loaded on the ship. Another classification is 'stores' or 'consumables' which means items used up (over time) in production but which are not raw materials; an example could be tools.

Lower of cost and net realisable value

The note on inventory and the accounting policy note show that inventories are valued at the lower of cost and net realisable value. In the case of debtors and cash, the 'cost' value is usually the same as the market value (after allowing for doubtful debts). With inventory, market value should be well above cost as the entity makes money by selling inventory at a profit.

This puts us on the alert because the accounting policy note for inventory shows that when net realisable value (NRV) is less than cost, NRV is used. NRV is the selling price less the extra costs estimated for getting the items sold. This could be a special advertising campaign, shipment costs or fixing damaged or old inventory for a special sale.

Clearly the entity must be able to sell most of its inventory well above NRV if it is going to be profitable. We would be concerned if a significant portion of inventory was at NRV. My rule of thumb is that inventory at NRV should be less than 2.5 per cent (i.e. about one in 40 items are anticipated to be sold for less than cost).

The acceptable level of inventory at NRV will vary for different industries. For instance, those producing fashion goods face a higher risk of producing unsaleable lines (because they have not predicted the market trends). Success comes through producing the right proportion of successful stock lines.

Consider making films. Films are the film-maker's inventory. The big American movie studios are ecstatic if they have a few blockbusters. *Home Alone* is an example. It cost about $18 million to make and grossed over $500 million worldwide. Twentieth Century Fox made a huge proportion of that year's profit on this one success. A year without at least one box office success is a disaster!

Unfortunately the typical disclosure is a mixture of cost and NRV. It would be an advantage to users if they were disclosed separately because it would enable you to see what proportion of inventory is not expected to recover cost. The user cannot tell what portion is not expected to recover cost.

An example of comparing cost with NRV:

	Cost of making one gloop (fictitious product)	$25
	Current selling price per unit	28
less:	Estimated selling expenses of special newspaper ad and distribution costs per unit	5
gives:	NRV	$23

NRV is less than cost so use NRV for this inventory item.

Items of inventory cannot be included twice. So inventories included at NRV are different items from inventories included at cost.

A proposed amendment to the standard, if adopted, will require disclosure of NRV separately from cost. If adopted, the amendment will be effective from 30 June 1998.

What is cost?

Imagine a factory bustling with activity, the noise of the machines, the conversations of the workers, goods in various stages of production. The materials used in production are brought to the start of the production line. The finished goods are loaded onto pallets and taken by forklift to the warehouse. The building is made of metal with a high roof. Electricity is used to power the machines and provide lighting.

The production manager and staff determine which items to make and how many at a time. On their computer screens they can find out current levels of finished goods inventory and estimated sales in the near future. The manager liaises with the warehouse and sales managers to develop the production schedule. Each of the three production lines is producing a different item.

Out on the factory floor, supervisors oversee the work, quality control checks output, and twice a day there is the change of shift. This factory is busy working three shifts a day round the clock.

And through all this activity the cost of producing each item is calculated. 'How can this be done?' you ask. With great difficulty. There is much activity to monitor and many items adding to the cost of production. In the end the costs can only be estimated. So we have run into a limitation on accuracy. Cost is not always easy to measure. Estimations mean that assumptions must be made on how the goods are produced, the amount of labour and raw materials required and the amount of wastage and rework due to errors in production.

An additional problem is that costs include some items which relate to production of individual products and some relate to many or all products.

The costs which relate to more than one product line have to be allocated over all the production lines involved—more estimation.

Now that we perceive how hard measuring cost can be, let's see what the broad approach is.

Elements of cost

The only costs included as part of the cost of inventory (for valuation on the balance sheet and in calculating cost of sales) are the costs of manufacture for a manufacturer or the costs of getting the inventory into store for a wholesaler or retailer. Other costs such as distribution, selling and administration are not included. True, they are overhead costs, but the practice in management accounting is to treat them as facets of the operation beyond the production or inventory purchase cycle. This was discussed in chapter 4 under the explanation of Alba's detailed profit and loss statement.

So the parts of cost in determining a manufacturer's cost of inventory are:

■ raw materials—cost of bringing them in which is the cost charged by the supplier plus freight inwards and, if imported, customs and excise duties;

■ labour used directly in the production process, i.e. the people working on the production line;

■ manufacturing overheads such as rent of the factory (or depreciation, council rates and land tax for owned premises), power, lighting, supervisors' wages and all other costs associated with running the production facility.

The manufacturing overheads are classed as either variable or fixed. 'Variable' means the expense varies with the level of production—such as electricity costs which vary with use of machines and lighting. 'Fixed' means the expense remains constant and is not affected by changes in level of production, e.g. council rates on owned premises. There is some overlap between fixed and variable costs which makes the measurement a little more complex. We will leave that to the management accountants as we only need to understand the general principles. Fixed and variable costs can be represented diagramatically as in figure 5.1.

So for each product the costs of raw materials and direct labour are established and assigned together with a proportion of manufacturing overhead. The overhead is the most difficult to apportion. The calculation must allow for factors such as total estimated overheads for the year, time taken on production line by each product, and how overheads vary with level of production.

The inclusion of fixed manufacturing overheads (as well as raw materials, labour and variable manufacturing overheads) is known as 'absorption' or 'full absorption' costing. It must be used by manufacturers in Australian and New Zealand accounts and tax returns. (Excluding fixed manufacturing overheads in valuing inventory is called direct or variable costing.)

Two other matters need to be considered: costs of labour and raw materials vary over time, and amount of time and raw materials used in

Fixed

$

production

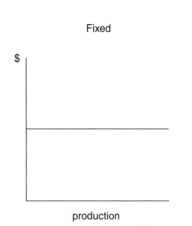

Variable

$

production

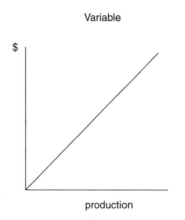

Figure 5.1

Manufacturing overheads

producing an item will vary up and down. Assumptions used in allocating costs will affect determination of what is cost. Users need to understand that different cost assignment rules are used and each one will give a different inventory cost value. Sets of accounts should disclose which method has been used, but will not (and are unable to) disclose the difference in inventory value using one method compared with another.

The four cost assignment methods allowed in Australia are set out below.

1 Specific identification, which is the actual cost of making each item or batch and keeping track of the item or batch from production through warehousing to sale. The cost of monitoring can be prohibitive, so this method is generally used with large or expensive items.

2 First-in, first-out (FIFO), which assumes the first items or batches purchased or manufactured are the first ones sold. The actual situation in the warehouse may be the opposite, but the situation in the warehouse is not considered. The cost of each item or batch is monitored so that as each item or batch is sold, the cost assigned to it is the cost of the oldest inventory on hand at the time of sale.

3 Weighted average cost, where the cost of making each new item or batch is added to the existing inventory on hand and a new average calculated. Each item or batch sold is assigned the average applicable at the time of sale.

4 Standard cost, where a standard is set for production of each item or batch. It involves the standard amount and cost of raw material plus the standard time required to make the item at the standard hourly rate plus an allocation of manufacturing overhead. Standard cost is allowed to be used where it approximates actual. Thus a standard would be expected to be a realistic 'close to balance sheet date' measurement.

In the international accounting standard, FIFO and weighted average cost are the preferred approaches with specific identification allowed when the inventory items are unique and are specific projects (or jobs). An alternative called LIFO (last-in, first-out) is allowed to accommodate the USA. New Zealand follows the international approach except LIFO is not permitted.

Alba's accounting policy note states raw materials are valued using FIFO, and finished goods and work in progress include raw materials, labour and manufacturing overheads.

Provision for obsolescence

Alba has allowed a small provision for diminution in value of raw materials. This is like the provision for doubtful debts. Inventory has to be at the lower of cost or net realisable value. A provision can be used to approximate or allow for obsolete or slow moving (selling) items of inventory for which a realisable value cannot be determined readily.

The provisions are more common in some industries than others. They are often used for fashion or entertainment industry goods where sales are limited to a short period. Consider popular rock'n'roll—songs last only a short time on the hit parade. Provisions are based on a projected period over which the inventory will be sold, e.g. if last quarter's sales were 300 units and 1000 units are on hand (valued at a cost of $1.00 each), then inventory will take almost a year to sell. Let's say the provision is based on none required for first three months, 25 per cent for second quarter, 50 per cent for third quarter and 100 per cent for fourth quarter—this gives:

| | Sales last 3 mths | Stock total | Provision calculated by projecting sales in months ahead | | | |
			1–3	4–6	7–9	10–12
Item	300	1000	300	300	300	100
Provision		(325)	(0)	(75)	(150)	(100)
Net inventory		675	300	225	150	0

Non-current inventory

Sometimes you see some inventory classed as non-current. It is probably work in progress which will take more than twelve months from balance sheet date to complete and sell. It is probably large scale projects.

An example is a property developer which makes money from building and selling property. The development takes more than twelve months. Another example (as mentioned in chapter 2) is ship building.

These types of projects, because of the money and risk involved, are closely monitored. Specific identification is the appropriate cost assignment method. All costs are carefully recorded. We would expect that a comprehensive contract has been signed which covers the price and procedures for variation in contract and price.

The companies with projects such as these have budgeted their revenue and expenses and profit. When should the profit be recognised? Accounting standard AASB 1009, *Accounting for Construction Contracts*, requires the recognition of profit earned over the period of the contract. The profit recognised is proportional to the stage of completion and, so, if half the contract has been completed, half the expected profit should be recognised. This is known as the 'percentage of completion' method of profit recognition.

Sometimes contracts are completed at a loss. The rule for recognition of losses on contract is that the entire anticipated loss expected on the contract should be recognised as soon as it is foreseeable.

Companies with these types of business prudently arrange for progress payments to provide the cash flow needed to pay the outgoings on the contracts. An invoice for a progress payment reduces the value of the work in progress (because part of the work in progress has become a sale) and increases the value of debtors—which is then reduced when the cash is collected. The total amount of the work in progress with the amount invoiced to customers (which is deducted to obtain net work in progress) must be shown in the accounts.

INVESTMENTS

	1997 $	1996 $
Total value of investments at cost	121 104	63 904

Read Alba's accounts notes 9 and 1(f).

Investments are shown as non-current assets, except for any investments expected to be sold within twelve months which should be included as current assets.

Investments are additional assets not needed for the main part of the business. They are generally acquired using surplus cash the business is not using to buy plant and equipment or fund the working capital necessary to keep production going. They can also be a strategic linking with other businesses, e.g. investing in the business of an important customer or supplier to foster the continuation of the relationship. Another reason for investing in other businesses can be the eventual expansion of activities through buying existing entities.

Alba's investments are included in the balance sheet at cost.

Alba has typical investments. Note 8 segregates the investments into listed and unlisted ones. Most are in listed companies and some in unlisted. Accounting standard AASB 1033, *Presentation and Disclosure of Financial*

Instruments, requires disclosure of net fair values of each class of investment. (See chapter 8.)

The quoted market value net of selling costs of each type of listed investment is given at the end of the note. The net market value of the listed shares which cost $62 465 is $75 874. This uses the market value at balance date and is calculated by finding the balance sheet date Stock Exchange share price for each listed company in which Alba holds shares, multiplied by the number of shares held in each company less the brokerage costs.

Under AASB 1033 an estimated fair value of the unlisted shares and units is given. There is no readily available market value. Alba's directors assessed current values of the underlying major assets and liabilities. This assessment could be difficult and time consuming.

Value of Alba's investments

The net market value of the listed shares and fixed interest securities exceeds the cost value, however the net market value of listed debentures and unit trusts is below cost.

Should Alba have valued these debentures and unit trusts at net fair value instead of cost? Recoverable amount (explained under valuing non-current assets—see above) and market value net of disposal costs should be considered in answering this question.

■ The cost of listed debentures is $2874 compared with market value of $2674, only a small difference. On maturity, the amount received will be the face value of the debenture, which is probably a round amount like $3000 and is higher than either value. The small difference and future amount to be received is a situation where leaving debentures at cost is reasonable.

■ The cost of the listed unit trusts is $4741 compared with market value of $3874. This is a larger difference and future value depends upon the market reaction to the trusts. So there is a stronger case that cost may be an unrealistic value. However, the difference of $867 is small when compared with the total value of investments and the operating profit. It is an insignificant and immaterial amount. On this basis, it is reasonable not to take any action.

If the market value was substantially lower than cost or recoverable amount, then I would prefer the investments to be shown at the market value.

To conclude on the information shown in Alba's investment note we can divide the total investments into those listed and those unlisted and compare the listed with the total net fair value:

	Cost $	Net fair value $
Listed investments	105 656	120 462
Unlisted investments	15 448	17 008
Total	121 104	137 470

This shows that for listed investments the market value comfortably exceeds cost and that unlisted investments are not major. The assessed net market value of unlisted shares is not much above cost. The use of cost on the balance sheet for listed investments does not result in a major undervaluation of the asset, especially as investments are not a main asset of the business.

PROPERTY, PLANT AND EQUIPMENT

	1997 $	1996 $
Total book value of property, plant and equipment	988 256	900 425

Read Alba's accounts notes 10, 1(d) and 1(e).

The major issues to consider here are the different kinds of property, plant and equipment (including leased assets); depreciation (recognising that items wear out over time); and aspects of valuation. In the past and in many other countries the term fixed assets is used instead of property, plant and equipment.

The total book value of each class of fixed asset must be shown. Within each class the gross value of assets, the depreciation and the net value (written down value) must be shown. These assets can be valued at cost, directors' or independent value or a mixture.

The basis of valuation used and the year in which it was done must be disclosed. So sometimes you will see land, for example, under each of cost, directors' and/or independent valuation. This means that different parcels of land are recorded in the books using different valuation methods. The year of the directors' or independent valuation must also be shown. Thus if parcels of land, for example, were revalued in different years, each year and the total directors' or independent valuation for that year must be disclosed. The approach to valuation is explained under 'How are non-current assets valued?' above. This approach and the disclosure requirements apply to all non-current assets.

Thus, in Alba's accounts, note 10 shows land and buildings 'at cost' for 1996 and 'at directors' valuation 1997' for 1997. Note 16 (Asset Revaluation Reserve) shows that land and buildings were revalued in 1997 and note 4 (Abnormal Items) shows property was sold in 1996. Thus the reason for the change from cost to directors' valuation is that the land and buildings were revalued during 1997. So it is the same property in each year, but valued in different ways. (If it had been an independent valuation, the name and qualifications of the professional valuer would also have to be disclosed.)

Classes of property, plant and equipment

A class is a group of like items combined for accounting disclosure purposes. Alba shows four classes—freehold land, freehold buildings, plant and equipment and plant and equipment under lease.

Other possible classes are leasehold land, buildings on leasehold land, leasehold improvements and equipment/premises under construction (used sometimes when major equipment/plant/factory is being built).

Accounting standard AASB 1021, *Depreciation of Non-Current Assets*, requires land and buildings to be shown separately. So the cost or revalued amount has to be apportioned between the two (paragraph 5.1). In some accounts land and buildings are combined and called 'property'. This is allowed for investment properties only, i.e. where the company does not occupy most of or use the property itself.

Leasehold land is that which is acquired on a long term lease basis (e.g. a 99 year lease). In Australia, places such as Canberra and parts of Queensland, the land is not sold freehold, but held by the government and leased long term generally without the expectation that the government will take over the land at the end of the lease. So, mostly, though it may be leasehold, it is as good as freehold.

Leasehold buildings are usually buildings erected on leasehold land where the same company owns both. Sometimes, leasehold buildings are buildings erected by a company on another entity's land. The company acquires a leasehold right to erect and use the building. The lease payment consists of an upfront lump sum and/or annual rent. The property generally reverts to the landowner at the end of the lease.

Leasehold improvements are internal walls and other improvements built to make leased premises usable by the tenant, e.g. fitting out offices in a city office block. They are usually built at the tenant's expense and required to be removed at the end of the lease unless the lessor agrees otherwise. The accounts of the tenant will include these leasehold improvements as part of its property, plant and equipment and depreciate them over the shorter of the useful life or lease period.

Plant and equipment under lease

Plant and equipment under lease is plant and equipment which is being acquired through leasing. Legally, leased items are owned by the lessor (the financier leasing the assets to its customers), but the accounting treatment is determined by the substance of the transaction. So leases are classified as either finance or operating leases.

Finance leases are those in which, in reality, the rights, duties and privileges of ownership reside with the lessee (the party using the assets). In other words, the lessee is really buying the asset over time and has borrowed finance in the form of leasing. Operating leases are those leases which are purely renting of the items. The lessee will not end up acquiring the asset. A typical example is the leasing of office space in a building—it is unlikely the tenant will gain an interest in the building—the tenant would have to pay a much higher level of rent.

As you can imagine, sometimes it may be hard to determine whether a lease is an operating or finance lease. In fact, you will learn when reading about lease liabilities in the next chapter why many preparers of accounts want leases to be operating rather than finance leases!

Any property, plant and equipment which is being acquired under a finance lease is accounted for in exactly the same way as any other property, plant and equipment, i.e. the initial recorded value of the asset is its cost (at date of acquisition), it can be revalued to directors' or independent values, and it is depreciated. So the following information applies to these leased assets as well.

Depreciation

Property, plant and equipment wear out over time, they are not eternal. The principles of depreciation discussed here can (and are required to) be applied to all non-current assets by AASB 1021, *Depreciation of Non-Current Assets*. The term amortisation can be used instead of depreciation, typically for intangible and leased assets. Assets which do not decline in value, such as land, are not depreciated.

The limited life of these assets is recognised by depreciating them over their useful life. Useful life is defined (in paragraph 12.1) as:

(a) the estimated period of time over which the future economic benefits embodied in a depreciable asset are expected to be consumed by the entity; or

(b) the estimated total service, expressed in terms of production or similar units, that is expected to be obtained from the asset by the entity.

This definition was introduced in 1996. The depreciation period is linked to the use of the asset by the entity. Previously it was linked to the physical life of the asset. This change meant an adjustment to depreciation for some listed companies. Alba was not affected.

There are a number of ways of calculating depreciation. Two common methods are 'straight line' and 'diminishing value' (or reducing balance). Straight line means the same amount of depreciation is charged each year. Diminishing value gives a reducing charge over the life of the assets. Diminishing value recognises that costs of maintaining the asset are likely to be higher as the asset ages and to even the total cost of the asset (depreciation and maintenance), greater depreciation is charged in the early years. Diminishing value is also useful for assets which are subject to early obsolescence because of technological advances (e.g. computers).

Let's learn these methods through an example. Smash-Em-Up, a scrap metal dealer, buys a new metal compacter for $225 000. The machine is estimated to have a useful life of five years. The useful life was determined by the financial controller in conjunction with the yard manager using the supplier's technical specifications. After the five years, the machine will have a scrap metal value of $25 000 (this is called the residual value). So the depreciation required is that which reduces the value to $25 000 over five years—a total depreciation of $200 000. The machine was acquired on 1 October 1996 and the financial year end is 30 June.

Using the straight line method the depreciation required each year is $40 000, but the machine is only held for nine months of the first year which means depreciation would only be $30 000 in that year. In table form we can show this as follows (amounts in dollars):

Date	Original cost $	Depreciation charged in P&L $	WDV $	Accumulated provision for depreciation $
1/10/96	225 000	—	225 000	—
30/6/97	225 000	30 000	195 000	30 000
30/6/98	225 000	40 000	155 000	70 000
30/6/99	225 000	40 000	115 000	110 000
30/6/00	225 000	40 000	75 000	150 000
30/6/01	225 000	40 000	35 000	190 000
30/6/02	225 000	10 000	25 000	200 000

WDV stands for written-down value, which is the net value of the asset at the end of each financial year. In 2002 only $10 000 depreciation is charged because we only depreciate to the residual value. The asset is reported in the balance sheet at its original cost less provision for depreciation:

Each year end	30/6/97 $	30/6/98 $	30/6/99 $	30/6/00 $	30/6/01 $	30/6/02 $
Cost	225 000	225 000	225 000	225 000	225 000	225 000
Provision for dep'n	30 000	70 000	110 000	150 000	190 000	200 000
WDV	195 000	155 000	115 000	75 000	35 000	25 000

We have considered one asset. Each asset is accounted for in the same manner. The figures included in the accounts (as in Alba's note 10) are the aggregation of assets held in each class of asset.

Let's look at the same example using diminishing value (reducing balance). In diminishing value we compute depreciation on the written-down value, which is a declining amount. Therefore the depreciation rate needs to be greater to achieve a final net value approximating the residual value over the same period of time. We will use 40 per cent.

Date	Beginning WDV $	Depreciation charged in P&L $	Closing WDV $	Accumulated provision for depreciation $
1/10/96	225 000	—	225 000	—
30/6/97	225 000	67 500	157 500	67 500
30/6/98	157 500	63 000	94 500	130 500
30/6/99	94 500	37 800	56 700	168 300
30/6/00	56 700	22 680	34 020	190 980
30/6/01	34 020	9 020	25 000	200 000

Using a depreciation rate of 40 per cent results in $200 000 depreciation charged in less than five years. A depreciation rate of 30 per cent takes about seven years.

The presentation for the balance sheet is the same no matter what method of depreciation is used, i.e. the book value (cost) less the total provision for depreciation.

If the directors decided to revalue this equipment, the new value would be substituted for the old cost and depreciation would start again over the useful life. This results in greater depreciation being charged than the original cost of the asset.

Tax depreciation

Accounting depreciation is based on useful life whereas tax depreciation is that specified in the depreciation schedules. The schedules may or may not be based on useful life. The schedules are varied from time to time. For example, in part of the 1980s we had accelerated depreciation which allowed companies much improved rates, and in the early 1990s an economic life concept and increased specified rates were introduced. Governments can change these at any time.

Larger corporations tend to follow the accounting concept, usually resulting in the accounting depreciation being different from the tax depreciation. Smaller businesses generally follow tax depreciation rates, as it is easier than keeping two sets of records and creating more adjustments to be made between accounting profit and taxable income. Aspects and implications of these differences are considered in the 'income tax' section of chapter 8.

Profit or loss on disposal

Profit or loss on disposal of non-current assets is calculated as the difference between selling price and book value. Using the Smash-Em-Up example, let's say that the metal compacter was sold on 31 October 2000 for $60 000 and that the straight line depreciation method had been used. The profit or loss on disposal is calculated as:

		$
	Selling price	60 000
less:	WDV at 31/10/00	61 667
gives:	Loss on disposal	(1 667)

WDV at 31/10/00 is calculated as:

	Book value (WDV) at 30/6/00	75 000
less:	Depreciation for four months to 1/10/00	13 333
gives:	WDV at 31/10/00	61 667

Profit or loss on disposal is always calculated as the selling price less the book value even when assets have been revalued. This creates opportunities for massaging reported profits, as explained under valuation of non-current assets.

Valuation

The importance of this area was explained earlier in this chapter. We, as financial statements users, are interested in the current market value of the assets. Land and buildings are usually the fixed assets that need to be revalued. (Large companies are required to obtain an independent or directors' valuation every three years and report the valuation in the accounts.) The written-down value of plant and equipment is usually a reasonable enough approximation of market.

In Australia, the location of owned or leased properties does not have to be reported but listed companies generally report their office locations. Companies do not indicate whether the properties are owned or leased. However, in some Asian countries this valuable information is reported, including whether owned or leased. This enables a user to obtain approximate values. Naturally this is limited to larger users as it is beyond the reach of the 'mum and dad' shareholders. The addition of this information in Australia would be useful.

INTANGIBLES

Alba does not have any intangible assets, but they are a very important type of asset. (You can skip this section if you wish without losing continuity of understanding of Alba.) Intangible assets have featured in a number of recent corporate collapses. Prices paid for them or valuations assigned to them were proven to be far too high when these corporations faced tougher times—they could not make enough money out of the assets to justify the price paid or cover the borrowings incurred to finance them.

The meaning of the word 'intangible' should be implanted firmly in our minds when assessing the substance of intangible assets. *Webster's New Collegiate Dictionary* simply says intangible is 'not tangible'. Its definition of tangible is 'capable of being perceived especially by the sense of touch, substantially real, capable of being precisely realized by the mind, capable of being appraised by an actual or approximate value'. So, if intangible is 'not tangible', its meaning is the opposite of this.

The very definition of intangible must make any prudent user of financial statements sceptical of any intangible assets included in a balance sheet. I am very wary of all intangible assets.

Intangible assets include brand names (or trade names), mastheads (i.e. newspaper titles), television and radio licences (the right to broadcast), patents and franchises, to name the more common ones, and goodwill. All, except goodwill, are known as specifically identifiable intangible assets. Goodwill is like a leftover intangible—the one left after identifying all the ones you can.

There is AASB 1013, *Accounting for Goodwill*, but none specifically governing other intangible assets. This situation's effect on Australian reporting has been very significant. The introduction of the goodwill accounting standard in 1987 led to many companies 'discovering' specifically identifiable intangible assets. The reason for this was that the goodwill accounting requirement of compulsory amortisation did not apply to other intangibles. A proposed accounting standard was developed for intangibles, but was withdrawn early in 1992. There was strong resistance to its requirement to amortise intangibles. Australia will consider a standard on intangibles when the International Accounting Standards Committee does.

In Australia, intangibles other than goodwill can be revalued or a value can be created for previously unrecognised specifically identifiable intangibles. The USA does not allow revaluation or recognition of intangibles not purchased from another party; and it also requires them to be amortised over a period up to 40 years. The period seems excessive—see below.

We will consider goodwill first and then other typical kinds of intangibles.

Goodwill

As stated above, goodwill is the unidentifiable intangible. Some see it as the magic ingredient which enables a business to make superior profits and later be sold at a profit. Some see it as the savings from not having to establish the operation yourself. Some see it as the value of established customer relationships and other important business relationships. The financial statements user needs to assess this asset carefully in the light of what is known of the entity's current situation and bearing in mind the general lack of solidity of intangibles.

Figure 5.2

Jopewi Pty
Ltd example

	Fair value $	Book value $
Assets		
Cash	15 839	15 839
Trade debtors (net of provision for doubtful debts)	231 847	238 458
Inventories	294 330	307 487
Prepayments	34 278	34 278
Investments	29 441	12 883
Property, plant and equipment	449 835	386 992
Future income tax benefit	55 490	55 490
Total assets	1 111 060	1 051 427
Liabilities		
Trade creditors and accruals	305 823	298 644
Loans	250 000	250 000
Provision for income tax	34 905	35 314
Provision for employee entitlements	178 436	178 436
Total liabilities	769 164	762 394
Net assets	341 896	289 033

Goodwill can only be recognised on the acquisition of an entity or business. Goodwill is calculated as the difference between the purchase price and the fair value of the assets acquired net of the liabilities acquired. Typically the fair value is the market value at the time of acquisition.

This is logical in the historical cost context because the cost to the purchaser is the market value at time of acquisition, not the values as recorded in the accounts of the entity or business acquired.

In 1998 Alba purchases another company. It pays $550 000 and acquires Jopewi Pty Limited which has assets and liabilities as shown in figure 5.2.

The goodwill is $208 104, being purchase price of $550 000 less the fair value of the net assets of $341 896. As in this example, there are often differences between fair value and book value. Debtors and inventories were reduced because some debtors were unlikely to pay and some inventory was obsolete. Property, plant and equipment increased because of higher market value of the property. The greatest risk with liabilities is that they may be understated. A review of trade creditors showed a small amount had been omitted.

So Alba has been prepared to pay $208 104 extra to obtain Jopewi. Why are they prepared to do this and what do they gain? Gains include the acquisition of an established business, saving them the time and cost of establishing it from nothing. Sometimes it provides diversification into new products, skills and technology, a new market, the profit already being generated. Sometimes it removes a competitor or secures a permanent customer. Management should always carefully consider what they are gaining from paying more than the fair value of the net assets and decide how much extra they are prepared to pay.

Obviously there seems to be some gain and so an element of goodwill is probably reasonable. The vendor will want to maximise selling price and the purchaser should want to minimise purchase price. As discussed in chapter 1, people often pay too much for businesses. Purchasers need to be more astute. Let's hope Alba has been wise!

How long does goodwill last?

There are three main arguments—it lasts forever, it has limited life or it has no continuing value and is simply the extra paid to gain the business. The accounting standard takes the view of limited life with some situations existing where it has no life. So the accounting requirement is to amortise the goodwill over the period of future benefit. Future benefit is linked to the ability of the goodwill to produce income—this is hard to assess. The Australian and international standards impose a maximum amortisation period of twenty years. (The USA allows 40 years while New Zealand limits it to ten and advocates five years.)

The goodwill gained at acquisition can only be maintained or increased depending on the skill of the new managers. In twenty years' time any goodwill will be due to the standard of management at that time, it will not have anything to do with the goodwill at the time of acquisition.

The author's view is that goodwill should only be considered to last for a maximum of five years and a shorter period, even immediate write-off, can be more realistic.

Some of us may remember when Melbourne's Myer group acquired Farmers department stores in New South Wales. Initially the name was changed to Myer, but it quickly reverted to Farmers because New South Wales people wanted to buy from a New South Wales owned department store—how easily pleased we are! Later, after about seven years, the name was changed to Myer. Then Myer bought Grace Bros in the 1980s and overnight New South Wales Myer stores became and remain to this day Grace Bros. This shows there is some value in the goodwill established, but surely the goodwill of Grace Bros today is due to the competence of current management?

Only straight line method of amortisation allowed

In 1996 the goodwill accounting standard was amended to allow only the straight line method of amortisation. This amendment followed a consensus view to this effect issued previously by the Urgent Issues Group.

A number of well-known Australian listed companies used the Inverted Sum Of the Year's Digits (ISOYD). The sum of the year's digits is similar to the diminishing value method in that depreciation is higher in earlier years. Basically to depreciate over twenty years you allocate twenty to the first year, nineteen to the second, eighteen to the third and so on. The sum of the digits for twenty years is 210 (20 + 19 + 18 + . . . + 3 + 2 + 1). The amount to be depreciated is then allocated in portions: 20/210 to the first year, 19/210 to the second and so on to 2/210 for nineteenth and 1/210 to twentieth year.

The ISOYD method reverses this resulting in a very small initial amortisation charge. Not until near the end of the twenty years are there large charges for amortisation of goodwill. This makes the profit much higher in earlier years.

Internationally the straight line method has generally been applied. Australia has now mandated the same.

Companies which were applying other methods were required to change to the straight line method for the unamortised goodwill existing at the time the revision came into force (which was for accounting periods ending on or after 30 June 1996).

Why do companies want to amortise for twenty years?

The accounting standard's requirement to amortise using the straight line method means there is an annual amortisation expense included as part of the calculation of operating profit. If we take Alba's goodwill of $208 104 and amortise it over twenty years there is an annual expense of $10 405. If it was amortised over five years the annual charge would be $41 621. Therefore reported profits remain higher the longer the period. And to write off the whole expense in one year would have a dramatic effect on reported profit.

The standard requires management to reassess the goodwill each year. If the continuance of future benefits has diminished or disappeared then there must be extra amortisation expense charged or the whole amount must be written off.

Amortisation is treated as a normal expense. It may be highlighted as abnormal if unusually large. The writing off of amortisation in the year of acquisition is treated as abnormal. (See chapter 8 for an explanation of abnormal items.)

Generally management wants to report results which are as good as possible. Thus the tendency is to amortise over the maximum period of twenty years. The lower the goodwill, the lower the amortisation expense. So if other assets can be identified which reduce the goodwill, this will help. And, wonder of wonders, other specifically identifiable intangible assets were discovered by many companies in 1987, the year the goodwill standard took effect!

Can we revalue goodwill?

The accounting standard only allows the recognition of goodwill as an asset at the time of acquiring an entity or business. The goodwill can only be reduced in value, through amortising. The standard does not allow goodwill to be revalued upwards. This means that any goodwill amortised cannot be recreated. Nor can any goodwill perceived to exist, but which was not acquired, be created.

So what do companies do if they want to recognise an intangible element but have not acquired a business or have already amortised it? They can recognise a specifically identifiable intangible such as trade or brand names.

Rheem example

In 1987 Rheem discovered that the major part of what was previously thought of as goodwill was in fact a specifically identifiable intangible asset—brand names, namely, the different product brands they made such as Rheem hot water systems, Vulcan heaters and Dishlex dishwashers. This was not a change in accounting policy as the remaining goodwill was amortised as previously, but it altered reported profits and assets enormously. Figure 5.3 summarises the effect of the shift in recognition of intangibles.

In the 1986 annual report, the whole $8 972 000 was called goodwill. In 1987, $19 307 000 would have been called goodwill if 'brand names' had not been discovered as a separately identifiable intangible asset.

The effect on Rheem's reported profit in 1987 was that instead of amortising almost $20 million over twenty years, which is about $1 million a year, only $28 000 amortisation expense was incurred. On top of this reduced expenditure, which continues for the next twenty years, there is the additional gain of $947 000 being goodwill previously amortised which was found to be brand names which should not be amortised. So 1987 profit was almost $2 million higher than it would have been if brand names had not been identified.

The amount allocated to establishment costs might have to do with the costs of establishing the brands, businesses or values of the brands. These costs are amortised.

An interesting secondary issue is the write-back of $947 000. Should items previously expensed be later reversed as income if the assessment of

	Consolidated	
	1987 $000	1986 $000
Profit and loss note extract		
Goodwill amortisation	28	480
Abnormal item—prior years amortisation of brand names written-back (i.e. recognised as income in 1987)	(947)	—
Balance sheet effect—extract of intangibles note		
Brand names	18 838	8 455
Goodwill	197	258
Establishment costs	272	259
	19 307	8 972

Figure 5.3

Rheem example

the situation has changed? There is no guidance in the goodwill accounting standard, but AASB 1011, *Accounting for Research and Development Costs*, states in paragraph 1011.50 that 'research and development costs . . . [which] were charged to the profit and loss account shall not be written back in the light of subsequent events'. This view is that what's done is done and should not be undone.

Goodwill and tax

The general principle is that goodwill is not an income tax deduction against revenue. It is deductible in the calculation of capital gains tax liability in that on the sale of the business or company, the goodwill is included as part of the original cost of the acquisition.

The amortisation of goodwill is not a tax deductible expense. So the accounting recognition is different from the tax recognition. These differences and the allowance for these differences in accounting for income tax are explained under the section on income tax in chapter 8.

What if the purchase price is less than the fair value of net assets?

Congratulations are in order! It is a good buy of some sort if you pay less than the fair value of the net assets. It is the opposite of goodwill. Well, shouldn't we recognise it in the opposite way as income? We could have deferred income on the balance sheet and recognise it gradually over a period of up to twenty years or recognise it immediately. Isn't it logical to treat it the opposite way?

The accounting standard on goodwill does not allow this. The standard uses the term 'discount on acquisition' and requires it to be accounted for by removing it from existence. This is done by proportionally reducing the value of non-monetary assets to eliminate the discount. Monetary assets such as cash and debtors cannot be reduced because the cash exists and payment will be received from debtors.

Non-monetary assets such as property, plant and equipment can only be reduced to zero value. Any remaining discount on acquisition after reducing non-monetary assets to zero is recognised immediately as revenue in the profit and loss. How realistic is it to state real non-monetary assets at zero or reduced from their fair value at date of acquisition?

This inconsistent treatment arises because of the doctrine of conservatism, where all known losses are recognised but unrealised gains are preferred to be treated as other than income.

How can a company overcome this problem? The law requires that standards be followed. Simple—proportionally reduce the non-monetary assets and then revalue them to the fair value. A complicating factor may be the need to revalue all similar assets held as the revaluation standard requires a class of assets to be revalued or revalued systematically over time.

Specifically identifiable intangibles

These may come into existence because money is paid to acquire the item or a valuation of the asset is done. Some intangibles obviously have limited lives and others are perceived to be everlasting.

Patents

Money is spent developing and lodging a patent or perhaps an entity buys a patent from another organisation. The costs are treated as an asset. The asset's life is limited to the life of the patent which is usually a maximum of fifteen years. At the end of the patent other people can obtain the patent information and manufacture the product.

A patent is very similar to plant and equipment except that it is a privileged right to make a product rather than a physical machine which is used to make products.

As with other non-current assets, directors should consider at the end of each year whether the asset value still reflects benefits of future use. For instance, if a new product has entered the market which makes the product covered by the patent obsolete, then there is no future benefit in the patent and it should be written off.

Brand or trade names

These are examples of assets arising out of the power associated with the name of the product or service. Coca-Cola® and McDonald's™ are household brand names throughout the world. People buy the product simply because of the name. There definitely is value in the product name. How these sorts of items are valued is discussed earlier in this chapter in the section on Valuation of non-current assets.

The important issue for readers to consider is the reality of the assessed value. You should always be sceptical of these values. Value is lost if products are not properly maintained in the eyes of the public. Sometimes better products replace them. Sometimes the mix of products sold changes and the value once associated with a product falls off.

An interesting aspect to think about is that until a separate asset was identified, we probably thought that the goodwill included the element of the entity's good name and that of its products and services. The Rheem example given above shows why companies may want to create a specifically identifiable intangible asset.

Television and broadcasting licences

There is value in the right to broadcast by television or radio. Such rights are subject to compliance with the conditions in the legislation and regulations granting the rights.

In Australia the federal government controls broadcasting rights and establishes tribunals to police the industry. Television licences are granted for a period of three years and can be renewed if the licensee is assessed at a public hearing as having complied with the rules. So if a significant amount is paid to acquire a media company with a right to televise, there is a risk of losing it all at the time of renewal of the licence.

Some other intangibles

Other intangibles such as mining and logging rights are like television and radio broadcasting licences. The rights continue subject to compliance with the requirements but are generally for longer periods than television and radio licences. Mining and logging rights would normally be amortised over the period of the rights unless it was very probable that the rights would be extended.

Ownership of franchises is like owning brand names and could have similar problems as to their real value. The franchise business must continue to be successful at two levels to maintain value—the franchisees must be able to have successful businesses and the franchiser must continue to be well managed, promote its product effectively and understand and adapt success-fully to the changing market.

Mastheads are another media intangible but are like product brand names—they are the brand names of newspapers, magazines or publishing houses.

DEFERRED EXPENSES

This category covers assets that cannot be categorised as cash, receivables, inventories, investments, property, plant and equipment, or intangibles. The typical items are prepayments, under current assets, and future income tax benefits, under non-current assets. The latter type is complex and is explained in the context of the topic of income tax (see chapter 8).

Sometimes cash on deposit is included as a current other asset. This is discussed under the section on Cash earlier in this chapter.

We are left with the significant items of prepayments and other kinds of deferred expenses.

Prepayments

	1997 $	1996 $
Prepayments	6 984	6 475

See Alba's balance sheet.

Prepayments arise from money paid in advance for a service, but the benefit of the service is still to be fully utilised at balance sheet date. Generally a refund of some kind is available if the service is cancelled or no longer required. Typical expenses which may involve prepayment are insurance, interest, local government charges (e.g. council rates) and rent.

At balance sheet date, prepayments are recognised by treating the portion of the payments which relate to services to be supplied after the balance sheet date as an asset instead of as an expense. In the next financial year the prepayment will be treated as an expense and at the next balance sheet date, that year's prepayments determined.

Consider this example. Alba pays a premium of $42 000 on 27 November 1997 for insurance cover from 1 September 1997 to 31 August 1998. What is the prepayment at 30 June 1998?

The benefit of the service lasts one year. If the policy is cancelled during the year, a refund is received for the months of the policy not required. On a monthly basis the cost is $3500 ($42 000/12). At 30 June 1998 there remains two months insurance cover which means a prepayment of $7000 ($3500 × 2). The expense in the profit and loss for the year ended 30 June 1998 is $35 000 plus the last year's prepayment (at 30 June 1997). The cash flows statement for the year ended 30 June 1998 will include $42 000 within the payments to suppliers and employees under operating activities.

Interest paid in advance often occurs with bill facilities. Here the company receives money less a discount, being the interest rate, and at the end of the period it must repay the bank the full amount. With ongoing facilities, the principal is not repaid until the facility is terminated, but each time the bills are rolled over (renewed) the company pays the interest. So the interest is paid in advance. When the bill period overlaps the balance sheet date the interest is apportioned by days between the days before and the days after. The apportionment to the days after represents the prepayment.

Some people used to arrange loans where interest was paid in advance covering a long period, e.g. three years. Why would an entity want to outlay so much in advance? The answer is for tax reasons. A tax deduction was allowed for prepayment in full to be claimed in the tax year in which it was paid. So these advance interest payments were tax deductible but were recognised for accounting profit purposes on the basis discussed above.

In the mid-1980s the government stopped this practice by limiting the prepaid interest deduction to a maximum of thirteen months from the date of commencement of the service. For advance payments of more than thirteen months, the deduction is apportioned over the period covered by the payment—that is, the same as for the accounting profit calculation. This tax rule applies to all prepayments, not just interest.

Deferred expenses

Other types of expenditure can also be deferred—a common one is research and development. Accounting standards covering specific areas of deferred expenditure give specific guidance; other areas are covered by similar principles.

The usual principle is that deferral is only allowed to the extent that future benefits arising from the expenditure will exceed the expense cost deferred and related annual costs and this situation must be assured beyond reasonable doubt. Remember, any deferral of expenses reduces the expenses included in the calculation of profit and so increases reported profits. Thus it is logical that deferral should only occur in valid circumstances. A user should consider carefully any deferred expenses.

When expenses are deferred, an entity should provide an accounting policy note explaining the basis of deferral, report the amount deferred and report the amount of deferred expense amortised each year.

Most deferred expenses will be shown under other assets, current or non-current. Some of these expenses may be shop fit-out costs, advertising costs for advertisements not to be used until after year end or, sometimes, any expense at all for which the directors can think up a reason to defer.

One way users can monitor whether the level of deferred expenses is reasonable is to measure the proportional change and compare this with the change in level of sales and profit. As a rule of thumb, the proportional change should be similar. A greater rate of increase in deferred expenses compared with sales or profit is a strong indication that excessive expenses are being deferred in order to report artificially higher profits.

Some deferred expenses are added to the value of fixed assets or inventory being constructed. Upon completion and use in production the fixed assets are depreciated and the inventory is (hopefully) sold for more than the accumulated costs (see non-current inventory in the section on Inventories in this chapter).

The types of expenses deferred for these projects include interest incurred to fund the project, local government and state government charges on properties being developed and, for mining and oil and gas, the costs of search and development.

You should carefully consider the information provided about expenses deferred in this manner. Users should endeavour to satisfy themselves that the asset will be used successfully or sold. In chapter 10 (Ratios) interest paid is an important element in the measurement of profit performance. Interest paid which is added to asset values should be considered when applying ratios; thankfully, it has to be reported.

POINTS TO REMEMBER

✔ The simplest description of assets is that they are items owned which can be sold to another party. Assets appearing in the balance sheet may not be readily saleable (such as future income tax benefit) or may simply be deferring of costs (such as prepayments) to match expenses with the period in which they provide benefit.

✔ Assets which will be realised (converted into cash), changed into other assets or used up within twelve months of the balance sheet date are included as current assets. All other assets are included as non-current assets.

✔ Cash represents the bank accounts, petty cash floats and cash in the till floats of the entity or group. If there is doubt the cash at bank may not be recoverable, a provision must be created to recognise the extent of the potential loss. Cash on deposit is considered in the same way but may be included under cash, other current receivables or other current assets.

✔ Receivables consist of money owing to the entity. The most common one is trade debtors which represent the amounts owing by customers for goods and services sold on credit terms. These are generally current but in an industry like the finance industry are mainly non-current. Other kinds of receivables are loans to third parties, loans to directors and other debtors. A provision for doubtful debts is required so as to show the net balance sheet value as the best estimate of the cash anticipated to be collected.

✔ Inventories are the products (stock) purchased or made and held for sale to customers. Inventories are valued at the lower of cost and net realisable value. Costs of manufactured inventory include raw materials, direct factory labour and manufacturing overheads. The acceptable cost assign-ment (measurement) rules are first-in, first-out (FIFO), weighted average cost, specific identification and standard cost. Inventory is shown under three main categories, being raw materials, work in progress and finished goods. Other categories can be goods in transit and stores. Inventories are classed as non-current when the production of the job takes more than one year.

✔ Investments are items such as shares, fixed interest securities and invest-ment properties. They are generally held for the long term. They, like other non-current assets, may be valued at cost, directors' or independent valua-tion, but they must not be valued above recoverable amount.

✔ Recoverable amount is the net of projected future cash inflows less cash outgoings of those assets, usually (but not always) discounted to current values.

✔ Property, plant and equipment consists of items such as land, buildings, leasehold land, leasehold buildings, leasehold improvements, plant and equipment, and plant and equipment under lease. All these assets, except land, wear out over time. This usage is recognised by depreciating to residual value over their useful life. Two of the most common deprecia-tion methods are straight line and diminishing value (reducing balance). The asset at valuation (cost, directors' or independent) less the accumu-lated provision for depreciation is called the written-down value (WDV). The asset value, provision for depreciation and WDV must be shown for each class of assets.

✔ Intangibles represent money paid for or valuations of items perceived to have a long term benefit. Examples are goodwill (which can only be purchased), trade and brand names, patents, television licences, franchise rights and logging rights. The dictionary definition shows intangible assets are not capable of being perceived (touched) or being precisely realised by the mind. More careful assessment should be paid to entities with greater proportions of intangible assets.

✔ Cost of an asset should include all costs of buying or creating the asset. For imported assets this can include foreign exchange movements, freight and handling charges and import duties. For self-constructed assets it can include wages. For property development and construction it can include local government taxes, land taxes and interest on borrowings.

✔ Assets are generally valued at cost whereas the relevant value to users of financial statements is market value. Market value represents what the entity can obtain for the asset in the normal course of business between a willing seller and willing buyer. One reason a user examines financial statements is to see how close asset values are to market value and so to their true worth.

✔ Assets, especially major non-current assets such as properties and intangibles (other than goodwill), may be revalued to directors' or independent valuations which are often based on market value. However there are other acceptable valuation methods such as replacement price and economic usage. The basis of valuation is not reported, nor is there any limitation on acceptable bases of valuation.

✔ Valuations of non-current assets such as properties and intangibles are based on projected revenues and expenses divided by a capitalisation rate or discounted to today's dollars. Revenues, expenses, capitalisation rates and discount rates are based on extensive assumptions. An allowance for the element of risk in obtaining the yields envisaged in the valuation is usually not included. This means the valuation tends to reflect maximum future profit. The valuations may not reflect the price likely to be agreed between a willing seller and willing buyer.

✔ Profit or loss on disposal of non-current assets is the net proceeds (selling price less selling expenses) less the book value (WDV) at time of disposal. Revaluation gains are generally added directly to asset revaluation reserves and are not included in the calculation of profit even on disposal, whereas devaluations are generally treated as an expense. This inconsistency distorts reported profit.

✔ When non-current assets are revalued upward the amount added to the revaluation reserve is the difference between the new valuation amount and the WDV. Depreciation of the asset begins again based on the new valuation over the useful life. This means that depreciation charged through the years on revalued assets can substantially exceed the original cost.

✔ Tax treatment of assets often varies from the accounting treatment. Differences occur in depreciation, revaluation and calculation of profit or loss on disposal.

6 Liabilities

This chapter describes and explains typical liabilities. Most of the liabilities are included in Alba's accounts, but additional provisions and unearned income are added. The challenge for preparers of financial statements is to ensure all liabilities are included. The challenge for users is to discover the liabilities that have been taken 'off balance sheet'.

WHAT ARE LIABILITIES?

The Statement of Accounting Concepts SAC4, *Definition and Recognition of the Elements of Financial Statements*, defines liabilities (paragraph 48) and when they should be recognised (paragraph 65) as:

> 'Liabilities' are the future sacrifices of economic benefits that the entity is presently obliged to make to other entities as a result of past transactions or other past events.

A liability should be recognised in the statement of financial position when and only when:

(a) it is probable that the future sacrifice of economic benefits will be required; and
(b) the amount of the liability can be measured reliably.

We are looking at more than legal obligations as it includes 'obligations imposed by notions of equity or fairness' (paragraph 57). The word 'probable' is stated to be 'that the chance of sacrifice of service potential or future economic benefits occurring is more likely rather than less likely' (paragraph 67).

A trend is to value non-current liabilities by discounting future projected payments rather than what is best estimate of the amount that would be paid at balance date to extinguish the liability. This has been incorporated in the accounting standard on employee benefits.

These aspects are not necessarily what preparers or users associate with liabilities and will be commented upon as necessary in the discussion of different types of liabilities.

There are four main kinds of liabilities—creditors, borrowings, provisions and deferred income. Those expected to be paid or extinguished within twelve months of the balance sheet date are classed as current liabilities and the rest as non-current. Sometimes deferred income is classed as part of equity. In addition to these actual liabilities, this chapter will deal with commitments and contingent liabilities which exist but are not liabilities owing at balance date.

The minimum liability categories listed on the balance sheet under AASB 1034, *Information to be Disclosed in Financial Reports*, (both current and non-current) are:

■ creditors;
■ borrowings;
■ provisions.

Valuing liabilities

The amount shown for a liability from the user's perspective is the amount owing or expected to be paid based on the current situation. The current conceptual thinking among the standard setters is the non-current liability values should be based on projected cash outflows discounted to current dollar values (now incorporated for recognition of certain employee entitlements). Two serious shortcomings of this approach are, firstly, for items such as provisions, these are merely futuristic estimates and, secondly, the discount rate used is based on future changes in the purchasing power of money.

Contrast this with the best estimate of the actual liability based on what would have to be paid today to extinguish the liability. Wouldn't this be the basis of negotiation if you were acquiring the liability as part of the purchase of a business? This is usually a simpler approach.

Missing liabilities

One of the most difficult things for management to do in preparing financial statements is to ensure that all liabilities are included. This is usually not a significant risk with assets, as money is spent acquiring or creating them. But with liabilities, the money is paid out at a later date. The task is to find all the liabilities created through conducting the business of the entity. Thus a user of financial statements needs to consider the risk of unrecorded liabilities.

There is another way liabilities are not recorded on the balance sheet. This is the creative accounting technique of placing them 'off balance sheet'. This means that amounts owing are massaged or placed in a legal form that means they do not have to be shown as liabilities of the enterprise. They are shown as some other entity's liabilities or simply avoided being classed as liabilities. We will consider the simpler examples of this in this chapter. Chapter 12 (section on consolidations) presents another aspect.

Entities want to keep liabilities off balance sheet due to how performance is assessed.

■ One measure of assessment is the proportion of liability to equity, known as debt to equity. If the proportion is not within the analyst's acceptable rule of thumb, the entity is perceived as being more risky. The rule of thumb may change with changing circumstances and vary between countries.

■ Another measure is solvency, the ability of an entity to pay its debts, where current assets are compared with current liabilities. The higher the current liabilities the worse the measure appears. This ratio is used in trust deeds and legislation and obviously becomes critical for those entities affected by the levels set.

Ratio formulae and acceptable levels are discussed more in chapter 10. The effect on measurement of performance is illustrated in figure 6.1.

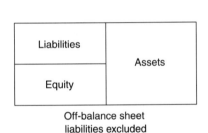

Off-balance sheet
liabilities excluded

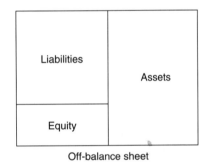

Off-balance sheet
liabilities included

Figure 6.1

Effect of putting liabilities on balance sheet

The left-hand picture is much more pleasing to analysts as it appears the entity has fewer liabilities and therefore less exposure to interest payments. The greater the interest payments, the greater the exposure to reduced profits or even losses due to adverse changes in the interest rate.

But the real picture is on the right-hand side. You will notice that with the recognition of the liabilities comes additional assets because the liabilities are used to finance the acquisition of assets. So a further temptation to exclude liabilities from the balance sheet is the advantage to an entity of showing *lower* assets. This, as you may remember from the preceding chapter, is that return on assets appears higher the lower the asset value.

A typical area of off-balance sheet financing is leasing, which is discussed later under borrowings.

CREDITORS

	1997 $	1996 $
Trade creditors	284 874	259 341
Accrued expenses	93 461	87 815
Other creditors	3 821	6 872

See Alba's accounts note 11.

In Australian accounts, information on creditors will be shown in the notes supporting the 'creditors and borrowings' liabilities shown under current and non-current liabilities in the balance sheet. These items are mainly current liabilities.

Creditors may be described as trade creditors, other creditors and accrued expenses (also called accruals or accrued liabilities).

Trade creditors

Trade creditors are the opposite of trade debtors.

Alba can use several checks to ensure that all creditors are recorded. The best method is to compare, for each creditor, the amount Alba shows as outstanding with the creditor's statement. Common reasons for differences are: payments sent have not been included on the statement (the cheque is in the mail—or drawer—syndrome); claims for credits not yet processed or agreed to by supplier (due to supply of faulty goods, wrong goods sent or wrong prices charged); and suppliers invoiced for goods or services not yet received by Alba. Staff at Alba would analyse the differences and Alba's trade creditors figures would be adjusted for differences where suppliers' information was correct.

Other creditors

Other creditors are creditors like trade creditors, except that they are creditors for the supply of goods and services which are not usual purchases. For instance, the purchases could be for plant and equipment. Usually there is no real difference from trade creditors. The distinction is arbitrary and best analysis is achieved by combining them with trade creditors.

Australian accounts do not usually give additional information about the nature of other creditors. In other countries more information might be provided which enables the user to assess if they are really creditors. Sometimes other creditors represent advance payments received from debtors where the entity has an obligation to provide a service or supply goods to remove the liability (the amount received in advance). In Australia these would be more likely to be shown as a type of deferred income or, maybe, a reduction of debtors. These are a different kind of creditor and would normally not be combined with trade creditors when analysing performance.

Accrued expenses

Accrued expenses are the opposite of prepayments. It is the recognition of use of services or receipt of goods where the invoice has not arrived. The event or transaction occurred in the financial year in question.

An example is the use of utilities such as electricity, which may be billed once every three months. Say the last bill received for the three months to 15 May was $6000. It was paid on 25 June. At a balance sheet date of 30 June there has been 1.5 month's subsequent usage of electricity. The next bill will not be received until after 15 August. The usage can be estimated as half of the previous three months, i.e. $3000. But perhaps in winter more electricity is used for heating. Comparison with last year's winter bill will reveal if an additional amount should be allowed.

This is an example of the logical approach that should be adopted in estimating figures in financial statements. Fundamentally the accounts are endeavouring to represent the situation of the entity expressed in dollar terms.

Another example of an accrual can be wages. If wages are paid fortnightly there is usually a pay period that spans the balance sheet date. The pay is often made at the end of the fortnight and needs to be apportioned between the current and the next financial year.

Let's consider an example:

Balance sheet date	30 June
Pay for two weeks ending 8 July	$24 000
Pay period would commence two weeks earlier	25 June
Number of days to accrue 25–30 June inclusive	6 days
Accrual is calculated as $24 000 × 6/14	$10 286

This has been based on the full fourteen days and assumes a seven day working week. The computation should be based on the actual working week. If we use a five day working week and assume the fortnight end is a Wednesday we have the following calculation:

Number of days to accrue allowing for weekends on 27 and 28 June and 4 and 5 July	4 days
Accrual is calculated as $24 000 × 4/10	$9 600

This demonstrates the effect based on different sets of circumstances. Management is responsible for ensuring accrued expenses are logically and accurately calculated.

Another very typical accrual is accrued interest. Interest expense is incurred daily on liabilities. Interest is paid in accordance with the requirements of the loan. Usually, this means interest is paid at the end of the month or quarter, but not necessarily. Whether paid or not, all interest incurred should be recognised in the accounts. So all unpaid interest due up to and including the balance sheet date will be estimated and included as part of accrued expenses. It is not added to the borrowings which reflect the principal outstanding.

Calculating these accrued expenses adds to the liabilities stated on the balance sheet and increases the expenses by the same amount. The accruals are estimated each year and should be estimated on a consistent basis. So Alba, like any entity, can look at last year's accrual calculations to check that they have considered at least the items considered then.

How the items are described in the accounts

All creditors and accrued expenses are required to be included in the accounts, but the descriptions may vary between entities. Some may use the three categories explained above. Others may combine them as one item. Other variations can be:

■ trade creditors and accruals plus other creditors;
■ trade creditors plus other creditors and accrued liabilities;
■ trade creditors plus accrued expenses (in this example what others might call 'other creditors' has been included as part of trade creditors).

If the evidence is that other creditors and accruals are basically like trade creditors in nature, then all should be added together when users calculate ratios which include creditors (see 'Days creditors' in chapter 10).

BORROWINGS

Alba has two kinds of borrowings which appear under current and non-current and three kinds of borrowings which appear under only one of these. They are grouped under secured or unsecured and the extent of security is described. See Alba's accounts notes 12, 14 and 1(i). Accounting standard AASB 1034 requires this information to be provided, including the extent of the security which, unfortunately, is not always given.

When you see the same descriptions listed under current and non-current it frequently means they are the same loans. This is the situation for Alba. The total principal outstanding is split between current and non-current—current is the amount of principal which will be repaid in the loan repayments made in the twelve months after the balance sheet date. The balance of the debt must be non-current.

Those of you who have a car loan or house loan will have experienced this. Your monthly loan repayments include principal and interest—not much principal in the early days of the loan! At the end of each year you owe less than at the beginning provided your loan repayments are higher than the interest charged on the loan during the year.

The due periods of the non-current loans are not shown. This disclosure is limited to borrowing corporations, being those companies which have borrowed from the public. An example is a finance company issuing debentures to raise funds to lend. This information would be useful in the projection of future demands on cash.

Bank overdraft

	1997 $	1996 $
Bank overdraft	50 382	56 810

The bank overdraft is secured by a floating charge over the assets of the company. Interest rate is variable. Average interest rate during the year 7.8% (1996—8.5%).

This is a very common lending facility. The overdraft facility is negotiated for a period of time, often two to three years, with an upper overdraft limit. Technically the overdraft is repayable on demand but, generally, provided the borrower complies with the terms of the facility, the overdraft is more like a medium term borrowing. It is included as a current liability because of the legal right of repayment on demand.

Individual companies and groups of companies often make arrangements with a bank where they have a number of bank accounts which are offset against each other and charging or receiving interest is based on the net balance owing or on hand. This means the amounts on hand or in overdraft in the individual accounts do not matter—it is the net situation from adding them together that does. Naturally this situation only exists for accounts held with one bank and within one country.

Alba has shown cash and bank overdraft. This indicates the two are not offset. They would be paying higher interest on their overdraft than the interest, if any, they are receiving on the cash on hand. Alba also has $150 000 on deposit. Why not pay out the overdraft and reduce overall interest costs? Perhaps they want the cash and overdraft facility to allow the purchase of assets without having to arrange additional borrowings—this ability may be worth more than the additional marginal interest cost.

Bank loans

	1997 $	1996 $
Bank loans — non-current	150 000	150 000

The bank loans are secured by a first mortgage over the land and buildings. The interest rate is reviewed annually at 31 December in line with prevailing market interest rates. The effective interest rate at 30 June 1997 is 9.95% (1996—10.45%).

This loan was raised in 1996 to help finance the purchase of the new property. This fact is revealed in the cash flows statement where $150 000 is shown as 'proceeds from borrowings' under the part on 'cash flows from financing activities'. The description 'first mortgage' on the property also supports this view.

The fact that it appears only under non-current means that none of the principal is repayable within twelve months of the balance sheet date. The loan may be for, say, a five year period during which only interest payments are required and at the end all the principal is due.

Other loans

	1997 $	1996 $
Unsecured		
Other loans—current	5 600	5 600
Other loans—non-current	16 800	22 400
Secured		
Other loans—non-current	20 000	20 000

Other loans are secured by a second mortgage over the land and buildings. (Note 14 includes information on interest and fair values.)

The unsecured other loans are shown under current and non-current because $5600 of principal is repayable within twelve months of the balance sheet date. This was the case in both years and is probably the annual principal repayment for the term of the loan.

The $5600 reduction is reflected in the reduction in the non-current portion. It looks as though the loan will be fully repaid within four years (as the non-current portion of $16 800 is three times the annual repayment).

The secured other loan seems to be on a similar basis to the bank loan. However, this loan appears to have existed prior to 1996 as in the cash flows statement 'proceeds from borrowings' only mentions the bank loans. The security of a second mortgage was probably transferred from the old property to the new property.

Lease liabilities

	1997 $	1996 $
Lease liability—current	37 471	35 917
Lease liability—non-current	135 742	129 841

The lease liability is secured over the assets leased.

In addition to this extract from notes 12 and 14, read note 20.

Lease liabilities as stated in the balance sheet are the amount of principal repayable on all assets being acquired by finance lease.

Yes, it is true that a lease is not legally a borrowing. Legally it is a means of acquiring use of property (e.g. buildings, motor vehicles and computer equipment) over a period of time. Legal ownership only passes upon payment of the residual. But financial statements are to present the substance, not the form, of events.

Accounting standard AASB 1008, *Accounting for Leases*, prescribes how to determine whether the lease is really the means used to finance acquisition of an asset or not, and describes how to account for the lease and what information must be given in the accounts. These notes explain the principles but do not give the detailed tests used to classify leases.

Leases which are a means by which the lessee acquires an asset are called finance leases. A finance lease is where the rights, duties and obligations of ownership are really borne by the lessee (party leasing the assets from the lessor) rather than the lessor (who legally owns the assets until the end of the lease when the lessee has the right to pay out the lease and acquire legal title). The accounting standard gives rules for assessing this, e.g. the lessee having to insure the assets is an indication of 'ownership'.

Other leases are called operating leases. These are supposed to be leases which represent simple rental of a building or equipment. At the end of the lease the lessee is not expected to acquire legal title to the asset. A straight-forward example is the lease of office space. Tenants would have to pay substantially higher rentals for them to be actually the repayment of principal and interest.

Finance leases are included in the balance sheet, i.e. the cost of the asset is included in property, plant and equipment and the principal outstanding is included as borrowing (as for Alba).

As illustrated in figure 6.1, finance leases increase the proportion of liabilities to equity. Preparers prefer not to have to show too much debt, therefore they are frequently interested in having operating rather than finance leases. This is achievable for situations which are really finance lease ones by structuring the lease document in such a way that it conforms with the technical description of an operating lease as presented in the accounting standard—another example of creative accounting. The argument is centred on the form of the lease rather than the substance!

Figure 6.2 shows how finance and operating leases are recorded.

For finance leases the cost of the asset and the lease liability is determined at the time of the commencement of the lease from information in the lease agreement.

■ The asset is depreciated (the term amortised is often used instead because the asset is not owned in a strict legal sense) over the lease term down to the lease residual value. However the entity's useful life is likely to be longer than the lease period. Thus the asset should then be depreciated over the useful life for the entity down to the estimated residual (e.g. trade-in) value.

■ The liability is the principal proportion of all future lease payments plus the lease payout amount (residual) at the conclusion of the lease. At the beginning of a lease this is the same as the cost of the asset. The liability

Figure 6.2		Finance lease	Operating lease
Finance and operating leases	**Balance sheet** *Asset*—non-current under property, plant and equipment	Plant and equipment under lease less Provision for depreciation	Not applicable
	Liabilities Current Non-current	Lease liability Lease liability	Not applicable
	Profit and loss statement Disclosed *expenses*	Depreciation on leased assets Finance lease charge	Lease payment
	Cash flows statement	Lease payment (under investing or financing)	Lease payment (under operating)

is split between current and non-current. The liability is reduced by the amount of principal within each lease payment made. As with other loans, the proportion of principal repaid is small in early repayments and increases to be almost all principal at the end of the loan period.

■ Each year the amount depreciated (amortised) is included as an expense.

■ The amount of interest paid in lease payments during the year is included as an expense and described as something like 'finance lease charge'.

At an early stage of a finance lease the depreciation plus the finance lease charge is greater than the lease payment. The situation is the opposite towards the end of the lease term.

The lease payment is allowed as a tax deduction, which means there is a difference between accounting expense and allowable tax deduction. (These differences pop up all over the place!) By the end of the useful life of the leased asset the depreciation plus interest is the same as the lease payments.

Alba's note 20 'expenditure commitments' shows the future lease payments contracted for at balance date split between finance and operating leases. The future payments are split into time periods specified by the accounting standard. The payments for finance leases cover the principal (including residual value) and interest. The note shows the deduction of future finance charges to give the principal outstanding at balance date, allocates this between current and non-current and references back to the borrowings notes 12 and 14.

PROVISIONS

Provisions are liabilities estimated to allow for events or transactions that have taken place but are not legally due and payable until some time in the future. The estimation may not be that refined because of limitations of information at the time of estimating.

Provisions relating to specific assets are deducted from those assets (and not included in liabilities). They provide a way of recognising that there is a reduction in the value of the assets. Typical examples (which were discussed in chapter 5) are:

- provision for doubtful debts, to recognise that not all debtors will pay;
- provision for obsolescence, to allow for stock subject to obsolescence;
- provision for depreciation or amortisation, to allow for fixed assets, intangible assets and deferred expenses being used up through wear and tear or by the transition of time.

All other provisions are in nature like liabilities and are included under current or non-current liabilities. Some occur under both when the anticipated timing of payment spans both classifications.

Provisions do not mean there is cash set aside. They merely recognise a liability to be paid at some future date. The actual cash is shown under assets in the balance sheet and the use of cash is shown in the cash flows statement.

We will discuss Alba's provisions and other provisions which occur quite commonly in larger or certain other types of companies.

Provision for dividend

	1997 $	1996 $
Dividends (from note 13)	30 000	30 000

This is the amount of final dividend declared by directors out of profit which will be paid after approval by the shareholders at the annual general meeting.

Larger corporations often pay their dividend in two instalments known as interim and final dividends. The interim dividend is usually paid in the second half of the financial year (around March or April for June year end companies). Alba pays interim and final dividends as shown in the directors' report in chapter 4.

Provision for income tax (current) and deferred income tax (non-current)

	1997 $	1996 $
Income tax—current (from note 13)	110 819	95 521

Alba only has a current liability. This is the best estimate at the time of preparing the accounts of the liability for income tax owing to the government. The accounts are prepared before the tax return. On preparation of the tax return there may be some adjustments to the liability.

Both income tax provisions are explained under 'income tax' in chapter 8, Profit and loss.

Provision for warranty

	1997 $	1996 $
Warranty (from note 13)	12 000	11 000

Entities selling goods with a warranty know at the time of sale that some warranty will be payable. They even know the typical amount involved because of past experience.

Consider a car. The selling price of the car is set to cover all expenses including estimated warranty costs and provide profit for the manufacturer and dealer. The price is subject to competition and the state of the economy.

Although the warranty costs will actually be paid in the future when the car is brought to the dealer for service, the cost relates to the production and sale of the car, not the running of the car. Warranty covers a fault in the production process not detected by quality control. So the warranty expense is matched to the sale of the car, not the cycle of servicing the car.

The warranty provision is determined by monitoring actual warranty costs and comparing them as a percentage of the sales on which the warranty was incurred. This percentage is then applied to the sales made and for which the warranty period has not expired at balance sheet date. If it is a twelve months warranty it means the last month's sales have full warranty exposure, the previous month's about eleven months and so on to the year's first month's sales where almost all warranty claims have arisen.

Alba has a very small provision for warranty of $12 000. Sales, as shown in note 2, are $3 399 504. The accounts have been audited so we should be able to rely on the figures. Possible explanations are that statutory warranties are not provided for; only some of the goods are sold with warranty; the quality is so good that there are very few, and only small, claims. If we were looking to buy Alba, or a significant part of it, then it would be sensible for us to investigate the reasonableness of this figure as part of the due diligence process. On the surface the liability does seem small.

Employee entitlements

	1997 $	1996 $
Current—annual leave	51 493	46 332
Current—long service leave	6 804	5 639
Non-current—long service leave	59 194	46 945

From note 13 and the balance sheet. Read notes 1(j) and 23.

This is the estimated amount owing to employees at balance sheet date for entitlements to annual leave and long service leave not taken by the employees at that date. The current liability portion (mainly annual leave) is estimated using salary and wage rates at the balance sheet date. For the non-current liability (generally long service leave) future payments are estimated, time of payment predicted and the amount discounted to present value using the Commonwealth bonds interest rates (for the same period of time as estimated when payments will be made). This approach is required by AASB 1028, *Accounting for Employee Entitlements*, which applied for years ending on or after 30 June 1995.

In Australia, under some awards and labour agreements, untaken sick leave entitlements are accumulated and paid out to employees on termination. In this situation the employee entitlements provision will include sick leave.

This is known as vested sick leave in that entitlement vests with the employee and any untaken sick leave must be paid on termination. The accounting standard requires it to be estimated in the same way as annual leave. The accounting standard requires estimation for total untaken non-vesting sick leave at reporting date which is expected to be taken. Non-vesting means the employee is not entitled to be paid out any untaken sick leave on termination. This estimation is based on past experience of actual sick leave taken.

In Australia, employees earn entitlement to annual leave at the rate of four weeks (twenty days) per year as a minimum. They are not able to take leave (except as agreed by the employer) until completing one year's service. However, if they left during the year they would receive a pro rata payment (e.g. if they worked six months they would be paid two weeks' annual leave). Thus entitlement commences from the first day.

Employers maintain employee records for all employees. These records include annual leave, long service leave and sick leave entitlements. At balance date the annual leave entitlement is calculated for each employee and the total for all employees becomes the balance sheet liability. Figure 6.3 shows how the liability can be calculated.

Figure 6.3 shows the calculation of liability at each balance sheet date from 1995 to 1997. The calculation is straightforward when records are adequately maintained. Australian workers under awards may be entitled to an annual leave loading of 17.5 per cent of normal salary. This additional calculation would be required in the example if the person was entitled. The person might not be entitled if paid above award and it was not company policy.

Figure 6.3

Annual leave entitlement record for BYU leave

Dates and description	Days earned	Days taken	Days owing	Wage rate per day $	Liability $
1/4/95 — employed					
30/6/95 — balance date	5	—	5	150	750
1/4/96 — anniversary	15	—	20		
3/5/96 — leave taken	—	10	10		
30/6/96 — balance date	5	—	15	170	2 550
8/8/96 — leave taken	—	7	8		
1/4/97 — anniversary	15	—	23		
30/6/97 — balance date	5	—	28	200	5 600

Under AASB 1028, *Accounting for Employee Entitlements*, the liability estimation approach just described is to be adopted for calculating accruals and provisions for wages, annual leave and sick leave and for 'other employee entitlements expected to be settled within twelve months of the reporting date' (paragraph 11).

All employee entitlement estimations must allow for associated costs such as workers compensation insurance and payroll tax. Previously most companies did not allow for these. Thus many companies had a retrospective increase in the liability in the first year the standard was adopted. This retrospective increase was adjusted against retained profits at the beginning of the financial year. This is explained further in chapter 8.

Other employee entitlement liabilities expected to be settled in more than twelve months 'shall be measured as the present value of the estimated future cash outflows' (paragraph 12) anticipated as a result of the arising of the liability. This applies to long service leave expected to be paid in more than twelve months time. The estimated future cash outflows are projections of the amount of liability payments allowing for increasing wage rates and estimating when the payments will actually be made. The discount rate to be used is the interest rate on national government guaranteed securities (paragraph 13) for the same period when the payments are expected to be made.

The approach for estimating the non-current portion is a very complex method. People are guessing the future. In the sale of a business the liability would probably be estimated similarly to annual leave, as it used to be. The standard (commentary, paragraph (xxx)) allows a short-hand method where it is not materially different from the standard's method. If I were the financial controller of a company I would be advocating this. It means a continuation of the old method with allowance for the associated costs. Alba has adopted the short-hand method.

The short-hand method for long service leave is the same as for annual leave except that the time from when the liability is recognised needs to be considered. Employees are required to serve the period of time specified under the award which provides for their long service leave entitlement. This is usually five years service and sometimes ten years. The leave is generally earned at the rate of thirteen weeks for every fifteen years service. It is a leave entitlement additional to annual leave. Between five and ten years, employees may in any case be entitled to long service leave in certain circumstances such as involuntarily leaving the employer.

Recognition from date of employment or after just one or two years service is probably creating too large a liability. It assumes everyone will continue in employment until entitled—which is not likely for new employees. Most tend to adopt recognition after five years service.

Why there is no provision for superannuation

Superannuation schemes are established to provide retirement benefits for employees. They must be set up independent of the entity in a separate trust. Trustees are appointed in terms of the trust deed and are responsible for the administration of the trust in accordance with the requirements of the trust deed. The government has established a set of laws and a supervisory body to ensure that superannuation schemes are valid and operated for the benefit of their members. The abuse of superannuation schemes in the past and a policy of encouraging all employees to have superannuation are the reasons why the government has increased and is still increasing regulation of this multi-billion dollar industry.

Superannuation benefits for an employee are built up by the contributions made by the employee and/or the employer. Most schemes are funded by both, while some are funded by employers only. Once the money is paid across to the superannuation scheme, it is the responsibility of the trustees. The government limits the freedom of lending back to or investing in the employer, in order to reduce the ability of employers to control funds in superannuation schemes.

Employee contributions are deducted from wages each month and paid to the scheme, together with the employer's contribution, in the following month. So at balance sheet date, there is generally only one month's contributions not paid. This liability is included in trade creditors or accrued expenses. Some companies may be further behind which may be of concern to the employees.

Legally a company has no further liability once it has paid its contributions. Management may see themselves as having a moral responsibility if the scheme is unable to pay the benefits specified.

There are two basic kinds of benefits.

■ Accumulated funds where the entitlement is simply the employer and employee contributions plus the investment gains earned on the contributions during the time in the fund. So if the scheme's investment strategy has been successful, the member will reap rewards; if not, the member suffers the consequences. In this situation there is definitely no further liability from the employer.

■ Defined benefits where the benefits are linked to wage levels, e.g. a lump sum payout of seven times the last three years' average salary. The investment strategy and the contribution levels are set and monitored to check that the scheme is generating sufficient funds to pay the defined benefits. This checking is done by actuaries reviewing the scheme every three years. They consider the existing funds, future contributions and investment earnings to see if they cover projected future benefits payments. When there is a shortfall, the employer company will often contribute additional funds over the next three years to reduce the gap. This is a moral and not a legal response.

Accounting standard AASB 1028 requires that for each defined benefits plan information should be given for each and in total. Information required includes accrued benefits, the net market value and the difference between the two plus the amount of vested benefits. The employer's accounting policy and amounts in its accounts must be given. Alba's information is shown in note 22.

Other provisions

The remainder of this section provides information on other types of provisions found in financial statements, and looks briefly at the question of monitoring the level of provisions.

Provision for maintenance

A maintenance provision aims to recognise significant maintenance required on large plant and equipment items over time rather than just in the year when the money is spent. This provision is used in mining companies and heavy manufacture production such as steel making.

The nature of the machinery held requires substantial overhauls from time to time. The plant may have to be closed to allow the work to proceed. The use of the machinery over a number of years causes the need for this work. So the provision is created to allocate the cost against revenue as earned rather than against revenue in a year in which the machinery is producing less revenue due to the overhaul.

This is a reasonable approach but may be abused by excessive provisions being created. If the entity has a number of units of this type of plant, then the cycle of major overhaul in itself may be a sufficient spread of the cost without the need to create a provision.

Provision for restoration

Some businesses such as mining are required, by the mining lease agreements, to restore the land to its natural state. The money will be spent after the mine is closed, but the action causing the restoration is that of mining. The revenue from the mining operation must allow for the cost of restoration as it is really part of the cost of running the mine.

This cost is typically allowed for by allocating a cost for each tonne of ore extracted. The amount allocated per tonne is added to the provision for restoration. By the end of the life of the mine, the amount in the provision should cover the estimated cost of restoration. The build-up of the provision should be reviewed at least annually to see if it is sufficient. The amount allocated per tonne of ore can be increased or decreased to make the build-up of the provision more realistic.

You should note that the build-up of the provision allows for a cost which will be spent in the future. It allows for it in the sense of creating a liability. It does not allow for it in the sense of setting aside money—no cash is physically set aside as the provision is built up. The payment of the liability will be funded at the time of the restoration. Hopefully the mining operation will have generated cash as well as profit! But if the cash has been used in developing new operations, the entity can borrow cash to meet the payments.

Provision for loss on disposal and provision for rationalisation

These provisions are created upon the decision of the directors either to sell a part of the business at a loss or to rationalise their operations. The actual sale or rationalisation will take place later but the financial consequences of the decision are recognised now.

These situations are problematic for an organisation if they occur too frequently. They indicate that earlier decisions to establish or buy certain businesses were not good and could indicate that the response to changing economic and market forces was too slow—earlier rationalisation or sale would have been less costly. These situations are often recognised in the depressed cycle of the economy but the seeds of the problems are sown earlier.

So we see down-sizing, right-sizing, extinction-sizing—all sorts of euphemisms are used to explain what usually are the consequences of earlier, inappropriate management decisions.

A provision for loss on disposal is estimated by considering the likely selling price on disposal less the selling expenses and less the book value of the assets being sold or scrapped. Estimates are allowed for retrenchment and redundancy payments. The trading profit or loss between the time of the decision to sell and the projected sale date is also estimated and included in the calculated loss. This provision is hard to estimate exactly and so there will probably be quite a variation which will be recorded as an additional loss or a profit at the time of actual sale. (This will not occur of course when the transaction is finalised prior to the preparation of the accounts, because then the final situation can be reflected in the accounts.)

A provision for rationalisation is similar to loss on disposal except that no-one is taking over the disposed-of items. Factories may close, employees may be retrenched or redeployed. Factory properties might be sold—but just the property and not the business which was operating in it. So the same sorts of items are allowed for in the calculation of the likely cost of the rationalisation.

The loss on disposal or cost of rationalisation is usually included as an abnormal item within operating profit. The significance of these and how they are considered in measuring profit performance is discussed in chapters 8 and 10.

You should always consider how frequently some of these items appear. A company rationalising and taking losses on disposal of parts of the business regularly over a number of years cannot be said to be very successful. These costs will be shown as abnormal and typically not included in calculating profit performance. Is this a wise approach to analysis? Companies know how performance is assessed; they present their results in the best way they can to maximise their performance.

When the stock market perceives a company to be experiencing difficulty and is looking for recovery in the future, it may be tempting for directors to 'drop a bucket' of bad news so that such costs are removed from future profit calculation. Indeed the more cynical may take the view that directors are sometimes extremely pessimistic so that, in the following year, they can find that they have significantly overestimated the losses. This means the overestimate is reversed in the next year and so causes the profit to be higher by the amount of overestimation.

Provision for claims

General insurance businesses make money by selling policies for more than the cost of claims plus cost of operations and by investing the premiums received (until claims have to be paid). Insurance companies make most of their profit on investments and often incur losses on the policies.

At the end of the year they have a number of claims still unpaid. The event leading to each claim has occurred and so the claim should be recognised. This is done by estimating the liability on known but unpaid claims at balance date.

There are several acceptable means of estimating claims. A company's statement of significant accounting policies should explain the method used. One method is to estimate on a 'claim by claim' basis where the amount likely to be paid out on each claim is individually determined and they are added to give the total provision for claims. Another method is to have an actuarial estimate of the future payments based on trends with past claims and current circumstances.

In addition to known claims at balance date, there are situations where the event giving rise to a claim has occurred prior to balance date, but a claim has not been received. These claims are known as 'incurred but not reported'. An estimate is made for them at balance sheet date. Like the warranty provision, the estimate is based on past experience. If there was a natural disaster such as a hailstorm near the balance sheet date, a higher than normal allowance would possibly be required in order to recognise it.

This reflects the principle that in estimating using past trends, you must allow for known different circumstances.

Monitoring the level of provisions

Provisions can be subject to manipulation. Increasing the level of provisions at a greater rate than really needed increases expenses and so reduces profit. Conversely, increasing the level of provisions at a slower rate than really needed reduces the level of expenses and so increases profit.

Over time, growing entities will have increasing levels of provisions. However, the prudent user should monitor the rate of increase to see if there is evidence of profit manipulation. Most provisions can be related to sales and operating profit. The simplest means of monitoring is to check that provisions are increasing or decreasing in proportion with increases and decreases in sales (in the first instance) and with profit (as a second comparison).

Some provisions relate better to other items. These are usually associated with assets. So the provision for doubtful debts can be monitored as a proportion of total debtors, as can provision for obsolete inventory. Provisions for depreciation of buildings, plant and equipment will increase as a proportion of the asset the older the asset becomes—they will remain more consistent if the assets are being renewed. Provision for amortisation of goodwill follows a similar pattern to that for fixed assets—the more recent the acquisition of the new business, the smaller the proportion the provision is of the asset.

Some other provisions occur more intermittently and cannot be logically related to other items. Two examples are provision for loss on disposal and provision for rationalisation.

Thus by understanding relationships between items you can monitor the reasonableness of the level of the provisions. But remember these are only a check. When there are changes in circumstances, provisions will change at rates different from normal. You need to allow for this. You cannot blindly assume the relationship should always be the same. Your skill at monitoring will improve with practice.

DEFERRED INCOME

Deferred income arises when income is received in advance of the period in which it is earned. It is usually included in liabilities and sometimes in equity on the balance sheet. Deferred income is usually included as a liability when the amount is refundable if the goods or services are not eventually supplied, but is often treated as equity when refunding does not exist.

Deferred income is like a liability because the taking of money in advance brings with it the obligation to provide the goods or services to satisfy the reason for the advance. Here the liability is discharged by supply of goods or performance of service instead of payment.

Premiums paid in advance (example)

General insurance companies always have deferred income. They receive premiums in advance. This is the other side of the coin from insurance prepayments which were considered in chapter 5 in the section on 'Deferred expenses'. The premium income is recognised month by month as the income is earned. So at the end of a month all premium income received—which provides cover for future months—is treated as deferred income.

This liability is usually a current liability as most insurance policies are for periods of a year or less. It is usually shown under the category 'other' or separately highlighted on the balance sheet. The term 'unearned premium' is a usual description.

Profit on sale and lease-back (example)

Many companies have raised needed cash by selling property or large equipment to finance companies and leasing it back. They remain as the tenants and to their customers there appears to be no change. Have you noticed the number of banks that have been selling their branch premises and remaining as tenants?

There is a profit on sale (often a big one) as the agreed value exceeds the book value. How should this profit be recognised? One method is to recognise the profit in the year of the sale. However, the property or equipment is still being used and rent is payable for as long as it is. The profit can be considered as a reduction in true rent cost. Under this approach the profit is recognised gradually over the period of the lease. The true rent cost is actually the rent paid less the proportion of profit allocated to that period. These leases can often be for ten years or more.

In this situation there is no refunding of the profit to the purchaser. So the profit is not a liability. It is typically included at the end of shareholders' equity with an accounting policy note explaining how it is being treated in the accounts.

COMMITMENTS AND CONTINGENT LIABILITIES

These are situations that exist at balance sheet date which may or will become liabilities in the future, but are not liabilities at that date. They are shown as notes in the accounts but not included in liabilities in the balance sheet. The three typical items are commitments for capital purchases, lease commitments and contingent liabilities. Accounting standard AASB 1034 requires these disclosures.

Capital purchases

Alba's accounts provide information in note 20 on expenditure contracted for at balance date but not included in liabilities. In 1997 the amount was $26 347. This represents orders for plant and equipment but the items are not received until after the balance sheet date. So there is really nothing on site against which to establish a liability. As soon as it is received, the liability will be recognised.

As you can imagine, this will be a normal situation for a business. A user of financial statements will only be interested in this item if it is unusual compared with what one would expect. For instance, for Alba, we could well be surprised if the amount was $250 000 or more. After all, Alba's plant and equipment at cost is just over $400 000 (see note 10). Why would they have ordered so much?

Lease expenditure commitments

These represent the future lease payments on all leases in force at the balance sheet date (as referred to in the discussion of leases under 'borrowings' in this chapter). Operating leases are purely rental and no liability is recognised for them. However, finance leases are recognised as a liability. The information in Alba's note 20 shows the time periods in which the payments will be made in the future.

Leasing is common and so the note will not be of great concern to a user unless there is reason to believe the lease commitments are excessive considering the financial situation of the company. An example could be leasing of a lot of floor space with a shrinking business in economic conditions that prevent subleasing.

The operating lease commitments might include finance leases disguised as operating leases. This is always worth considering for large operating lease commitments other than property rental.

Contingent liabilities

This note to the accounts is always important and should be considered carefully. All companies, whatever their size or type, are required to produce this note.

Contingent liabilities refer to situations that exist at balance sheet date but where liability to pay funds will occur after the balance sheet date only if another event occurs. At balance sheet date this occurrence is considered to be unlikely and so a liability does not exist now or in the future. If the matter is likely to become a liability it should be included on the balance sheet as a provision.

Alba's note 21 shows two contingent liabilities.

- Guarantees of other people's debts, e.g. a parent may be a guarantor for a child on the purchase of their first car. The parent does not owe the money, the child does, but if the child defaults on repayment the debt becomes the parent's. Thus the amount of $24 000 in 1997, shown in note 21 is not owed by Alba at the moment. Another consideration is that it is a small, insignificant amount. In consolidated group accounts you will usually see that companies within the group have guaranteed repayment of each other's borrowings. This gives lenders access to other companies in the group if the company to which they lent becomes insolvent.

■ Capital gains tax liability that would be payable if Alba's revalued property were sold for the revalued amount. Alba claims no intention of selling the property and so has decided not to recognise this amount in the accounts. If it had decided to recognise it, it might have been included as a reduction from the asset value or as a deferred tax liability.

Another item frequently found in contingent liabilities is information on litigation proceedings. Suppose a matter is still in dispute and the outcome is unknown. If the company expects to have to pay some amount, the best estimate should be included as a provision rather than leaving the item as a contingent liability. If the result is unknown or the company expects to win, it should be shown as a contingent liability.

On the one hand, the company may be concerned about giving too much disclosure for fear of pre-empting the result. It may feel that by recognising a liability it will be admitting too much. Alternatively, the user wants the best information and the law requires it. The directors may spend quite some time considering what to do!

The note is supposed to include an estimate of the maximum potential liability. There may be reluctance to disclose this. The company's lawyers may believe it cannot be reasonably estimated. Yet another potential difficulty!

Finally, how can the entity be sure all contingent liabilities are included? This is probably not a difficulty for small companies, but for large companies and groups it can be very difficult to ensure the information is accurately compiled. Yet users are very interested in this note to the accounts because of the valuable insight it can provide into situations which may have detrimental financial consequences.

POINTS TO REMEMBER

✔ Fundamentally, liabilities are amounts owing or anticipated to become owing in the future as a result of transactions and events of the entity. They are generally valued at the amount which would be required to pay them out if they were paid at balance sheet date.

✔ Liabilities are classed as current liabilities if they are expected to be paid or extinguished in some other way within twelve months of the balance sheet date. Other liabilities are classed as non-current.

✔ There are really four kinds of liabilities—creditors, borrowings, provisions and deferred income.

✔ There are two significant risks facing a user when considering liabilities. The first is that some liabilities are not included on the balance sheet (e.g. due to the preparer's difficulty of finding them all). The second is that liabilities are deliberately created to be off balance sheet (e.g. where a finance lease is made to look like an operating lease).

✔ Creditors are suppliers of goods and services received but not paid for by balance date. Accrued expenses can be the same, except that an invoice is not received prior to the preparation of the accounts and the amount owing is estimated. Accrued expenses also allow for items such as wages which may be paid in the next financial year, but part of the payment is for the last few days of the current financial year. Another typical accrual is unpaid interest on borrowings. Creditors might be shown as trade creditors and other creditors.

✔ Borrowings is the principal owing to lenders at the balance sheet date. These borrowings may be secured or unsecured. Typical borrowings are bank overdrafts, bank loans, other loans, loans from shareholders, lease liabilities. Leases are treated as a liability when classed as a finance lease—that is, the lease is really an arrangement to finance the purchase of an asset.

✔ Provisions are a means of recognising an event or transaction that has occurred before the balance sheet date, but are not legally due and payable until some time in the future. Provisions relating to specific assets are shown as deductions from those assets (e.g. provision for doubtful debts). All other provisions are shown as liabilities. Typical provisions are for dividends, income tax, employee entitlements, deferred income tax, warranty rationalisation, maintenance, restoration, claims.

✔ Provisions, being estimates, provide an opportunity for manipulation. Excess increases reduce profit whereas insufficient increases increase profit. A user can monitor potential manipulation by monitoring the change in level of the provision against the appropriate item to which the provision relates.

✔ Information on commitments is of interest when they are unusually large in relation to the size, activity and normal situation of the company.

✔ Contingent liabilities should always be considered by the user for revealing items which may become significant liabilities in the future.

7   Equity

This chapter describes the two components of equity: the owners' contribution (e.g. share capital) and the reserves (gains and losses made by the entity over time). Alba's accounts show typical items found in companies. These and other fairly common equity items are explained.

WHAT IS EQUITY?

Equity represents the shareholders' or other owners' (e.g. proprietors, government) interest in the entity. The Statement of Accounting Concepts SAC4 (paragraph 78) defines equity as 'the residual interest in the assets of the entity after deduction of its liabilities'. Total assets less total liabilities is known as net assets. Therefore equity is equal to net assets.

As we have seen in the previous two chapters, the difference is determined by what are considered to be assets and liabilities and how they are valued. Assets, especially significant non-current assets, are not generally valued at market, the most useful value for a user. This means equity is over- or under-stated to the degree that assets are over- or under-stated.

Equity as shown on Alba's balance sheet consists of three main items, being share capital, reserves and retained profits. In consolidated accounts (see chapter 12) there can be a fourth item called outside or minority shareholders.

There are basically two parts to equity, being the contributions made by shareholders in the past and the gains made by the entity through all aspects of its operations. Share capital is contributions by shareholders. Retained profits is some of the gains made; you would expect reserves to be the same, but they may not be.

SHARE CAPITAL

	1997 $	1996 $
Share capital	400 000	400 000

Alba's share capital is shown in note 15. The authorised capital is the maximum amount of share capital that can be issued under the company's articles and memorandum of association. This can be increased by a shareholders' meeting. Authorised capital no longer has to be disclosed.

Alba only has one type of share, being ordinary shares. But companies can issue either ordinary or preference shares. Each of these can be divided into different kinds with different rights attaching to them. For instance a class A ordinary share may have voting rights while a class B share does not. The choice is the company's and is stated in their articles and memorandum of association.

Preference shares differ from ordinary shares in that the shares are usually repaid before ordinary shares in the winding up of a company. They normally do not have voting rights. They usually have a set rate of dividend which is paid before ordinary share dividends. Sometimes the dividend is cumulative which means that if there is insufficient profit to pay dividend this year it will be paid, all being well, next year along with next year's dividend.

Redeemable preference shares are those which are repaid to the shareholders as specified in the setting up of those shares. The redemption may be at a specified date or as requested by shareholders after a specified date has passed. Redeemable preference shares turned into a means of borrowing during the 1970s and 1980s. Finance companies subscribed for redeemable preference shares with dividend rates based on interest rates. The dividends were received free of tax so the interest rate was reduced by the tax rate to give the same after-tax income to the finance company. The government became concerned that this method of financing was being used to avoid paying tax, and severely restricted it. This aspect is less important to a user than the fact that a borrowing was being treated as equity. This again affects the relationship of liabilities to equity. In reality redeemable preference shares had become borrowings but by law they could only be shown as equity. Today, you will only occasionally see redeemable preference shares and there is a slight return to offering them as a means of shareholder investment.

Alba has issued 400 000 ordinary shares at $1.00 each fully paid. Alba can only issue the kind of shares allowed by its authorised capital, but it can vary the amount at which they are issued. The $1.00 is the par value, i.e. the nominal value of the shares. The shares can be issued partly paid with calls being made for further payments on the shares at later dates. The shares can be issued at a discount which means the full amount does not have to be paid—this can occur when the shares are not worth their par value on the Stock Exchange. And the shares can be issued at a premium—that is, where subscribers for shares are willing to pay more than the par value. This is possible where the shares can be disposed of for more than the par value.

Alba has a share premium reserve of $100 000 which was created when they issued 100 000 shares in 1996 (see cash flows statement) for $200 000, that is par value of $100 000 plus share premium of $100 000.

In the event of the winding up of the company, shareholders of limited liability companies can only be called on to pay any unpaid amounts on issued shares. For instance, if a company had issued $1.00 shares paid to 80 cents, and it collapsed, shareholders could be asked to pay the additional 20 cents per share.

In the note on issued shares, the shares can only be issued and paid up to the maximum of the par value. Any additional amount paid on the issue of shares is called share premium and must be shown under the 'share premium reserve'. The share premium is really a contribution of capital but, because the law still follows old concepts of what is capital, it must be included in a separate reserve. The use of share premium is limited to such things as issuing of bonus shares and repayment, in certain circumstances, to shareholders. The aim of the restrictions is to protect shareholders' capital, but this approach does not achieve the aim.

When shareholders subscribe funds to a company the company receives the funds and deposits them in a bank account. It uses the cash in the bank to acquire things needed such as fixed assets and inventory. Money does not necessarily remain in the bank. So neither the share capital nor share premium reserve is represented by cash in the bank. It is represented by all the assets less the liabilities. The shareholders' interest is protected to the extent that assets exceed liabilities. Over time the difference should increase in a healthy company as profit is used to fund the growth of the business. The company must have real net assets for there to be any valid equity. Therefore the legal concept of maintaining capital (equity) through creation of special reserves such as share premium is ineffective.

The Second Corporate Law Simplification Bill removes the concept of par value. (At July 1997 this legislation is still to pass through Parliament and the government is conducting a broader review.) This legislation would bring Australia in line with changes in New Zealand and follows the same approach as the USA.

Shares would be issued at any price. Par value is not used. This means the share premium account would disappear. As explained above, share premium is the difference between the par value of the shares as specified in the articles of association and the actual issue price. If the legislation becomes law share capital will reflect the actual issue price being the contribution received from the shareholders.

I think this is a welcome change as equity only really consists of either contributions made by shareholders or gains made by the company kept by the company.

Dividends, as now, will only be allowed to be paid out of profits. They can be paid in cash, transfer of assets or by issue of shares. This means that dividends will not be paid out of the issue of shares to shareholders for a consideration. This has been possible in certain circumstances in the past through the use of share premium accounts for dividend. How this is done is explained under 'Dividends' in chapter 8.

I believe it is illogical to pay a dividend from what has been a contribution from shareholders. In reality it is really a return of contribution and should be called that.

Convertible notes—are they debt or equity?

Convertible notes start as a borrowing and finish by being either repaid or converted to shares. Listed companies sometimes raise funds by issuing convertible notes. Subscribers to the notes receive interest at the rate specified and, at the date specified in the convertible notes, are able to convert the notes to shares. The notes are converted at the price per share set in the note. If subscribers do not convert the notes to shares at the end of the period, the company repays the principal to them.

In practice there are variations on these characteristics of convertible notes, but this does not change the general concept. The issue for a user of financial statements is when the notes should be treated as liabilities and when as equity. The treatment of them affects the comparison of liabilities to equity.

Once notes are converted to shares they must be treated as equity; but at what point along the way should they be shown as equity rather than borrowings? The Statement of Accounting Concepts SAC4 uses the term 'probable' to help decide if an item should be included as a liability. Applied in this situation, it means that notes should be shown as equity when it becomes probable that they will be converted to shares. However, the conservative approach is to treat them as borrowings until actually converted.

In exploring the probability of conversion, it is certainly reasonable to treat notes as equity when it is highly likely that holders will convert them. Holders are likely to convert to equity when the market price of the shares on the stock exchange is greater than the price at which the notes would be converted. The bigger the margin, the more likely they are to convert because of the greater potential profit through selling the shares.

A user's aim is to treat convertible notes in the most realistic way considering the circumstances. When examining financial statements which show unconverted convertible notes as equity, and when you are satisfied from the evidence that they are not very likely to convert to shares, then treat them as liabilities when using ratios to measure performance. A user can always treat items shown on the financial statements differently from the way they are shown—analysts frequently do.

From financial years ending on or after 31 December 1997 AASB 1033, *Presentation and Disclosure of Financial Instruments*, governs classification as equity or a liability. See 'Reporting on financial instruments' in chapter 8.

RESERVES

All reserves can be classified as one or other of three kinds: contributions by the shareholders, realised gains and unrealised gains. Alba's reserves are shown in note 16.

Share premium and other 'contribution' type reserves

	1997 $	1996 $
Share premium	100 000	100 000

We have seen how share premium is really a contribution by shareholders. I suggest that another example of this kind of reserve is options, where shareholders subscribe funds to acquire an option which gives them the right to acquire shares at a later date. In this situation the options are issued at a price. Shareholders are willing to pay the company to gain the right to an option which can be converted to a right to buy shares later. On exercising the option they will have to pay more money to subscribe. Some contend the option price is more like revenue as it does not actually constitute part of the issue price of the share.

A further example is a forfeited shares reserve. This occurs when shareholders fail to pay a call on partly paid shares. The shares are forfeited by these shareholders but the company is not required to return money paid. The shareholders lose their investment. In fact the company can reissue the shares again at full price. So the company gains additional contribution which is usually described as a forfeited share reserve.

Asset realisation and other realised gains reserves

	1997 $	1996 $
Asset realisation	306 346	279 532

The asset realisation reserve represents gains made on the disposal of what are called 'capital' types of profit. The profit is initially recorded on the profit and loss statement and then transferred from 'retained profits' to this reserve. Some companies leave this kind of profit within retained profits and do not create the reserve.

Alba's reserve increased by $26 814 during 1997, which was the profit on selling investments. This profit was shown as an abnormal item in note 4. The reserve increased by $254 296 in 1996, being $184 722 shown as abnormal profit from selling the old property (note 4) and $69 574 transferred from the asset revaluation reserve. This transfer is the amount the property had been revalued in prior years. As discussed under 'Valuation of assets' in chapter 5, this gain is never recorded as profit.

Other typical reserves arising from realised gains are:

- retained profits—yes, retained profits is a reserve but it is shown separately on the balance sheet;
- general reserve, which is simply the allocation of some of the retained profits under a different name; it was more popular in earlier years and was seen as a reserve that would not be used for the distribution of dividend;
- capital profits reserve, which is usually another name for asset realisation reserve.

Asset revaluation and other unrealised gains reserves

	1997 $	1996 $
Asset revaluation	111 512	—

As discussed in chapter 5, the asset revaluation reserve is the gain from revaluing non-current assets. This gain is never recognised in the profit and loss but simply added to the revaluation reserve. In 1997 Alba added $111 512 to the reserve, being $71 529 from revaluing the land and $39 983 from revaluing the building.

There is no requirement to do anything with amounts allocated to this reserve. Typically, on *disposal* of the revalued asset, the applicable revaluation amount is transferred to the asset realisation reserve as shown in Alba's 1996 movement in that reserve.

The asset revaluation reserve can be used to distribute dividend. This has normally been done by using it to issue bonus shares. In the 1990s, bonus shares are less frequently issued out of asset revaluation reserves because they have lost their tax free status. This is connected with the change in approach to taxing dividends known as dividend imputation. Dividend imputation is commented upon in the 'market performance ratios' section of chapter 10.

Another common unrealised gains reserve is the exchange fluctuation reserve. This is the accumulation of gains and losses from converting the financial statements of overseas subsidiaries into local currency for the purpose of producing consolidated accounts. This reserve will be a negative reserve when there are more losses than gains. See the 'all-inclusive profit concept' in the next chapter.

Why are there so many different kinds of reserves?

These different reserves have developed over time. Each reflects the kind of items involved. The share premium reserve has been required by law.

A major reason why capital reserves such as asset realisation were created was that bonus shares issued out of profits of an untainted capital nature were tax free. The asset revaluation reserve used to also have the benefit of tax free bonus issues. It is required for upward revaluations of non-current assets under AASB 1010.

The foreign currency translation reserve is required under AASB 1012, *Foreign Currency Translation*, for gains or losses from translating self-sustaining foreign subsidiaries.

So many of these distinctions are arbitrary. From the users' point of view, the key issue is whether all gains and losses are recognised in the equity. My view is that changes in market value of non-current assets form part of these gains and losses and should be regularly recognised. The failure to do this is a major reason why shareholders' equity does not usually show the full interest of shareholders in the business.

Just like provisions, reserves do not represent cash. Any cash flow coming through realised profits is added to cash at bank at the time received, and then used to buy other assets, pay expenses or pay liabilities. The cash is used in the business.

POINTS TO REMEMBER

✔ Equity represents the interest of shareholders and consists of both contributions for shares and gains made by the company. The extent to which the equity shows the full interest of the shareholders is dependent on the extent to which significant non-current assets are valued at current market values.

✔ Share capital is the issued and paid up capital of the company. There are ordinary and preference shares. Preference shares give preference for payment of dividends and are usually at specified dividend rates. Redeemable preference shares mean the shareholders receive their money back at the time of redemption, and have often been used as a means of borrowing.

✔ Shares have a par value which is their nominal value. Shares can be: issued as partly paid with calls for additional contributions from time to time; issued at a discount when shareholders would not be prepared to pay full value; and issued at a premium when shareholders are willing to pay more than par value to subscribe. The maximum liability of shareholders in the event of the collapse of a company is for any unpaid amount on the shares.

✔ Reserves can be divided into three categories: contributions by shareholders (such as share premium reserve); realised gains (such as retained profits and asset realisation reserve); and unrealised gains (such as asset revaluation reserve). The share premium reserve has been required by law and the asset revaluation and foreign currency translation reserves by accounting standards. Other reserves have evolved for historical reasons.

✔ In the final analysis, the shareholders only possess value in the entity to the extent that the assets exceed the liabilities.

8   **P**rofit and loss

This chapter explains what profit is considered to be in terms of the Statement of Accounting Concepts SAC4 and the 'all-inclusive profit concept'; describes extraordinary and abnormal items; shows what revenues and expenses are disclosed; analyses the idea of 'normal' profit; and covers specific items—foreign currency gains and losses, financial instruments, income tax, dividends and segment results.

REVENUE AND EXPENSES

The Statement of Accounting Concepts SAC4 does not define profit or loss, but defines revenue and expenses as follows and explains when they should be recognised. Profit exists when revenues exceed expenses and losses are the opposite situation. The difference is added to or subtracted from the equity.

> 'Revenues' are inflows or other enhancements, or savings in outflows, of future economic benefits in the form of increases in assets or reductions in liabilities of the entity, other than those relating to contributions by owners, that result in an increase in equity during the reporting period. (Paragraph 111—Definition of revenues.)
>
> A revenue should be recognised in the operating statement, in the determination of the result for the reporting period, when and only when:
> (a) it is probable that the inflow or other enhancement or saving in outflows of future economic benefits has occurred; and
> (b) the inflow or other enhancement or saving in outflows of future economic benefits can be measured reliably. (Paragraph 125—Criteria for recognition of revenues.)
>
> 'Expenses' are consumptions or losses of future economic benefits in the form of reduction in assets or increases in liabilities of the entity, other than those relating to distributions to owners, that result in a decrease in equity during the reporting period. (Paragraph 117—Definition of expenses.)

An expense should be recognised in the operating statement, in the determination of the result for the reporting period, when and only when:

(a) it is probable that the consumption or loss of future economic benefits resulting in a reduction in assets and/or an increase in liabilities has occurred; and

(b) the consumption or loss of future economic benefits can be measured reliably. (Paragraph 132—Criteria for recognition of expenses.)

These definitions are saying that all changes in equity other than contributions by or distributions to owners are to be treated as revenues or expenses in the profit and loss statement. This is quite revolutionary as it means items excluded under the all-inclusive profit concept would be included. I agree with this in principle as it gives more consistency of treatment of gains and losses. You have seen the inconsistency in treatment of revaluation gains under revaluations of non-current assets in chapter 5.

Revenues and expenses can only be recognised when it is probable that they have occurred and they can be measured reliably. These points were discussed in chapter 6.

The implementation of these definitions and recognition requirements will require the revising of certain accounting standards to enable the recognition of all gains and losses through the profit and loss statement, and remove the requirement that some gains and losses be recognised as additions or subtractions directly against reserves. This chapter is based on the accounting standards in force at 30 June 1997 (i.e. any required revisions to accounting standards had not been made by that date).

ALL-INCLUSIVE PROFIT CONCEPT

The fundamental doctrine is that all profit, from whatever source, should be recognised. This is done by starting with the premise that all revenues and gains and all expenses and losses incurred during the reporting period should be included in the determination of profit unless specifically excluded. This is called the 'all-inclusive profit concept'.

Australia has followed the all-inclusive approach in the accounting standard for companies, AASB 1018, *Profit and Loss Accounts,* and for other entities in AAS 1, *Profit and Loss or Other Operating Statements.* However, the approach is not quite all-inclusive (as stated above, this would need to change to comply with SAC4), as there are three exceptions: revaluation of non-current assets, currency translation and new accounting standards.

Revaluation of non-current assets

Gains from revaluing non-current assets such as land and buildings are added to the asset revaluation reserve and not recognised as revenue under AASB 1010, *Accounting for the Revaluation of Non-Current Assets.* These gains are unrealised as there has not been a sales transaction with a third party. The gain arises from reassessing the value of the asset. Will the gain be enduring? Will it be realisable in the future? The typical accounting approach adopted by this standard is to be conservative and wait and see.

Gains and losses are reported following these rules:

■ most revaluation gains are added to the *asset revaluation reserve*;
■ to the extent a revaluation gain reverses an earlier devaluation, then it is recorded as revenue in the profit and loss statement;
■ most devaluations are recognised as an expense in the profit and loss statement;
■ to the extent a devaluation loss reverses an earlier revaluation, then it is recorded as a reduction from the *asset revaluation reserve*.

See chapter 5 for more commentary on the valuation of and accounting for non-current assets.

Currency translation

Gains or losses arise from converting the financial statements of self-sustaining overseas subsidiaries into local currency for the purpose of preparing consolidated financial statements are added to or subtracted from a reserve usually called *currency fluctuation reserve*. 'Self-sustaining' means the overseas operation is operationally and financially independent, e.g. more than just a company used to import the Australian parent company's product into the overseas country.

The argument for not including them as part of profit and loss is that fluctuations in exchange rate are beyond the control of management. Management are not trading or dealing in currencies, but operating their business in different countries. So it is considered better to eliminate this gain or loss from profit reporting.

This is inconsistent with revaluations. With currency translation, both gains and losses are taken direct to the reserve whereas with revaluations the general principle is to take only gains to the reserve.

Accounting for foreign currency is discussed in more detail later in this chapter.

New accounting standards

Gains or losses from adjusting previously reported profit and loss can arise from applying a new accounting standard or statutory requirement. In the year that a new accounting standard is applied, there is often an effect on that year's reported profit and an accumulated effect on prior years' profits as a result of changing the way revenue or expenses are recognised. The effect on the current year is reported as part of profit but the cumulative effect is adjusted against retained profits at the beginning of the financial year.

An example for many companies during 1995 was the introduction of the revised requirements for accounting for employee entitlements (discussed in chapter 6). This required the inclusion of on-costs such as payroll tax and workers compensation and the reassessment of the non-current liability to be an estimate of future payments discounted to today's value. Mostly this resulted in an increased liability. The cumulative retrospective effect was adjusted against retained profits.

For Country Road the cumulative effect appeared in the 1995 consolidated profit and loss statement as follows:

	Note	1995 $000	1994 $000
Operating profit	2	16 344	4 129
Income tax attributable to operating profit		(452)	(3 692)
Operating profit after income tax		15 892	437
Retained profits/(accumulated losses) at the beginning of the financial period		1 604	(22 787)
Adjustment to retained profits on adoption of AASB 1028—Accounting for Employee Entitlements		(816)	—
Aggregate of amounts transferred from reserves	18	—	26 951
Total available for appropriation		16 680	4 601
Dividends provided for or paid		7 314	2 997
Retained profits at the end of the financial period		9 366	1 604

The cumulative retrospective adjustment reduces retained profits by $816 000 but is never reported as part of an annual profit.

The 1995 profit is calculated using the revised accounting policy which appears to lead to a higher employee entitlement expense whereas the 1994 profit was calculated under the previous rules. Therefore, the two profits are not calculated on the same basis. The financial effect is not disclosed. It is probably much less than the cumulative effect.

CLASSIFICATION OF PROFIT

Revenue and expenses are classified as either operating or extraordinary. Most items are part of operating profit. These are revenue and expenses that are part of the ordinary operations of the business. See the detailed profit and loss statement for Alba Manufacturing in chapter 4. Items within operating profit can warrant disclosure due to their nature and amount—these are called abnormal items. Alba had one abnormal item in 1997 and two in 1996. Users of financial statements should pay attention to extraordinary and abnormal items which are defined as follows.

Extraordinary items

In Australia, extraordinary items are revenue and expense items caused by transactions or events outside the ordinary operations and are *not* of a recurring nature. This means that such transactions or events which do recur, though extraordinary in nature, are included as part of operating profit.

The limitation of extraordinary items to make them rare has been an international trend. Accounting standards in some other countries might treat *recurring* extraordinary items as extraordinary. In some countries extraordinary items are called unusual items. Countries which do not follow international accounting standards or have not followed current accounting trends may not even distinguish extraordinary or unusual items from ordinary operations.

Because extraordinary items are defined as not likely to recur, they are expected to be rare. Examples of extraordinary items are the gain or loss on sale or abandonment of a significant business or its associated assets and losses from the condemnation, expropriation or unintended destruction of property (AASB 1018, Commentary, paragraph (xv)).

Accounting standard AASB 1018 requires disclosure on the profit and loss statement of extraordinary items after the 'operating profit after tax'. The extraordinary items can be included with before tax, tax on extraordinary items and extraordinary items net of tax. This disclosure must be supported by a note listing each extraordinary item and the tax applicable to each. There can be a mixture of gains and losses which can total a net gain or a net loss.

In 1996 Alba Manufacturing reported the gain of $184 722 from sale of its property as an abnormal item. The commentary at the beginning of chapter 4 explains this was the sale in December 1996 of its first owned premises which they bought in 1983. Thus it was thirteen years from purchase to sale. They now have a new property that might be sold in the future.

Accounting standard AASB 1018 allows that what is extraordinary for one entity is not necessarily so for another. Perhaps an argument could be mounted that the gain on sale is extraordinary for Alba (the position taken in the first edition of this book). However, this seems unlikely given that the Australian Securities Commission has approached several listed companies, having them reclassify extraordinary items as abnormal items. The example of CSR under 'Dividends' later in this chapter was such a situation.

To demonstrate how extraordinary items are presented on the profit and loss statement let's treat Alba's gain on sale of the inner city property as extraordinary. The following is a recasting of the profit and loss statement from operating profit to profit after extraordinary items and the associated note in the accounts.

	Note	1997 $	1996 $
Operating profit before abnormal items	3	302 502	287 645
Abnormal items	4	26 814	(26 841)
Operating profit after abnormal items and before income tax		329 316	260 804
Income tax attributable to operating profit before abnormal items		(117 612)	(114 805)
Income tax attributable to abnormal items		—	9 663
Income tax attributable to operating profit	6	(117 612)	(105 142)
Operating profit after income tax		211 704	155 662
Profit on extraordinary item		—	184 722
Income tax attributable to extraordinary item		—	—
Profit on extraordinary item after income tax	5	—	184 722
Operating profit and extraordinary profit after income tax		211 704	340 384
Note 5 Extraordinary item Profit on sale of property (no tax effect)		—	184 722

Abnormal items

Within operating profit, from time to time, revenue and expense items vary from the normal pattern. These revenues and expenses which are considered abnormal by reason of their size and effect on the operating profit or loss after income tax (AASB 1018 paragraph 9) are termed abnormal items and must be reported in the accounts. They are also items which might be regarded as outside ordinary operations but are of a recurring nature. Note 4 of Alba's accounts shows different abnormal items in each year.

■ In 1996 inventory was reviewed and $26 841 worth of old and obsolete inventory was written off. Each year the company would allow for this, but in 1991 it recognised that a significant amount of worthless inventory had built up over recent years and should not be included any longer as an asset. The company could claim this write off as a tax deduction. So the expense, net of tax, was $16 373. The tax effect of abnormal items must be reported.

■ In 1996 Alba sold its inner city property and purchased a larger outer suburban property. Accounting standard AASB 1010 requires the profit or loss on disposal to be calculated as the sale proceeds less the book value at the time of disposal. This profit on sale was $184 722. The property was purchased in 1983 which was before capital gains tax was introduced in September 1985. Thus there is no tax payable on profits. In earlier years the property that was sold had been revalued. The amount in the asset revaluation reserve at the beginning of 1996 was $69 574 (see note 16 in Alba's accounts). This amount was transferred to the asset realisation reserve on disposal of the property. Thus the total gain on the property was $254 296 ($184 722 plus $69 574). As discussed earlier in this chapter and in chapter 5, AASB 1010 requires revaluation gains to be generally recognised through the asset revaluation reserve and never recorded as part of profit.

■ In 1997 Alba sold some shares which it had held for many years. The profit of $26 814 is free of tax because the shares were purchased prior to the introduction of capital gains tax in September 1985. It has been many years since the company sold any of its investments. It could be argued that the gain is an extraordinary item—however, there are likely to be future disposals of investments from time to time, so it is treated as an abnormal item. Of course, a company engaged in share trading or regular realisation of investments would not treat it as abnormal, but as an operating item.

Alba shows the totals of abnormal items and related income tax on the profit and loss statement (see chapter 4). This enables us to clearly distinguish between what is regarded as ordinary operating profit and what is regarded as abnormal. This form of presentation is not required. An acceptable alternative is to show just the operating profit after abnormal items. The amount of the abnormal items is shown in the note. Alba's profit and loss statement would then look like:

	Note	1997 $	1996 $
Operating items after abnormal items and before income tax	3, 4	329 316	445 526
Income tax attributable to operating profit	5	(117 612)	(105 142)
Operating profit after income tax		211 704	340 384

This conveys the impression of a substantial fall in profits. However, when the abnormal items are removed, there is actually a small increase in profit of $14 857, just over 5 per cent.

Companies can vary from year to year as to whether or not the abnormal items are shown separately on the profit and loss statement or not. This can be done to create an impression of profit change. For instance, if profit after abnormal items had increased but profit before abnormal items had decreased, then showing the after abnormal items only gives the sense of improved profit performance.

DISCLOSURE OF REVENUE AND EXPENSES

The statutory profit and loss statement provides only summary information, as shown for Alba Manufacturing. Further information is disclosed in supporting notes to the accounts. The information reported is what the Corporations Law and accounting standards require and consists of the following.

■ Sales and other significant items of revenue adding to total revenue (note 2 of Alba). This disclosure is required by AASB 1004, *Disclosure of Operating Revenue*.

■ Certain expenses such as interest, depreciation, lease payments and profit or loss on disposal of property, plant and equipment (note 3).

■ Additional disclosure of certain expenses, being details of defined benefits superannuation schemes (note 22), payments to auditors (note 25), remuneration of directors, including those employed by the company as well as any others (note 24) and, in listed, borrowing and a limited number of other companies, the remuneration of executives. Fees paid to professional consultants such as lawyers and management consultants do not have to be disclosed. There has been increased disclosure of the level of payments to directors and executives because of perceived excessive payments and growing shareholder interest in having this information. However, the information is limited to numbers of people paid within $10 000 bands. Names are not given, though people generally assume the chief executive is the highest paid executive.

■ Abnormal items and the tax pertaining to each of them (note 4).

■ Extraordinary items and the tax pertaining to each of them.

■ Information on current and deferred income tax and tax losses (note 5).

■ Reconciliation of income tax expense (when the difference between the accounting profit multiplied by the tax rate and the reported tax expense is greater than 15 per cent—note 5).

We will use some of the information disclosed as revenue and expenses in calculating ratios, especially ratios about profitability and financing structure, in chapter 10.

Items listed under note 3 of Alba are explained in the comments on the relevant assets and liabilities.

There has been increasing interest in transactions with related parties. The accounting standard AASB 1017 requires disclosure of transactions with related parties (see receivables—'loans to directors' in chapter 5). Related party transactions on a commercial basis can be perfectly satisfactory. So when reading information on related party transactions think about how valid it seems for the types of business in which the entity is engaged. Alba's note 29 and related notes indicate that the company's related party transactions are reasonable.

WHAT IS 'NORMAL' PROFIT?

Measuring profit performance is one of the important aspects of analysing a business. What profit should be used in this calculation? How should we consider abnormal and extraordinary items?

The aim is to use 'normalised' profit. This is the profit resulting from ordinary revenues less ordinary expenses. Financial statements analysts like to eliminate 'out of the ordinary' items. The important issue is to distinguish ordinary from out of the ordinary items.

Imagine you are a preparer of financial statements. Wouldn't you like to remove all the unfavourable items you can from being considered as 'ordinary' profits? The three possibilities are to allocate them as:

■ abnormal;
■ extraordinary;
■ something else such as adjustment to retained profits.

The tightening of requirements in Australia has limited the choice mainly to abnormal items. In other countries, there is still more scope—consider this example from a Singapore listed group's consolidated accounts.

	1990 $000	1989 $000
Operating profit before taxation	9 307	8 212
Taxation	1 939	1 708
Profit after taxation	7 368	6 504
Outside shareholders' interests	800	760
Profit before extraordinary items	6 568	5 744
Extraordinary items	88	(207)
Profit for the year	6 656	5 537
Dividends	1 596	1 019
Retained profit	5 060	4 518

This group seems to be making profits, paying dividends at only about 20 per cent of profit. So the group should be building a strong retained profits reserve. In the balance sheet retained profit is not separately disclosed. One figure for all reserves is given:

	1990 $000	1989 $000
Reserves	80	4 292

This shows a big drop from 1989, which surely cannot be due to profits, it must be some other reserve! The Singapore group's note 19 provides information about reserves and discloses the following interesting figures labelled *Movement in revenue reserve/(accumulated losses)*:

	1990 $000	1989 $000
Balance 1 January	(1 251)	(2 546)
Exchange adjustments	(96)	(40)
Goodwill on consolidation written off on acquisition of subsidiaries	(9 764)	(3 183)
Prior year adjustments	(211)	—
Profit transferred from Profit & Loss Account	5 060	4 518
Balance 31 December	(6 262)	(1 251)

Instead of retained profits they actually have accumulated losses which are rising primarily as a result of goodwill paid on acquiring subsidiaries. The $80 000 total in reserves is from share premium and asset revaluation reserves.

So what is the profit? The group has presented the information in a form to encourage users to think it is $5 060 000. Its note 19 includes an explanation that the prior year adjustments 'relate to expenditure of subsidiaries not previously recorded'. This is normal expenditure which has not been included in calculation of profit either in 1990 or in the prior year! The Australian standard requires it to be included in 1990 profit. It can be highlighted. The international standard IAS 8, *Unusual and Prior Period Items and Changes in Accounting Policies*, encourages either the Australian approach or the retrospective adjustment of the prior period reported profit. These accounts have done neither.

Does the approach adopted provide scope for forgetting expenditure each year and recording it in the next year as an adjustment? I hope that is too cynical a view.

The goodwill represents the excess paid above the net assets to acquire new businesses during the year. Goodwill is discussed in chapter 5. The adjustment to retained profits means that shareholders' equity has been reduced but not treated as an expense. It is never reported as part of operating profits or as an extraordinary item.

The international standard IAS 22, *Accounting for Business Combinations*, allows goodwill to be adjusted against shareholders' equity (as in this example) or treated as an asset and amortised over the period of future benefit. The latter method reduces reported profit each year in which goodwill is amortised, while the former method avoids any effect on reported profits.

Australia, New Zealand and the USA require recognition as an asset and amortisation (see chapter 5). When the goodwill has no future benefit, it is written off as an expense immediately.

In our example we have over $12 000 000 adjusted against retained profits in just two years! Other information in the accounts shows that the group spent $12 414 000 in 1990 on acquiring new subsidiaries, of which $9 729 000 was goodwill. Most of the cost paid was for an intangible asset of dubious value.

The exchange adjustment of $96 000 seems to be on translation of overseas subsidiaries into Singapore dollars. This treatment is in accordance with accounting standards discussed earlier in this chapter.

Subsequent annual reports showed a large downturn in profit, write off of intangibles, sale or close of unprofitable businesses (some bought in 1989 and 1990), completely new Board and new major shareholders.

We come back to the question—what is the profit? We may have differing opinions. The critical lesson to be learned from this example is that when interpreting profit performance *you* must consider carefully what you wish to include as 'normalised' profit. The accounts will present their view. You are able to make your own adjustments.

In chapter 10, Ratios, we remember this when assessing the profit performance of Alba Manufacturing where we have operating profit with three different abnormal items and a gain on revaluation of property. The most important component is the abnormal items.

Investment analysts tend to concentrate on the profit before abnormal items. The importance of abnormal items is discounted. Abnormal items are regarded as 'one off' items. For listed companies abnormal items are, unlike Alba's situation, often negative. The profit after abnormal items is worse than before. Thus it is favourable if analysts discount or ignore the abnormal items.

My experience is that we should examine the abnormal items. I make a practice of listing the abnormal items over time as part of my assessment. Frequently abnormal items can be prevalent or have a recurring pattern. In such situations the estimating of ongoing profit is more likely to be realistic if we allow for estimated recurrence of the abnormal items. I believe if analysts did this, then there would be lower expectation of future profit performance for a number of Australian listed companies. I am sure similar situations exist in other countries.

FOREIGN CURRENCY GAINS AND LOSSES

An entity which buys or borrows from, or which sells or lends to, an entity in another country, and makes the transaction in a currency different from its own, is subject to gains or losses. These arise from fluctuating exchange rates over the duration of the transaction. The longer the period, the greater the likelihood of gains or losses.

The accounting standard AASB 1012, *Foreign Currency Translation*, sets out how to account for and report this information. We will look at four typical situations:

■ borrowing from overseas;
■ capitalisation of exchange gains and losses;
■ protecting against exchange fluctuations;
■ converting foreign subsidiaries' financial statements into local currency (which was mentioned early in this chapter).

Borrowing from overseas

Here is a typical example of a foreign currency transaction. Imagine Alba's $20 000 non-current secured loan was a $US borrowing. On 1 October 1995 Alba borrowed $US15 000 interest-only (at 7.5%), the loan repayable in five years time. The exchange rate at the time was $A1.00 = $US0.84. This means that at the time of borrowing Alba owed $A17 857 ($US15 000/0.84).

At each balance sheet date the loan has to be shown in the accounts valued at the exchange rate of that date. The accounting standard is based on the premise that the best estimate and most relevant value is obtained by using the current exchange rate.

The following table shows the history of the loan over its life.

Date	Exchange rate $A1.00 = $US	Loan value $US15 000 $A	Gain or (loss) reported in P&L $A
1/10/95	0.84 date of borrowing	17 857	nil
30/6/96	0.78	19 231	(1 374)
30/6/97	0.76	19 737	(506)
30/6/98	0.65	23 077	(3 340)
30/6/99	0.72	20 833	2 244
30/6/00	0.79	18 987	1 846
1/10/00	0.74 date of repayment	20 270	(1 283)
Total loss on the borrowing over the five years			(2 413)

The greater the volatility of the exchange rate over the period, the greater the fluctuation in amounts reported as gains or losses on exchange. The overall loss of $2 413, which is the cumulative amount recognised over the five years, has varying gains or losses recognised in each year. However, the final loss is not known at the beginning of the loan. At any point in time the best estimate available is the exchange rate at year end.

The loss becomes realised when the loan is actually repaid. Income tax applies to realised gains or losses. This means that recognition of the unrealised gains or losses during each financial year is neither assessable nor deductible in the tax return. By the time of repayment of the loan, the tax and accounting recognition are the same—the difference is they are recognised differently over the period of the loan. This is known as a timing difference. See the section on income tax later in this chapter to learn how tax-effect accounting treats timing differences.

Lending is treated in exactly the same way except that we are looking at the opposite situation from borrowing. So if Alba had lent $US15 000 to another entity, it would have made a gain of $2 413 on exchange fluctuations over the five years.

The same principles apply for buying and selling except that the time between the beginning and end of the transaction is much shorter. For instance, the purchase of inventory from overseas is recorded in inventory at the exchange rate ruling when the inventory is received into store. Any difference between the exchange rate then and at the time of payment is recorded as a gain or loss on foreign currency.

Capitalisation of exchange gains and losses

Exchange gains or losses are capitalised (i.e. added to the value of assets) during the period when assets are being constructed. The asset can be for use by the entity itself, such as the building of a factory or large piece of machinery, or built for another entity, such as the construction of a ship. What this approach means is that any overseas borrowings used to fund the asset have both the interest and the foreign exchange gains and losses added to the value of the asset.

The amount at which these non-current assets are recognised in the accounts is subject to the upper limit of the recoverable amount discussed at the beginning of chapter 5.

Protecting against exchange fluctuations

It can be very expensive to use foreign currencies, particularly for borrowing, because of the risk of substantial loss. This is amply illustrated by the huge exchange losses suffered by borrowers who used foreign loans in the 1980s. Some borrowers have sued the banks for their losses, claiming the banks misled them. They assert they would not have borrowed had they understood the risks. Some found they had to pay back more than one-and-a-half times the amount borrowed, because the Australian dollar dropped so much in value in the mid-1980s.

The risk of loss can be eliminated or reduced by various measures. The practices used to reduce the risk are called hedging. Forward exchange contracts are often used. These contracts provide that the foreign amount will be paid at an exchange rate given in the contract. The actual exchange rate may be different at the time, but that is the risk of the financial institution providing the contract. The forward exchange contract rate may be different from the rate existing at the time of establishing the contract, but that is the price the buyer takes to have peace of mind on the amount to be repaid. The financial institution charges a fee for providing payment at a set rate.

When the exchange rate is set, any balance date asset or liability covered by the contract is protected from risk of loss arising from fluctuations in the exchange rate. When purchasing or selling goods and services, any difference between the exchange rate used to record the transaction and the contract rate plus the costs of the hedge are included in the cost of the item acquired or sold.

For other transactions the difference between the exchange rate and the contract rate at the time of the contract is recognised immediately. Any fee charged by the financial institution for providing the contract is allocated over the life of the transaction—that is, it is treated like an interest cost. So at the balance date there will be a prepayment for any unused forward exchange contract costs. This is the substance of what the accounting standard recognises, but the way it is expressed makes it seem more complex.

Another approach to hedging is commonly called a natural hedge. This is where a foreign currency borrowing is arranged to be paid from a foreign currency receivable. This practice is quite common in large multinational entities where they can plan their financial needs on a global basis. To the extent that the borrowings and receivables due dates approximate each other, exchange gains or losses on the payables and receivables can offset each other, leaving only a small net effect.

Converting foreign subsidiaries' financial statements into local currency

Each year entities with foreign subsidiaries must prepare consolidated accounts expressed in local currency. Foreign subsidiaries are classed as either self-sustaining or integrated. Self-sustaining foreign subsidiaries are defined as being 'not an integrated foreign operation, being an operation that is independent, financially and operationally, of the company and whose operations do not normally expose the company or group to foreign exchange gains or losses' (paragraph 1012.06). Integrated foreign subsidiaries are defined as the opposite, particularly that they are 'financially and operationally interdependent'.

For translating the foreign currency financial statements of self-sustaining subsidiaries into Australian dollars the exchange rates to be used are the balance date rate for the balance sheet and the average annual rate for the profit and loss. The gains or losses arising, because of the difference in exchange rate this year compared with the prior year, are added to or subtracted from the foreign currency translation reserve. As discussed at the beginning of this chapter these gains or losses are never treated as part of profit.

As an example, let's imagine Alba establishes a subsidiary, Jopewi Berhad, in Malaysia. It is a separate operation manufacturing light industrial machinery. Alba has invested in its equity and the company has obtained loans from Malaysian financial institutions. To keep it simple we will imagine the company does not trade for the first two years of its existence. The investment in the subsidiary gains in value when the Australian dollar falls because more Australian dollars are received for the same amount of overseas currency.

Date	Exchange rate $A1.00 = Malaysian Ringgit	Net assets $M200 000 $A	Gain/(loss) added reserve $A	Balance of reserve $A
1/9/97*	2.04	98 039	nil	nil
30/6/98	2.13	93 897	(4 142)	(4 142)
30/6/99	1.85	108 108	14 211	10 069

* date subsidiary created

For foreign subsidiaries classed as integrated foreign operations (e.g. it aids the importing of the Australian product into the foreign country) any gains or losses on currency translation are included in the profit. However, the basis of translation is different. All monetary assets and liabilities (e.g. cash, debtors, inventories and loans) are converted at balance date rates. All non-monetary assets and liabilities (such as fixed assets and provisions) are converted at the rates at the time they were first recognised or last revalued.

REPORTING ON FINANCIAL INSTRUMENTS

From 31 December 1997 AASB 1033, *Presentation and Disclosure of Financial Instruments*, must be applied. In chapter 4, Alba has complied early at 30 June 1997. The underlying purpose of these disclosures is to provide information on the risks of loss on financial assets, financial liabilities and equity instruments due to shifts in circumstances such as rising interest rates, adverse changes in foreign currency exchange rates on foreign currency transactions and borrowings, and exposure to losses on derivative financial instruments.

Some financial instruments can be very complex and difficult to understand. This section aims to provide you with some background information and to help you understand the kinds of disclosures this standard requires. The disclosures cover balance sheet items as well as profit and loss. The section is placed immediately after 'Foreign currency gains and losses' because foreign currency is one of the areas of financial instruments.

What are financial instruments?

The accounting standard defines a *financial instrument* 'as any contract that gives rise to both a financial asset of one entity and a *financial liability* or equity instrument of another entity' (paragraph 8.1).

A financial asset includes cash; a right to receive cash or another asset; be able to exchange it for another asset under favourable conditions; and ownership of some kind in another entity. Common examples are trade accounts receivable, notes receivable, loans receivable and bonds receivable (AASB 1033, Appendix, paragraph 4).

A financial liability is a contractual obligation to pay a liability by cash or from another financial asset; or 'exchange financial instruments with another entity under conditions that are potentially unfavourable' (paragraph 8.1). Common examples are trade accounts payable, notes payable, loans payable (borrowings) and bonds payable (AASB 1033, Appendix, paragraph 4).

Equity instrument 'means any contract that evidences a residual interest in the assets of an entity after deducting all of its *liabilities*' (paragraph 8.1). Examples include ordinary shares, preference shares which are not really a form of financing, and 'warrants or options to subscribe for or purchase ordinary shares' (AASB 1033, Appendix, paragraph 7).

Typical disclosures required

The Alba disclosures are spread through the relevant notes rather than accumulated in one note. Either Alba's approach or disclosing most in a separate note is acceptable.

Typical disclosures (reference to Alba chapter 4 notes included) resulting from this standard are detailed below.

- Accounting policy information on financial instruments such as cash at bank, trade debtors (note 1(g)) and borrowings (note 1(i)) and information on potentially adverse situations arising from the terms and conditions of the financial instrument.

- Reporting of 'net fair value' for each class of financial asset (notes 1(g), 6, 7, 9) and liability (notes 12, 14, 27). Net fair value is the market value of an asset or liability between a willing seller and a willing and informed buyer. For an asset, the costs of exchanging that asset are deducted. For a liability, the costs of exchanging the liability are added. Net fair value must be separately disclosed for readily tradable and infrequently traded financial assets or liabilities.

- For each class of financial asset carried in the accounts at an amount greater than the net fair value, the book value and the net fair value must be disclosed. The reasons for not reducing the book value to the net fair value must be disclosed. This includes 'the nature of evidence that provides the basis for management's belief that the carrying amount will be recovered' (paragraph 5.7 (b)).

- For each class of financial asset, whether recorded as an asset or not, the 'exposure to credit risk must be disclosed' (paragraph 5.5). It must be the maximum exposure to loss ignoring any underlying security. Thus for debtors it is the risk of non-payment which should be covered by the adequacy of the provision for doubtful debts (notes 1(g), 7). Perhaps a debtor has provided security which has reduced the estimate of the provision. This would have to be added back in reporting the exposure. If one or a few debtors make a large portion of the total trade debtors, this exposure must be disclosed including the estimated maximum possible loss excluding security.

■ Exposure to interest rate risk must be disclosed for each class of financial asset or financial liability whether on or off the balance sheet (notes 12, 14, 27). Disclosure includes the earlier of the loan maturity dates or review of interest rates. Fixed interest loans might have dates when that rate will be reviewed. Variable interest rate loans are usually subject to change at the discretion of the lending institution. Disclosure of the effective or weighted average effective interest rates is required for items such as debentures and notes receivable and payable. I would like to see disclosure required of actual interest rates incurred annually on each class of borrowings.

■ 'The entity's objectives for holding or issuing derivative financial instruments, the context needed to understand those objectives, and its strategies for achieving those objectives must be disclosed' (paragraph 5.3). The standard suggests the disclosure should be included with the note on the associated financial instruments (notes 1(c), 27).

I am not sure that the disclosures will necessarily be very readable or understandable. For instance, the disclosure of net fair value does not mean that the asset or liability will have to be finalised on that basis, e.g. a debenture might be held to redemption date and full recovery made. Doubtful debts net of the anticipated recovery from any underlying security is likely to be more realistic than adding back the security. The reader will need to carefully consider the information and think about the likely risk of loss. In Alba's situation none of the disclosures indicate a serious problem with the values used in the balance sheet or the profit and loss. (Please note that there might be some errors in the disclosures given in Alba due to this being a new and unused standard at the time of writing.)

Derivatives

Derivatives have received much publicity with events such as the collapse of Baring Brothers which resulted from trading in derivatives at their Singapore branch. The huge loss was caused by large volume speculative trading in a market where the price moved against the position held by the trader. Derivatives did not cause the problem, it was the trading in them.

Derivatives can be complex. At the fundamental level they are designed to provide a means of reducing the exposure to losses on financial assets and financial liabilities, e.g. a forward exchange cover to lock in the exchange rate to be used to pay or receive a foreign currency amount or an interest rate swap designed to reduce the overall interest rate payable on a borrowing. At the riskier end they can be traded on markets exposing the trading parties to shifts in pricing in the market.

Edna Carew in her book, *The Language of Money*, which consists of 'plain speaking' definitions of terms used in the financial industry, explains (page 97 of the 1996 edition) 'derivative products' as:

> contracts or instruments whose value stems from that of some underlying asset such as commodities, equities or currencies, or from an index such as the stock-exchange index, or from an indicator such as an interest rate. Derivative products include swaps, forwards, futures, options (puts and calls), swaptions, caps, floors and collars. The list is constantly evolving.

The name 'derivative' comes from 'derived'. The derivative product is derived from another item, typically a physical item. Ms Carew's explanation suggests some items from which derivatives are derived. It is beyond the scope of this book to spend much time on derivatives. Four common derivatives are detailed below.

- Forward exchange contracts which set the exchange rate which will be used at a set date for the payment of a foreign currency amount. This was included in the preceding section.

- Swaps which are to do with exchanging interest rates or foreign currencies. A typical one is the swapping of fixed interest rates with variable interest rates and vice versa. They do not swap the principal outstanding, they swap the interest rates. Imagine you have a variable interest rate loan and anticipate rising interest rates. To lock in a lower interest rate you find someone who is willing to swap their fixed interest rate for your variable rate.

- Futures are contracts concerning the buying or selling of commodities at an agreed price in the future. For example, gold miners or cotton farmers can choose to sell their product today for an agreed price in the future. They have to deliver the product in the future. This provides certainty on the price and the profits, provided the costs are incurred as expected. It is a protective technique if you expect the price of the commodity will be lower than the price being used in the futures contract. The gold miner or the cotton farmer must provide the product.

  People can trade futures on futures exchanges without the obligation of providing the commodity. When trading you are pitting your estimation of the future price with that reflected in the contract. Those buying are anticipating the price will increase; those selling, that it will fall.

- Options are a right to buy or sell an item at a certain price in the future. The option is exercised when the buying or selling takes place. People are more likely to exercise the option in favourable circumstances. For instance, an option to purchase a share is more likely to be exercised if the market price of the share is higher than any cost paid for the option and the share price specified in the option.

An 'American option' is one which can be exercised at any time up to the expiry date of the option. Whereas a 'European option' can only be exercised on the expiry date.

Options can be issued at a price. Thus, listed companies might choose to issue options as a means of raising some capital now while delaying the issue of shares (and rights associated with those shares) to a later date.

INCOME TAX

Income tax is a very complex area. This section covers how income tax payable is determined and explains tax-effect accounting. Tax-effect accounting is how income tax expense is recognised in the profit and loss and two related balance sheet items being the future income tax benefit and deferred tax liability. With tax-effect accounting one or both of these items must exist. The first part of this section covers calculating income tax payable and the balance deals with tax-effect accounting and associated issues. If you obtain a general sense of income tax and how it is represented through tax-effect accounting you are doing well.

How would you calculate your income tax expense? Say you are an employee who has tax deducted from each pay packet. At the end of the year you prepare your tax return. Using the tables in the tax form you can calculate the tax payable on your taxable income—your tax expense. You compare this amount with the tax you have paid through deductions from your pay as shown on your group certificate. If insufficient tax was deducted, you owe the government money. If more than sufficient was deducted, the government owes you money.

As individuals, we would count the estimated tax payable on the current year as our tax expense. This is what the application of the income tax legislation requires us to pay. This is called the 'tax payable' method of recognition.

Companies also pay tax but, unlike employees, they do not have tax deducted during the year. In Australia tax is payable as a lump sum in the next year or by quarterly instalments. The latter often means some of the tax is paid before year end. So all or most of the tax is owing at the end of the year. In simple terms, companies follow an annual cycle, which for Alba is:

	1997 $	1996 $
Amount of tax owing at the beginning of the year	95 521	65 914
less: Amount physically paid during the year (see cash flows statement)	112 984	86 948
	(17 463)	(21 034)
add: Estimated tax payable on current year's operating profit and extraordinary items (see note 5)	128 282	116 555
gives: Amount of tax owing at the end of the year (see note 13)	110 819	95 521

Accounting standard AASB 1020, *Accounting for Income Tax (Tax-Effect Accounting)*, requires the use of the 'liability method'. This is a much more complex method of determining tax based on the matching principle, i.e. matching expenses against revenue.

Tax-effect accounting assumes tax is an expense. However, tax can be viewed as an appropriation of profit similar to a dividend. Tax is not a voluntary expenditure incurred to generate revenue. Tax is an imposition by government to raise revenue to be used in carrying out its duties. If you adopt the 'appropriation' view, then the preferred approach to recognising tax expense is the 'payable' method which you and I use when considering our own tax situation. This is my preferred approach as it is simpler and more readily understandable.

Accounting profit and taxable income are different

Taxable income is different from profit because taxable income is prescribed by legislation, whereas profit is based on accounting concepts of revenue and expenses (or the all-inclusive profit notion). Throughout the world, income tax for businesses is based upon profit with additions, adjustments and

Figure 8.1

Comparison of accounting profit and income tax

Profit is an accounting concept	Income Tax Assessment Act
Revenue	Assessable income
(Expenses)	(Allowable deductions)
Profit	Taxable income
multiplied by	Income tax rate
gives Unadjusted tax payable	
	(Rebates)
gives	Income tax payable

Relationship		Alba's Situation $
	Accounting profit (from Alba's profit and loss)	329 316
add:	Income assessable in current year but not included as revenue in profit and loss, e.g. an insurance recovery loss recognised at time of loss but not assessable until received.	—
	Depreciation charged in accounts.	34 645
	Items never allowed as deductions such as entertainment expenses.	36 414
	Items not allowable or fully allowable as deductions this year but will be eventually fully allowable such as increases in provisions, e.g. doubtful debts allowed when bad debt written off, annual leave allowed when taken.	39 066
gives:	*Subtotal*	439 441
less:	Exempt income which is revenue for profit purposes but tax laws make it exempt from income tax, e.g. profit on disposal of shares which were bought prior to commencement of capital gains tax.	(26 814)
	Allowable depreciation using income tax regulations depreciation rates.	(31 917)
	Items allowed as a deduction when paid, not when provided.	(12 157)
	Deductions specified under income tax which would not normally be an expense in the profit and loss, e.g. the additional 25% deduction claimable on qualifying research and development expenditure. The business expense will only ever be 100%, not 125%.	—
gives:	**Taxable income**	368 553
times:	Income tax rate for companies of 36%	
gives:	Unadjusted tax payable	132 679
less:	Rebates such as dividends received from Australian domestic companies	(1 860)
add/less:	Underpayment/(overpayment) of income tax of prior years	(2 537)
gives:	**Tax payable** (see Alba note 5)	128 282

Figure 8.2

Calculating income tax payable from accounting profit

exceptions. This means there must be differences between the two, and so the income tax liability cannot be simply the accounting profit multiplied by the company tax rate.

We can compare the formulas for the profit concept and income tax as shown in figure 8.1.

In practice taxable income is determined by starting with the accounting profit and making all the adjustments for the differences between the two. Once the taxable income is determined, then the income tax payable can be calculated. The actual calculation of taxable income and tax payable is very briefly described in figure 8.2. Figures are provided for Alba. You will not be able to check all these figures against Alba's annual audited accounts. The accountants review the detailed profit and loss and other information to determine what adjustments need to be made.

Figure 8.2 is prepared for the Australian situation. Other countries will be similar though the actual specific examples will vary. For instance, in Australia the general rule is entertainment expenses are not deductible whereas in New Zealand 50 per cent is deductible.

Figure 8.2 shows how the tax payable is determined. However, the tax expense is $117 612 as included in the profit and loss statement rather than the amount payable of $128 282. The reason for this is the application of tax-effect accounting. The reason for the difference between the two figures is due to what accountants call timing differences. The remainder of this section explains tax-effect accounting.

The income tax payable of $128 282 is not the same as the income tax liability provision of $110 819 shown in note 13. Two items make up the difference being the overprovision (overestimation) of $2 537 for the previous year's tax and $20 000 paid by the balance sheet date against the current year's tax ($128 282 − $20 000 + $2 537 = $110 819).

Tax-effect accounting

What tax-effect accounting attempts to do is to create a tax expense based on accounting profit rather than taxable income. That is, it aims to take the accounting profit and multiply it by the tax rate to give tax expense. In looking at examples of the differences between accounting profit and taxable income we can group them under two categories:

■ permanent difference, which means that an item is always treated differently under accounting as compared with tax—like entertainment expenses which are never an allowable tax deduction, or exempt income which is never assessable;

■ timing difference, which means that the periods (years) in which items are recognised for accounting purposes vary from those under tax laws—like employee benefits where the liability and expense are recognised for accounting purposes based on entitlements arising from length of service, but a tax deduction is only allowed when the benefit is paid; or prepayments where the tax deduction is obtained before the expense is recognised.

It is not really possible to simply calculate tax expense as 36 per cent of profit when there are permanent differences, as taxable income never recognises them. So tax-effect accounting adjusts profit for permanent differences to give the tax expense. The difference between tax expense and tax payable are the timing differences. The relationship is demonstrated by figure 8.3.

	Alba's situation $
Accounting profit (being operating profit from Alba's profit and loss)	329 316
Multiplied by tax rate—36%—prima facie tax	118 554
+/– Permanent differences (including under/(over) provision from prior year)	(942)
= **Income tax expense**	117 612
+/– Timing differences	10 670
= **Income tax payable**	128 282

Figure 8.3

Tax-effect recognition

Note 5 of Alba's accounts shows the prima facie tax, income tax expense and income tax payable. In note 5 the four items between the prima facie tax and the income tax expense add to $(942). The timing difference is described as 'provision attributable to future years'.

Alba's note 5 shows how the income tax expense relates to the income tax payable ('provision attributable to current year'). This links the actual income tax payable and the tax-effect income tax expense. This disclosure is no longer required as it was a requirement of Schedule 5 which was not replaced in AASB 1034 and is not required by AASB 1020. Appendix 4 to AASB 1034 states this 'does not provide information of particular relevance'. I think it does; it shows us the situation under the tax payable method or recognition rather than tax-effect accounting. We could deduct the tax payable from the profit as an alternative view of the profit after tax. Without this disclosure, the tax payable information is lost.

Remember our balance sheet equation of E + L = A (equity + liabilities = assets)? Here we have a reduction in equity being the income tax expense and an increase in liabilities, but they are not equal. There is the difference of $10 670! Tax-effect accounting creates these differences each year. The differences are added to or subtracted from a non-current liability called Provision for Deferred Tax Liability (DTL) and/or a non-current asset called Future Income Tax Benefits (FITB). The question the user must ask is 'will the liability ever be paid or the asset ever be realised?'. The actual amount owing to the government is already recorded under current liabilities as Income Tax Provision. These are added extras for the sake of tax-effect accounting.

How do you choose whether to adjust DTL or FITB?

Deferred tax liabilities

Deferred tax liabilities (DTLs) are created when the tax deductions are allowed before the accounting expense is recognised, or when income is assessable after being recorded as revenue.

An expense example is mining companies developing mines. Costs of developing the mine such as labour and interest are added to the cost of the mine, i.e. treated as a fixed asset. When the mine is operational its cost is depreciated over its anticipated life, typically by allowing an amount per tonne of ore extracted. However, the tax deduction is available at the time the items are paid.

Prepayments is a common expense example where the tax deduction can be up to thirteen months prepayment but the accounting expense is recognised in the following years.

An income example could be an insurance claim. An insured loss has occurred and for accounting purposes there is no overall loss because insurance will be received. For tax purposes the loss might be claimed as a deduction in the year of the loss and the insurance payment treated as income in the year it is received.

For users the key question is 'will this liability ever be paid?'. In a growing company a DTL typically increases over time and does not reverse. An exception to this can be the mining companies mentioned above.

The international accounting standard states that timing differences may be excluded 'where there is reasonable evidence that these timing differences will not reverse for some considerable period (at least three years) ahead. There should also be no indication that after this period these timing differences are likely to reverse' (IAS 12, *Accounting for Taxes on Income*, paragraph 18). In such circumstances these timing differences would not be included in a DTL or FITB. The amount of timing differences excluded should be disclosed.

If we take the view that the liability is not a real liability we no longer want to recognise it. Reduction of liabilities means equity should be higher by the amount reduced, to keep our balance sheet equation correct. The gain in equity is allocated to retained profits because we are saying that too much was allowed as income tax expense when creating the liability.

Future income tax benefits

Future income tax benefits (FITBs) are created when tax deductions are allowed after the accounting expense has been recognised or when income is assessable before being recorded as revenue.

An expense example is employee entitlements such as annual leave. Employees earn their entitlement to annual leave over the period of their employment. The Australian rate is at four weeks per year of employment. The period of employment creates the entitlement. So the expense is recognised through a provision for annual leave. When leave is taken or paid out on termination of the employee, the payment is deducted from the provision as the expense has already been previously recognised. However, the amount provided for annual leave is not an allowable tax deduction. Only actual leave taken and paid can be claimed as a tax deduction.

An income example might be lease premium charged by a lessor on a well-positioned shop in a popular mall. The premium is received at the beginning of the lease period and is included as assessable income. However, it is recognised as revenue proportionally over the period of the lease.

Like a DTL, the FITB increases over time in a growing company. The same concern about the validity of the asset applies. In fact recognition of the asset can be said to be more dangerous than liability recognition—an amount recognised as an asset means that tax expense is not recognised.

My preference is not to consider an FITB as a valid asset. If we disregard the asset we need to decrease equity by the same amount. As for DTL, retained profits must be adjusted, except that this time profits are decreased because the view is that FITB should have been treated as part of tax expense in the past and not deferred as an asset. These assets can be millions, even hundreds of millions, of dollars on Australian listed companies.

Alba's tax-effect

Alba Manufacturing has an FITB of $73 250 (balance sheet) but not a DTL. Alba mainly has timing differences that create an FITB and has chosen to offset items which create a DTL against the asset. It has done this because they are much smaller than the items creating the FITB.

So in 1997 the timing difference of $10 670 has been added to the FITB.

Tax losses

Sometimes businesses have tax losses rather than taxable incomes. This situation arises when tax deductions exceed assessable income. Like an accounting loss, this is not a good situation if it occurs over a number of years with no real sign of change.

Under tax law, when a business returns to taxable income, it can offset tax losses against the taxable income. It will pay tax again after all the tax losses have been offset against the taxable income. There are rules to follow and restrictions on the use of tax losses but they are a subject for a book solely on income tax. For our purposes the general principle is what matters.

In certain circumstances company tax losses can be sold. Another company will pay up to 36 cents in the dollar if they can comply with tax law requirements and offset the purchased tax losses against taxable income. So tax losses can have a value.

Under tax-effect accounting, tax losses can be recognised as an FITB asset only if realisation is virtually certain. The accounting standard regards this level of certainty as likely to be met 'only in rare and exceptional circumstances'. Thus existence of these tax loss assets should be the exception rather than the rule. However many listed companies have these assets.

The Australian Securities Commission (ASC) operates a Financial Reporting Surveillance Program. The ASC became concerned at the number of companies carrying tax losses as part of the FITB. It was not rare. They issued Practice Note 36, *Future Income Tax Benefits*, in August 1993 providing guidance on factors to consider. The guidance for tax losses arising from trading, which I think are very reasonable, are (paragraph 9):

(a) has the cause of the losses ceased?
(b) were the losses incurred as a result of a 'one-off' event against a profitable trend?
(c) is the company earning profits and taxable income?
(d) does the company have a track record of budget reliability?
(e) is there a comprehensive budget showing a recoupment of the losses within, say, two to three years?

Companies which have incurred tax losses which have not been offset against taxable income must disclose the amount of the tax loss. This disclosure will be as part of an FITB and/or in the income tax or accounting policy notes to the accounts when not recognised as an FITB. So all tax losses, whether recognised as an asset or not, must be reported.

Information about tax losses, whether included in FITB or not, is required in the accounts. This is essential for understanding the profitability of the company and should be required whatever the method of calculating tax expense.

For mining companies tax losses usually exist during the time a mine is being developed and are reduced during the production life of the mine. This happens because allowable deductions occur throughout the development phase while no revenue is being earned. This is the opposite of the effect of the DTLs for mining companies discussed above.

Always consider the extent of tax losses. In the long run companies should generate accounting profits and taxable income because the aim is to be profitable. This is the general principle. There may be exceptions in the short to medium term such as mining companies which generate tax losses until the mine is operational. But be very careful in your assessment of companies or groups with large and rising tax losses relative to their assets or retained profits. Such situations can indicate that they will not be viable in the long run.

DIVIDENDS

The law allows dividends to be paid only out of profits (as defined over the years through case law, it is different from the accounting view). They can be profits of the current year or accumulated profits from prior years retained in the business. Generally all reserves other than share premium can be used to declare dividends. However, dividends are mainly declared out of retained profits.

The cash used to physically pay the dividends comes from the money in the bank. If there is insufficient cash available, the company may need to borrow to pay the dividend.

One of the best ways to grow a business is to retain as much of the profits as possible in it. As a rule of thumb, at least half the profit should be retained. However, listed companies also consider the dividend expectations of their shareholders. If the expectations are not met, the sharemarket will react negatively. So it is interesting to see what companies do to maintain the ability to pay dividends—as shown in these three examples.

1   In February 1992, CSR announced a huge write-down to comply with its interpretation of the requirement of valuation at no higher than recoverable amount (see 'Valuation of assets' and 'Investments' in chapter 5). The devaluation was so great that nearly all retained profits ($555.2 million at 31 March 1991) were eliminated, leaving just enough profits from which to pay dividend. CSR decided to apply to the court to allow them to transfer share premium reserves into retained profits to boost the reserve.

Initially the write-down was treated as an extraordinary item, but the Australian Securities Commission required them to treat it as an abnormal item. The ASC position makes sense in the light of information earlier in this chapter. Note 9 (Abnormal Items) of the accounts showed the write-down as consisting of:

	1992 $mill
Abnormal items (shown in note 9)	
Quarry and other raw material reserves	(68.6)
Plant and equipment	(193.5)
Growing timber and log licences	(44.9)
Goodwill	(215.9)
Patents and trademarks	(120.6)
Investments and other non-current assets	(16.5)
Total non-current asset write-downs	(660.0)
Plant closure costs and other expenses	(36.2)
	(696.2)
Income tax benefit	79.3
	(616.9)
Outside equity interests in abnormal items	58.7
	(558.2)
Amount added to capital reserve on revaluation of land and buildings (as shown in note 28)	186.4

Think of what this means! Nearly all the retained profits were deleted by this massive devaluation. The devaluation was largely of assets acquired in taking over companies for which, in the end, CSR had paid too much. It indicates that the company has ended up with no retained profits after paying 1992 dividends despite all its years of operations. $558 200 000 was transferred from share premium reserve to retained profits to cover the abnormal items. (Court approval is required for such transfers.) So at the balance date retained profits are shown as $564 100 000 being, in effect, contributions by shareholders, not true retained profits.

Page 4 of CSR's 1992 annual report states:

> With the exception of land and buildings, assets assessed as undervalued (and there were many) were not revalued upwards. This followed the strict application of accounting standards and reflected our wish to be conservative in the face of low growth prospects.

Revaluation gains cannot be included as profit. So $186 400 000 could not be offset against the write-down.

CSR devalued its assets to comply with the requirement to carry assets at no more than recoverable amount which was introduced into AASB 1010 at that time. Many other companies also announced large devaluations in order to comply with the recoverable amount requirements.

2   In 1987 M.I.M. Holdings changed the way it accounted for exchange losses to comply with a new accounting standard that was coming into force in the next year. This resulted in a massive write off of exchange losses of $545 211 000 against retained profits. The profit after tax, dividends paid, write off and transfer from assets revaluation reserve were:

	1987 $000	1986 $000
Operating profit after tax	48 490	48 265
Extraordinary losses after tax	(8 844)	(16 909)
Operating profit and extraordinary items	39 646	31 356
Retained profits at beginning of year	268 518	257 330
	308 164	288 686
Dividend paid and declared	(31 720)	(22 239)
Currency translation adjustment	—	2 071
Retained profits prior to adjustments	276 444	268 518
Write off of exchange losses	(545 221)	—
	(268 777)	268 518
Transfer from asset revaluation reserve	550 000	—
Retained profits at end of year	281 223	268 518

The transfer from asset revaluation reserve was necessary to maintain a positive retained profits reserve. The company really paid dividend out of asset revaluation surplus.

3   During 1988 and 1989 OPSM reported increasing operating profits and substantial extraordinary items. The extraordinary items arose from losses on acquired USA operations where too much had been paid for the assets. The following information taken from the profit and loss statement shows how a large part of dividend was really declared out of prior years' retained profits.

	1989 $000	1988 $000
Operating profit after income tax	23 226	18 458
Extraordinary losses after income tax	(17 545)	(13 904)
Profits from current year to cover dividend	5 681	4 554
Dividends paid and declared	(14 734)	(13 204)
Amount of prior years' profits used to cover dividends	9 053	8 650

These three examples show situations where dividend payment was a heavy drain on retained profits. They also show the effect that large losses or changes in accounting policy can have on the cumulative performance of a group.

We considered asset valuation and how it is accounted for in chapter 5. We have considered what profit is in this chapter. How profitable are companies? Is their performance being properly assessed? Does the sharemarket reflect the real value of the shares? We will consider these questions in chapter 10.

SEGMENT RESULTS

Alba's note 28 is a brief two line statement that the company only trades in Australia in light industrial machinery. The note does not add any information to that provided in the directors' report, but AASB 1005, *Financial Reporting by Segments*, requires it.

The note is of great value in the case of diversified groups—groups operating in different industries or different countries. These groups must disclose the sales, operating revenue and assets of each of their major industry and geographical segments. An industry segment is a particular industry, typically as defined in the Stock Exchange classification of industries. A geographical segment is a particular country or a group of countries in the one physical area with similar political and socio-economic conditions. A segment must be shown separately when it is responsible for more than 10 per cent of *any two of* sales, results and assets. Any smaller segments are lumped together under 'other'. The information compiled ties back into the accounts. Figure 8.4 gives an example.

Figure 8.4   Segmental information from James Hardie Ltd 1996 Annual Report

	Sales		Profit/(loss) before tax		Assets	
	31.3.96 $mil	31.3.95 $mil	**31.3.96 $mil**	31.3.95 $mil	**31.3.96 $mil**	31.3.95 $mil
Segment Reporting						
Industry segments						
Building Products	**686.9**	569.0	**94.2**	96.2	**609.8**	564.0
Plumbing & Pipelines	**349.6**	398.9	**(2.1)**	15.0	**285.7**	318.0
Building Services	**496.9**	533.0	**14.6**	7.4	**244.8**	241.7
Irrigation	**185.3**	193.1	**3.8**	9.4	**152.1**	162.9
Investments	**33.0**	31.4	**(4.1)**	(7.2)	**133.4**	151.9
Interest	—	—	**(27.5)**	(18.5)	—	—
Unallocated	—	—	**(8.1)**	(15.9)	**363.1**	428.8
Economic Entity, before abnormal items	**1 751.7**	1 725.4	**70.8**	86.4	**1 788.9**	1 867.3
Abnormal items						
Building Products			**(4.3)**	—		
Plumbing & Pipelines			**(4.1)**	—		
Building Services			**(25.5)**	—		
Irrigation			—	—		
Investments			—	—		
Unallocated			**(14.8)**	—		
			(48.7)	—		
Economic Entity	**1 751.7**	1 725.4	**22.1**	86.4	**1 788.9**	1 867.3
Geographic segments						
Australia	**1 140.5**	1 179.0	**33.8**	61.7	**1 115.9**	1 224.4
USA	**367.3**	339.9	**37.1**	21.0	**490.6**	461.1
New Zealand	**206.2**	176.6	**34.6**	28.3	**119.5**	122.9
Other countries	**37.7**	29.9	**(7.2)**	(6.1)	**62.9**	58.9
Interest	—	—	**(27.5)**	(18.5)	—	—
Economic Entity, before abnormal items	**1 751.7**	1 725.4	**70.8**	86.4	**1 788.9**	1 867.3
Abnormal items						
Australia			**(44.3)**	—		
USA			**(4.4)**	—		
New Zealand			—	—		
Other countries			—	—		
			(48.7)	—		
Economic Entity	**1 751.7**	1 725.4	**22.1**	86.4	**1 788.7**	1 867.3

Prior year segmental information has been restated to reflect the current industry segments. In the analysis by industry, cash deposits and future income tax benefits have been treated as unallocated.

The segmentation is for sales, segment results and assets. The profitability of each segment can be measured by comparing the percentages of *result over sales* and *result over assets* for the different segments.

The elimination items occur when there is some selling of goods and services between the segments and some joint use of assets by the segments.

In segmental information, the unallocated revenue, expenses and assets are items that apply to the whole group and cannot be assigned to just one of the segments. For instance, the group usually has a corporate headquarters which looks after the whole group.

The basis of pricing inter-segment sales is supposed to be disclosed. This may be sensitive information because of possible tax implications of what may be seen as artificial prices set to create higher profits in countries with lower tax rates. It is often not disclosed.

POINTS TO REMEMBER

✔ Under SAC4 all revenue and expenses should be included to determine profit.

✔ The accounting standards adopt the all-inclusive profit notion except for three items excluded from profit:
1 revaluation increases (except to the extent that they reverse a devaluation recognised in profit and loss) and devaluations to the extent that they reverse previous revaluations;
2 currency exchange fluctuations arising from translating self-sustaining foreign subsidiaries' accounts into local currency;
3 cumulative effects on retained profits up to the beginning of the current year caused by applying a new accounting standard.

✔ Revenue and expenses are classified as either operating (the majority) or extraordinary (the rare exception). Operating items which are unusually large or different from normal plus revenues or expenses outside ordinary operations which are of a recurring nature are reported as abnormal. Extraordinary items are gains or losses which are outside the ordinary course of business and are of a non-recurring nature.

✔ Items disclosed in the profit and loss statement and supporting notes are only those required to be shown by the Corporations Law and accounting standards. They include revenue, certain expenses, abnormal items, extraordinary items, income tax expense and some explanation of the calculation of income tax expense.

✔ In assessing profit performance, analysts want to use 'normalised' profits. The tendency is to use operating profits before abnormal items. A prudent user will consider the frequency and pattern of abnormal items, will have regard to extraordinary items and will carefully monitor adjustments to retained profits.

✔ The general rule is that all foreign currency gains and losses are recognised in the profit and loss statement in the year incurred. Gains or losses from translating self-sustaining overseas subsidiaries are added direct to the foreign currency translation reserve. The costs of purchased hedges are generally deferred and amortised over the period of the hedge. Purchased hedges and natural hedges protect against fluctuation in foreign currencies.

✔ Income tax expense is calculated by using the liability method of tax-effect accounting. The method's aim is to pretend, as much as possible, that income tax expense is calculated in terms of accounting profit rather than tax law. This causes the income tax expense to be different from the estimated tax liability for the year. The difference is added to or subtracted from the future income tax benefit and/or deferred tax liability. Users should consider whether these are real assets or liabilities.

✔ Related party information should be considered for what it may reveal about transactions which may be on terms more favourable than normal commercial practice.

✔ Dividends can be declared out of current year's and accumulated profits. Directors will endeavour to meet the shareholders' dividend expectations. This may conflict with retaining profits in the business, which is an effective method of funding expansion.

✔ Segmental information provides very valuable information about sales, profits and assets for each major segment of a diversified group. The information is produced for industry and geographical segments. The profit performance in terms of sales and assets can be compared across segments.

9 Cash flow

Annual reports of entities which are reporting entities are required to include cash flows statements. This has been required from financial years ending on 30 June 1992. Before that there were funds statements. The requirement for a cash flows statement follows a worldwide trend. Analysts have always wanted this information to help them better predict likely future cash flow, but the accounting profession took time to see it as being more useful than funds statements.

The accounting standard covering cash flow is AASB 1026, *Statement of Cash Flows*. The following commentary on Alba's cash flows statement considers the requirements of the standard; gives warning signals and desirable trends; and analyses Alba's cash flow performance.

WHY YOUR ORGANISATION SHOULD PRODUCE CASH FLOWS STATEMENTS

It is almost five years since I wrote the first edition of this book. In that time I have become more familiar with cash flows statements. They provide very valuable information. Unfortunately they take time to prepare as they must be prepared after the balance sheet and profit and loss statement. These two statements are generated from accounting systems but cash flows statements usually aren't. Thus, because of this difficulty of preparation they are not generally prepared for entities other than reporting entities. I would like to see general ledger accounting packages include the generation of cash flows statements as a matter of course.

In chapter 1 we saw how Sally used both a profit budget and cash flow forecast as part of her planning. Not only did Sally's Plantery need to generate a profit, it needed to have sufficient cash to be able to pay debts as they fell due and to remain viable. Typically, budgeting includes cash and profit forecasts. However, reporting to management of what has happened is usually limited to very detailed profit and loss statements and the balance sheet.

The historical detailed profit and loss statements usually show actual against budget and last year's actual. The historical information is used to help budget for the future. It helps management assess the reasonableness of the budget. But this is not done for cash flow forecasts! How can management assess the reasonability of cash flow forecasts if there are no historical ones for comparison? I think management and directors are at risk when they rely on cash flow forecasts which they cannot vet in any way.

Cash flow forecasts are usually in a format like:

	Cash at the beginning of the period
add:	Cash receipts
less:	Cash payments
gives:	Cash at the end of the period

The cash flows statement form is:

	Cash flows from operating activities*
	Cash flows from investing activities*
	Cash flows from financing activities*
gives:	Net cash movement for the year
add:	Cash at the beginning of the year
gives:	Cash at the end of the year

> * Each of these shows cash in and cash out and is subtotalled to give net cash movement under each category. The total of these three net cash movements gives the 'net cash movement for the year'.

From this chapter, especially analysing Alba's cash flow situation, you will see that this format is far superior. If Sally used this format for her cash flow forecast she would be able to see more clearly the cash generated from trading activities independently of other sources of cash. I am convinced that all organisations producing cash flow forecasts should use the cash flows statement format because it shows the projected pattern of cash flows better. If the forecast and the reporting of actual are in the same format, management and directors will find it easier to assess the reasonableness of the forecast. Unless there is a change in circumstance the patterns of the past are good predictors of the future.

Have you ever tried to sit on a two-legged stool? Impossible unless it is on a large base or you have a very good sense of balance. But we can all sit comfortably on a three-legged stool. In fact a three-legged stool will not rock! I believe using only the profit and loss statement and balance sheet is like sitting on a two-legged stool. To gain a comprehensive view of the financial situation we need all three financial statements: profit and loss statement, balance sheet and cash flows statement.

A simple way I think of a business is that it should generate revenue with profit. If there is real profit there will be strong net cash inflows from operating activities. If it is creative accounting profit, there will be a lack of cash inflows from operating activities.

WHAT DOES CASH FLOW SHOW?

The cash flows statement shows where the cash comes from and where it is used in the running of the business. Alba's cash flows statement contains typical items found in most cash flows statements for listed companies.

Australia and New Zealand require the use of the 'direct method'. This means the cash flows from operating activities must show the receipts from customers, payments to suppliers and employees and so on as Alba shows. The 'indirect method' reduces the cash flows from operating activities to being the reconciliation of profit after tax to cash flows from operating activities. In other words, if Alba was using the indirect method, something like what is shown as the reconciliation of profit and cash flows from operating activities in note 19 would be shown on the cash flows statement as the operating activities. This is far inferior.

Unfortunately many countries, such as the USA, allow the indirect method. Where there is a choice of methods most companies opt for the indirect because it is easier to calculate. This is the situation in Singapore, for instance. The use of the indirect method reduces how we can use cash flows information by removing one of the vital warning signals (see below) and by reducing possible cash flow ratios, introduced in chapter 10.

The cash movements are classified as operating, investing or financing activities. These are the three major arms of running a business.

1   Operating is the selling of the goods and services and costs associated with that. The typical items are:

Cash in
— Receipts from customers

— Interest received*
— Dividends received*

Cash out
— Payments to suppliers
    and employees
— Income tax paid
— Interest paid*

> * These items can be argued to fit under more than one category. The standard allows the preparers to decide which classification they want. Interest paid—is it operating or financing? It is part of the ordinary expenses of the business but it is only incurred because interest is payable on a borrowing raised to run the business. Dividends received can be argued to be operating or investing. Interest received certainly can be operating; it can be considered financing when it is merely an offset against interest paid or it can be considered investing if the entity has significant interest-bearing investments.
>
> Most Australian companies class them all as operating. In comparing one company with another you need to adjust for this if they show them differently. The New Zealand accounting standard requires them all to be shown as operating. In my analysis I always class them as operating.

2   Investing is the acquiring of fixed assets and other assets used to produce the goods and services. It is also the acquisition of companies and businesses plus the savings for a rainy day, like investing in shares and

fixed securities, putting surplus cash on deposit and so forth. The typical items are:

Cash in
— Proceeds from sale of property, plant and equipment
— Proceeds from sale of investments
— Proceeds from sale of companies and businesses

Cash out
— Payments for property, plant and equipment
— Payments for investments

— Payments for acquisitions of companies and businesses

3 Financing is how the business finances its investing and operating activities through raising funds from shareholders and borrowers. The typical items are:

Cash in
— Proceeds from new borrowings
— Proceeds from issuing shares

Cash out
— Payments on borrowings
— Dividends paid

The cash inflows and outflows are the gross movements—that is, it is the total cash received and paid. For example, details of new borrowings and repayments of existing borrowings must be shown rather than just netting them to show the end result.

Thus the standard requires the use of gross movements with only a few exceptions when net can be used; for example, in the finance industry the net increase or decrease is shown in deposits because the movements from receiving and repaying deposits are incidental to the major feature of how the deposits change in one year.

Reconciliation of cash

Cash at the end of the year shown on the cash flows statement must be reconciled to cash items in the balance sheet. Alba shows this at the bottom of the cash flows statement. The cash at the end of the year was $39 124. Note 6 includes cash at bank of $75 632; note 7 includes bills of exchange of $13 874; and note 12 includes the bank overdraft of $50 382. The totals of these three notes agree with the balance sheet for cash, receivables and borrowings respectively.

Under the accounting standard the definition of cash is broader than simply the cash at the bank. Accounting standard AASB 1026, paragraph 9, defines cash as 'cash on hand and cash equivalents'. 'Cash equivalents' are defined as:

> . . . highly liquid investments which are readily convertible to cash on hand at the investor's option and which a company or an economic entity uses in its cash management function on a day-to-day basis; and borrowings which are integral to the cash management function and which are not subject to a term facility.

In practice this means bank overdrafts are included in cash. All items which have been included as cash will be listed in the reconciliation note. You can trace from that note to where the items appear in the balance sheet. As for Alba, this is usually traced through some of the notes which support the balance sheet items.

Notice that the short term deposits of $150 000 are not included as cash under the definition. This is because they are not redeemable until a certain date. However, Alba probably thinks of them as cash but does not think of the bills of exchange as cash. (A proposed amendment to the standard for the definition of cash would probably mean that short term deposits would be called cash.) The bills of exchange are classed as cash because they can be discounted at the bank tomorrow.

The accounting policy note should include a description of what has been included as cash. Alba's is given in note 1(k).

Reconciling cash flow from operations to operating profit

Cash flow from operations is the movement of cash during the year on items related to profit whereas operating profit is the calculation of profit in accordance with accounting principles. The reconciliation lists the differences between the two. The differences are primarily the non-cash items included in the calculation of operating profit and changes in working capital (current assets and current liabilities) other than interest-bearing current liabilities.

Alba's reconciliation is shown in note 19. The reconciliation is divided into two parts: the first group are the non-cash items in the profit and loss; and the second group are mainly changes in current assets and current liabilities.

Generally, cash flow from operating activities is higher than profit after tax because of the non-cash items in profits. For Alba in 1996 it is the other way around because of the large gain from sale of the property. The cash flows statement shows the proceeds (not profit) under investing activities (not operating activities).

The following explains the other adjustments of different types of items.

■ Depreciation and amortisation expense in the profit and loss recognises the using up of an asset (as explained under 'depreciation' in the property, plant and equipment section of chapter 5). The cash relating to these assets moves with the method of payment (e.g. bought for cash, borrowings raised and repaid or leased). So the expense is not included as part of cash flow.

■ Provisions are recognised in profit calculation as the net change in the estimate of the amount of provision required in the current year compared with that required in the prior year. The cash is paid later on or during the year. Any cash paid is allowed for in the calculation of the amount of provision required at the end of the year. So the net change in the provision is not included as part of cash flow.

- Expenses associated with finance leases are (as explained under 'borrowings' in chapter 6) recognised in the profit and loss as amortisation of leased assets and finance lease charges. The cash movement is the payment of the lease payments. So the expenses must be removed from operating and the cash payments are included as part of financing.

- The disposal of investments and property, plant and equipment is included in operating profit as the gain or loss on disposal, whereas the cash movement is the cash received on their sale. So the gain or loss is not included as part of cash flow, but the proceeds are included as part of investing.

- The following listed items are accounted for in different ways for profit purposes compared with associated cash movements. The difference between the two is measured by the change in the balance sheet amount this year compared with last year, which is the adjustment made in the reconciliation.

Item	Included in profit and loss as	Included in cash flow as
Trade debtors	Sales	Receipts from debtors
Inventories	Cost of sales	Payments to suppliers
Trade creditors, other creditors and prepaid expenses	Expenses, cost of sales	Payments to suppliers
Income tax	Income tax expense	Income tax paid

Don't be too concerned if you find this difficult to understand. The explanation is difficult to grasp. The essential thing to understand is that cash flow is different from—though related to—profit. Cash flow shows where cash comes from and is used, whereas profit is accrual recognition of revenues and expenses. It is reasonable for a financial statements user to accept that adjustments are required between the two without having to know the detail of how and why it is done. A user should be able to assume that those preparing the accounts have done this correctly.

WHAT CASH FLOW DOES NOT SHOW

Cash flow shows cash in and cash out. It does not show non-cash items. So cash flow might look good, but not reveal some critical problems.

There are two key risks not covered by cash flows statements:

1 Liabilities, which are amounts owing and yet to be paid. Entities experiencing financial stress tend not to pay their debts. So the liabilities increase. This situation is seen on the balance sheet (unless the liabilities are not being recorded).

2   Assets losing value, which, if acquired with cash, appear in the cash flows statement when paid for. Losses of value recognised in the financial statements will appear in the profit and loss statement and/or as a reduction of the asset revaluation reserve. Over-valued assets can remain on the balance sheet. The over-valuation is often difficult for a reader to detect.

HOW IS CASH FLOW USED?

As stated previously, an entity must have a positive cash flow and earn profit over the long term in order to survive and grow. So just as we look at profit over time for a favourable trend, we can look at cash flow for positive signs. Favourable trends include:

- cash flows from operating activities are positive;
- cash is invested in the acquisition of assets used to produce income, such as property, plant and equipment, investments and acquisition of businesses (thus net cash flows from investing activities are normally an outflow);
- over time, cash to fund expansion is raised from a mixture of operating activities, borrowings and share issues;
- cash received on disposal of major assets seems to be used in sensible ways such as funding new major assets, repaying borrowings, invested to earn income or used to provide a return of capital to shareholders.

Unfavourable signs include:

- operating activities continually use up rather than supply cash—this can often be the case in the beginning of a business, but if ongoing it is a strong sign of impending business failure or cash from operating activities is small;
- cash received from borrowing or share issues is used to fund negative results in operations;
- cash received on disposal of major assets is used to fund negative results in operations.

Besides looking at past trends revealed from historical cash flows, a vital aspect for sophisticated analysts is to use the information to predict future cash flows. The trends revealed by the historical information are modelled (e.g. using computer spreadsheets) to project cash inflows and outflows into the future.

These techniques are beyond the scope of this book, but interesting issues arise in the endeavour to project cash flow. For instance, the timing of borrowing repayments is important as sufficient cash will be required or new borrowings arranged. Analysts want to know when these critical points will occur so they can predict the likely cash situation at the time and the likely need to arrange new funds. To project this they need to know the repayment schedules of borrowings. This information is only provided by borrowing corporations. So analysts scrounge for indications of timing of repayment of borrowings. This information would be a very useful new disclosure requirement.

Three warning signals

There are three warning signals of insufficient generation of cash from operating activities, being:

■ net cash flows from operating activities are an outflow (negative);
■ payments to suppliers and employees are higher than receipts from customers;
■ net cash flows from operating activities are lower than operating profit after tax.

The first two are very significant and would normally indicate a company is failing if they exist for a number of years. The third one can often indicate a lack of real profit being generated. However, remember for Alba in 1996 the operating cash flow was lower than profit after tax because of profit on sale of the property. It was included in the profit and loss statement but the proceeds from the sale are included under investing activities. Thus, it is not an indicator of a cash flow problem for Alba.

The trends we want to see

As mentioned at the start of this chapter, a simple overview of what we want to see is that a business should generate sales with profit and, if there is real profit, there will be a strong cash flow from operating activities.

A mature successful business will generate so much cash flow from operating activities that it will:

■ fund its investing activities;
■ fund the dividend;
■ provide funds to repay borrowings.

A growing business often has insufficient cash flow from operating activities due to the strain of growth. When sales are growing fast, then debtors and inventory grow, demanding cash to fund them. In the medium to long term this situation should be overcome. In the meantime the business needs to arrange sufficient cash through owner contributions and/or borrowings.

In assessing how an organisation is funded, the typical discussion is a choice of owner contributions or borrowings. But as we can see from the cash flow, a third source is cash flows from operating activities. I term this self-generation. It comes from real profits. Conceptually I think self-generation is the best. A great achievement is to fund your own growth from how well you are doing while paying dividends and meeting borrowing commitments.

WHAT DOES ALBA'S CASH FLOWS STATEMENT REVEAL?

Alba's cash flows from operating activities are strong in both years with 1996 being about $80 000 higher. The reconciliation of profit after tax to operating cash flows in note 19 shows this is primarily due to inventories. In 1996 inventories decreased by $60 391 which means more inventory was sold than made. This helps the cash flow. In 1997 inventories increased by $54 978 which means more inventory was made than sold. Cash is used to manufacture the inventory. The overall effect of this situation is a downward pressure on cash flows in 1997 compared with 1996, being the addition of the two amounts which is $115 369.

In 1997 the cash flows from operating activities of $259 948 were sufficient to cover investing activities outflow of $134 447 and financing outflows of $115 122 and still leave an increase in cash of $10 379. This is even stronger than it at first appears. When you examine investing activities you will see there were proceeds from sale of investments and almost twice as much spent on new investments.

Note 9, investments, shows that the main increases were in shares and fixed interest securities. The majority of both of these investments are traded on the stock exchange which means they are quickly convertible to cash. The market value information shows they are worth more than the cost.

The other interesting item under investing activities is $70 000 was placed on short term deposit. There is no inflow from short term deposit showing money was not withdrawn during the year. In 1996 $80 000 was placed on short term deposit. Note 6 shows how these deposits have increased to $150 000. All achieved in the last two years.

Thus, 1997 cash flow is very strong.

In 1996 the changes were even greater. As described above, there is much higher cash flows from operating activities of $337 190. The major change in financial situation for Alba in 1996 was the sale of the old property and purchase of a new one together with how it was financed.

The investing activities shows $484 560 was raised from the sale of the old property. The cost of the new property is included within the $777 915 payment for property, plant and equipment. Alba only held one property at the end of 1996 being the new one. Note 10 shows this property at cost. The cost is the addition of the land of $368 471 and the buildings of $297 154. This totals $665 625. The difference of $112 290 ($777 915 − $665 625) must be what was spent on plant and equipment. This is still more than twice 1997, probably reflecting some re-equipping upon moving into the new premises.

The new property was mostly funded by the proceeds from the old property. How was the shortfall funded? Under financing we can see that $200 000 was raised by issuing shares to owners and proceeds from borrowings were higher than repayment of borrowings. We can deduce that 100 000 ordinary shares were issued at $2.00 each. Note 15 shows there are

400 000 ordinary shares on issue. Note 16 shows the share premium is $100 000 and that it occurred in 1996. Thus, share premium is half, the other must be in share capital.

The proceeds from borrowings and repayment of borrowings is the new mortgage loan on the new property and payout of the previous mortgage loan on the old property. This is the most likely explanation and is supported by the description of mortgage security on the bank loan of $150 000 in note 14.

Did Alba need to raise $200 000 from shareholders and increase borrowings by $80 000 to finance the new property? The answer is no. The net change in cash in 1996 is a huge $155 709. How was this used? Notice that the cash at the beginning of the year was negative $126 964. How can you have negative cash? It means the bank overdraft was higher than the cash at the bank. The net change in cash was used to reduce the overdraft substantially. Remember under investing activities (discussed above, concerning 1997) that $80 000 was placed on short term deposit in 1996. This is more accumulation of cash. If the cash was not placed on deposit and the overdraft not reduced, Alba would not have needed to raise money from shareholders. They might have got by without increasing the borrowings.

So why has Alba accumulated so much cash over the last two years rather than retire debt or not raise share capital? As with all of the discussion so far, we can only surmise. We are attempting to work out the story from the information in the accounts. By thinking about the story ourselves, it means that if we went to Alba management and asked for an explanation, we can compare it with our own thoughts—a cross check. I think our story is fairly accurate, however, we will be guessing about why they have accumulated so much cash.

At the end of 1997 they have cash at the bank of $75 632 and cash on deposit of $150 000, a total of $225 632. But they have more cash available. Note 18 shows the overdraft limit is $200 000. Note 12 shows only $50 382 was drawn at year end leaving another $150 000 in available cash. So they have about $375 000 cash available to use without asking anyone's permission. But still more cash is available—note 9 consists mainly of investments which could be sold quickly for cash. Perhaps with the move into the bigger property there are more plans for expansion, e.g. purchase of more plant and equipment.

When we consider performance using ratios we can reflect on how effective the move of premises has been so far. A bigger premises means potential for expanded production. Expanded production should be reflected in increased sales. Note 2 shows sales increased under $300 000 or less than 10 per cent. Thus there is not evidence of a large increase yet. So will the expansion work? We will consider this when we calculate ratios, especially profitability performance.

Examples from Alba of the difference between cash flow and profit

Income tax paid is cash paid to the Australian Taxation Office during the year for the company's income tax. The profit and loss statement shows the calculated income tax for the current year's profit. The cash flows statement is mostly the payment of the liability remaining from last year plus some of this year's liability. In Australia (as in most other countries) companies pay most of their company income tax in the following year. Thus the cash flow moves about one year behind the recognition of the expense. So for Alba the situation is:

	1997 $	1996 $
Cash paid which pays out remainder of prior year's liability and some of this year's liability	112 984	86 948
Income tax expense shown in the profit and loss	117 612	105 142
Provision for income tax as shown in note 13	110 819	95 521

Dividends paid is the cash paid during the year, which usually consists of the prior year's final dividend declared plus the current year's interim dividend. The current year's final dividend will be paid to shareholders next year. In the current year accounts it is included as a liability on the balance sheet because it is unpaid. So for Alba the situation is:

	1997 $	1996 $
Dividends physically paid during year:		
Final dividend declared in prior year	30 000	25 000
Interim dividend paid during year out of current year's profits	30 000	25 000
Cash payments of dividend during the year	60 000	50 000

Compare this with the dividends paid and declared on Alba's profit and loss statement. Cash moves differently from recognition in profit!

Other information to be shown

Purchase or disposal of subsidiaries and businesses

In larger companies the purchase or disposal of companies or businesses can be fairly common. A note is required to be included in the accounts which shows the fair value of the assets and liabilities acquired or the book value of the assets and liabilities sold. The consideration paid or received must also be shown. This consideration could include cash and other kinds of payment such as issue of shares and giving of credit terms for deferred payments.

In the case of a purchase, the difference between consideration and fair value of the net assets will be goodwill. In the case of a sale, the difference between consideration and book value of the net assets sold will be the profit or loss on disposal.

The cash inflows and outflows are what is included on the cash flows statement. For the purchase of a company or business the cash paid during the year to buy the business is an outflow of investing activities. From this amount is deducted or added (and also separately shown) the kind of cash items acquired. These can be cash at bank and on hand, bank overdraft and bills receivable or payable. Any deferred payments to be made at a later date will be shown as an outflow of investing activities in the period in which the payment is actually made.

For the sale of a company or business the cash received from the sale is shown as an inflow of investing activities. Similarly to a purchase, cash items sold are deducted. Any deferred payments receivable in later periods are shown as inflows in the period in which payment is received.

Non-cash financing

Information on non-cash financing and investing activities is shown in note 17. Alba acquired plant and equipment through finance leases. The cash movement for these is the lease payments, which are included in outflows under financing activities.

Another situation could be the funding of part of the purchase of a company through the issue of shares to the former owners. This saves cash but reduces the original shareholders' ownership in the entity.

Standby credit facilities

The standard requires information on the standby credit facilities and used and unused loan facilities. This provides users with information on what additional sources of credit are already in place should there be a cash shortage in the near future. It helps users forecast the future cash flows.

Note 18 provides more information on Alba's overdraft (over and above the amount and kind of security shown in note 12). Note 18 shows the facility is in force until 31 March 1999 and is expected to be continued. It also shows the upper limit of the overdraft is $200 000.

POINTS TO REMEMBER

✔ Cash flows statements show the cash obtained and used by the entity during the financial year. This is shown under operating (buying and selling the goods and services), investing (buying and selling non-current assets) and financing (raising and repaying of borrowings and investors' contributions) activities.

✔ The gross amounts of cash flows are shown. For example, cash obtained from new or extended borrowings and repayments on borrowings are shown separately—they are not offset against each other to show only a net increase or decrease in borrowings.

✔ The net inflows or outflows from operating, investing and financing are added to give the net movement of cash for the year. This, in turn, is added to the cash at the beginning of the year to give cash available at the end of the year. Cash is cash at bank, bank overdrafts and other very liquid items such as bills receivable. Liquid items subject to set terms of settlement (like cash on deposit other than at call) are not counted as cash.

✔ Cash flows from operating activities are reconciled to operating profit after tax. The reason there is a difference is that profit measures revenue less expenses—these items mainly involve the movement of cash but not always.

✔ Other notes required which give additional information supporting the cash flows statements are details on purchase and disposal of companies and businesses, other non-cash means of investing or financing activities, and standby credit information.

✔ Analysts use cash flows statements to determine trends in the entity's use of cash and to forecast future cash flow. They do this to try to see if the entity will have sufficient cash to continue operations. An entity must have positive cash flow from operating activities and be profitable in order to survive and grow.

✔ There are three warning signals for cash generation from operating activities being: net cash outflow from operating activities; payments to suppliers and employees being higher than receipts from customers; and cash flow from operating activities is lower than operating profit after tax.

✔ A mature successful business will generate sufficient cash flow from operating activities to fund its investing activities, pay a dividend and repay borrowings. This is a sign of self-generation which is more powerful than borrowing or raising owners' contributions in order to fund the business.

10 Ratios

In chapter 1 we considered the importance of planning and budgeting. We mentioned how within an entity there are many ways of comparing actual results to budget. However, only those privileged to receive this information are in a position to do this. Those on the outside are limited to the information publicly available. Besides examining the financial statements, we can use ratios.

Ratios measure relationships between different elements of the financial statements. Ratios provide a means of converting raw figures into figures that can be compared for the one entity over a period of years and compared with ratios calculated for other entities. They allow us to see trends over time, trends between entities in the one industry and trends compared with other entities and other industries.

Norms have been established for industries against which individual entities can be measured. Rules of thumb of acceptable minimum or maximum ratio values can be used as checks of reasonability of performance. However the norms and rules of thumb are not absolute—wise users will consider each circumstance and draw their own conclusions.

In this chapter you will be able to learn what the typical ratios are, how they are calculated and what they tell you about performance. You will also be introduced to cash flow and segment ratios which are not as commonly used. The calculation of Alba's ratios for 1997 is set out. You can check your understanding by calculating the 1996 ratios. These are included, but not the details of the calculation. By being applied to Alba, you can see a practical example. Alba's performance is assessed over a five year period.

This chapter brings together the consideration of financial statements, what they mean and the way in which accounting policies affect the ratios. These matters are considered through the analysis of Alba's performance. (An Excel spreadsheet using these ratios is available from the author. See information on p. xiv.)

A BETTER APPROACH TO ANALYSIS

The first chapter of Fridson's book, *Financial Statement Analysis—A Practitioner's Guide*, is called 'The Adversarial Nature of Financial Reporting'—a telling commentary in the chapter title. The comments and examples given in this book reinforce Fridson's view. It means we must be thoughtful in our approach to analysis and not merely follow standard procedures. Entrepreneurs, directors and even government bodies know what users want to see and they supply it—they paint the best picture they can within the rules and regulations. We must read between the lines.

Fridson's suggested approach to analysis (Fridson 1991, p. 3) is worth following:

> Financial statement analysis is an essential skill in a variety of occupations, including investment management, corporate finance, commercial lending and the extension of credit. For individuals engaged in such activities—or who analyze financial data in connection with their personal investment decisions—there are two distinct approaches to the task.
>
> The first is to follow a prescribed routine, filling in boxes with standard financial ratios, calculated according to precise and inflexible definitions. It may take little more effort or mental exertion than this to satisfy the formal requirements of many positions in the field of financial analysis. Operating in a purely mechanical manner will not provide much of a professional challenge, nor will a rote completion of all of the 'proper' standard analytical steps ensure a useful—or even a nonharmful—result, but some individuals will view these problems as only minor drawbacks.
>
> [Fridson's] book is aimed at the analyst who will adopt the second and more rewarding alternative, namely the relentless pursuit of accurate financial profiles of the entities being analyzed. Tenacity is essential because financial statements often conceal more than they reveal. To the analyst who pursues this proactive approach, producing a standard spreadsheet on a company is a means rather than an end. Investors derive but little satisfaction from the knowledge that an untimely stock purchase recommendation was supported by the longest row of figures available in the software package. Genuinely valuable analysis begins *after* all of the usual questions have been answered. Indeed, a superior analyst adds value by raising questions that are not even on the checklist.

The present chapter's introduction to ratios cannot pretend to enable you to develop your skills to the level of those of a superior analyst. However, issues such as what is the real 'normal' profit are raised for you to consider when applying ratios; comparing cash flow with profit ratios.

Martin Roth, in his book *Analysing Company Accounts*, provides practical examples and insights in assessing listed companies. The book is written in a very readable style and provides another and extended view of ratios.

I want to conclude this section on a better approach to ratio analysis with Fridson's view—which I support—on the approach preparers of financial statements adopt (Fridson 1991, p. 4):

Corporations have substantial incentives to exploit the fact that accounting principles are neither fixed for all time nor so precise as to be open to only a single interpretation. Analysts who appreciate the magnitude of the economic stakes, as well as the latitude available under the accounting rules, will see clearly that a verdict derived by passively calculating standard ratios may prove dangerously naive.

And this comment was written in the land (the USA) with the most accounting standards, commentary and guidance on standards—also the land of the great Savings and Loans collapse, where reality was shown to be far different from what the financial statements had said. So, perhaps we should add to the old adage 'buyer beware', 'user (analyst) beware'!

INDUSTRY AND OTHER COMPARISONS AVAILABLE

No matter whether you are looking at a large, medium or small business, there is value in comparing that business's performance with industry averages. The challenge is to obtain industry information. Fortunately in Australia there is quite a lot of information available.

■ Industry groups often have information for their own industries.

■ The large accounting firms and other organisations analyse and publish surveys on major business and industry segments.

■ Chambers of commerce may have some general information on their members.

■ State government small business departments may have some general information.

■ Two private enterprise providers of performance information for small business are:

– Dr Keith N. Cleland, Pracdev Key Indicator Reports (PKIR), PO Box 678, Armidale, NSW 2350; phone (02) 6772 5076; fax (02) 6771 1745.

This annual publication provides a one page summary on over 150 small business categories covering manufacturers, wholesalers, retailers, trades and professions. Information on each industry includes average annual turnover (sales), major expenses such as wages as a percentage of turnover, key success factors and how to monitor the business. The book is compiled from information provided by accounting practices around Australia. Naturally, client confidentiality is not breached.

– Financial Management Research Centre (FMRC), *Small Business Profiles for Various Industries*, Beasley and Geddes Pty Ltd, Financial

Management Research Centre at the University of New England, Armidale, NSW 2351; phone (02) 6772 5199; fax (02) 6772 7607.

The FMRC profiles cover a wide range of small business segments. Each profile provides information derived from a survey of the industry and typically covers:

— industry overview
— discussion of key factors of success
— average figures for income and expenses
— average ratios
— discussion of the figures and ratios, including an expected rate of return on assets and equity
— figures and ratios further divided into three separate groups for small, medium and large turnover
— contrast of good and poor management performers
— layman's guide to interpreting ratios
— worksheet for examining a particular company.

In this book we are not comparing Alba with an industry average, but we are comparing performance over five years.

RATIOS USED

There are many ratios available and, for any ratios, analysts have their own preferences of what the formula should be. So we enter a minefield when advocating a limited group of ratios with specified formulae. However, I am confident that the ratios and the formulae used will provide you with the fundamental tools for interpreting nearly any business you may examine.

Some ratios are regarded as more useful for investors and others for lenders. I think it is best to have a broad look at performance. While it is true that an investor is concerned with profitability and security of investment, the company needs to be able to meet its obligations to lenders and creditors in order to remain in business. Likewise, while it is true that a lender is concerned with earning interest and being repaid, the company needs to be profitable and growing in the long run in order to maintain and improve its ability to service its borrowings.

The ratio groups and ratios used are detailed below.

■ Liquidity—testing if the entity will be able to pay its debts as and when they fall due:
  – current ratio
  – acid test.

■ Management efficiency—examining how well working capital is managed, that is how quickly cash is collected from debtors, inventory sold and creditors paid:
  – days debtors
  – days inventory

- days finished goods
- days creditors.

■ Financing—considering how comfortably the entity can meet its interest commitments, its level of debt financing compared with equity, the comfort of the term of borrowing compared with assets funded, and whether or not borrowings contribute to profit of shareholders:
  - interest cover
  - debt to equity
  - comparison of liability and equity financing of assets
  - comparison of rate of profit with cost of borrowing.

■ Profitability—checking how profitable the entity is from the perspective of profit on sales, assets and shareholders' equity:

  using before and after abnormal items
  - gross margin
  - return on assets (ROA)
  - return on equity (ROE)

  using cash flows
  - cash gross margin
  - cash return on assets (CROA)
  - cash return on equity (CROE)

  using segment information for each industry and geographic segment
  - net margin
  - return on assets.

■ Market performance—looking at the security of the value of the shares, what investors get for their money in terms of the profit attributable to them, the dividends received and the value of the shares:
  - net tangible assets per share
  - dividend per share (DPS)
  - earnings per share (EPS)
  - dividend cover
  - dividend yield
  - price/earnings (P/E).

When calculating ratios for a group of companies use the group figures. Ignore the holding company's figures because it is only one company in the group. It does not reflect how the group has fared. You may also need to consider profit from associated companies. The importance and meaning of groups and associated companies are explained in the next chapter.

The formulae and the calculation for Alba using 1997 figures are provided for each of the ratios except segment results.

When calculating any ratios you need to do the following.

■ Make sure you find the item specified in the formula. For each formula in this chapter, each item is referred to its location in the accounts. When looking at accounts, the location in the accounts will vary because different formats are used. Therefore look for the item specified carefully. In Australia a prescribed format was required from the early 1980s to 1996.

■ Check that the ratio result appears reasonable. If it seems unusually low or high check that you have calculated it correctly. If the calculation is correct, consider if the ratio is relevant for the entity you are examining. For instance, days debtors will be meaningless for a cash sale business and days inventory will be meaningless for a service business (because it does not sell goods).

■ Do not simply input the financial statements data into a ratio model. Where you find the figures do not really represent the story, input them in accordance with your view. For instance you might decide a current asset is really non-current, or an abnormal item is normal. You can always run the model twice: first using the figures as presented; second using your interpretation. Then you can analyse what the information shows.

■ You can vary the ratio formula. It is not sacrosanct. You should compute the ratio using a formula relevant to the situation. (This book uses typical formulae for the ratios chosen.)

■ When using ratios calculated by others you should not assume they have used the same formulae as you would. In legal documents (such as trust deeds), and when seriously comparing different companies, find out or establish what the ratio formulae will be so that there is common understanding between parties and a common basis for comparison.

■ The number of decimal points used in the ratios calculated should be limited to the least necessary to make the ratio sufficiently accurate and to be easily readable. Most of the ratios are limited to one decimal point. Those expressed in days are shown in whole days because a fraction of a day has no real meaning.

LIQUIDITY

Liquidity is the ability of the entity to meet its debts as and when they fall due. An entity can monitor this through its cash flow forecasts. Our review of Alba's historical cash flows statement shows Alba can pay its debts. Thus cash flows statements will help you assess the ability to pay debts as and when they fall due. As users we need to utilise liquidity ratios and the management of working capital.

Current ratio

Formula is

$$\frac{\text{Current assets}}{\text{Current liabilities}} = \frac{1\,175\,244}{686\,725} = 1.7\,\text{times}$$

Current assets and current liabilities are from the balance sheet.

Trend is

1993	1994	1995	1996	1997
1.1	1.2	1.3	1.6	1.7

Rule of thumb minimum level is 1.5.

This ratio shows the current assets available to cover current liabilities at the balance sheet date. There should be a reasonable buffer of current assets over current liabilities as an indication of the ability of the entity to pay its debts as and when they fall due.

Alba's situation has improved steadily over the five years, moving from an unacceptably low situation to being just above the minimum acceptable level. This indicates that management have taken action to overcome the low level of liquidity.

Acid test

Formula is

$$\frac{\text{Current assets less inventories}}{\text{Current liabilities less overdraft}} =$$

$$\frac{(1\,175\,244 - 508\,723)}{(686\,725 - 50\,382)} = \frac{666\,521}{636\,343} = 1.0\,\text{times}$$

Current assets, inventories and current liabilities are from the balance sheet.
Overdraft is from note 12 (if overdraft is shown under secured and unsecured add both together).

Trend is

1993	1994	1995	1996	1997
0.6	0.7	0.7	1.0	1.0

Rule of thumb minimum level is 0.7 or 0.8.

This ratio aims to show the more liquid current assets available to pay the more immediately payable liabilities. The rule of thumb is half the current ratio because inventory and debtors are usually the two major current assets. However, overdrafts are typically small in larger businesses and do not change the denominator significantly.

Inventories are deducted from current assets because when inventories are sold on credit they convert to trade debtors before becoming cash—so inventories are not necessarily very liquid. This does not apply in a cash sale business. The ratio formula can be altered so as not to deduct inventories for a cash sale business.

Prepayments and deferred expenses can be deducted from assets because cash will not be received from them; it has been paid out already.

Overdraft is deducted from current liabilities because, though legally payable on demand, the facility is usually for quite a reasonable period. This means the liability does not have to be repaid in the near term.

Bills payable facilities are often provided by banks in a similar manner to overdrafts. In this situation they should be deducted too. This does not apply to Alba because it does not have any bills payable borrowings.

Some provisions may not really be payable for several months after balance sheet date. These too can be deducted. For Alba, most of the income tax will be paid in July, the dividend around November and the employee entitlements throughout the year. Perhaps adjustment could be made for the last two.

Like the current ratio, Alba's acid test has moved from being too low to being above (indeed well above) the minimum rule of thumb.

General comment on Alba's liquidity

Alba's management has turned an unsatisfactory liquidity situation into a reasonably comfortable situation. Liquidity measurements use current assets and liabilities which are working capital items.

Working capital is current assets less current liabilities. Sometimes this amount is calculated and considered in the analysis of liquidity.

MANAGEMENT EFFICIENCY

Management efficiency measures control of specific parts of working capital. We will consider management efficiency and its relationship to liquidity.

Days debtors

Formula is

$$\frac{\text{Year end trade debtors}}{\text{Sales}} \times 365 = \frac{438\,569}{3\,399\,504} \times 365 = 47\,\text{days}$$

Trade debtors ($424 695) is the amount before doubtful debts because the gross amount is what is to be collected. Bills of exchange ($13 874) have also been included because some debtors have paid using a promissory note, but Alba is still waiting to receive cash until the bills due date. These figures are from note 7—receivables (current). (Any non-current trade debtors could be included or excluded.)

Sales is from note 2—operating revenue.

Trend is

1993	1994	1995	1996	1997
45	49	48	46	47

This ratio shows how quickly cash is being collected from debtors. A good way of considering how well the entity is collecting its debtors is comparing the ratio calculated with their credit terms. Unfortunately credit terms are not published in the annual accounts. So we can only surmise unless the information has been obtained in some other way.

Alba's credit terms appear to be 30 days. Is the collection time of 47 days reasonable? Credit terms of 30 days are interpreted as being that payment is required one month after the end of the month in which the goods or services were bought. Goods and services are actually sold throughout the month rather than at the end. Therefore the actual collection days must be greater than 30 even when payment is being received on time. Actual average collection of 45 days for entities with 30 days credit is a very good result. On this basis Alba is managing its debtors well.

If some of Alba's sales are for cash, then the real days debtors is greater. The greater the portion that cash sales are of total sales, the more understated is the days debtors figure. The accounts are not required to provide a split of cash and credit sales. If they did, then we could calculate the real average days debtors.

Another issue that can affect the validity of the ratio is whether the level of debtors fluctuates throughout the year. In all ratios we are using year end balance sheet item figures. The ratio can be calculated using the average debtors (or whatever balance sheet item it is) figure. The average is the sum of the balance at the beginning of the year (which is last year's balance) and that at the end of the year, divided by two. To use average balance we would need to have the 1995 accounts too. But this is still inaccurate where the level of debtors is substantially different at month ends during the year from what it is at year end. We do not have this information and so cannot allow for the situation should it exist. Alba's management can allow for it because they have all the information. Remember that these issues apply to all ratios using year end balances.

Alba's days debtors have remained fairly constant over the five years moving between 45 and 49 days. This consistency together with the closeness to the likely 30 day credit terms shows debtors are well controlled (assuming there are few cash sales).

Window dressing

An issue to remember with liquidity and management efficiency ratios is 'window dressing', a common practice. When calculating the ratios we are relying on the accuracy of the year end figures. However they can be 'dressed' to make them look better.

Days debtors is improved by taking the view that the actual cash received from trade debtors in the beginning of the month following year end belongs to the current financial year. This view is justified as 'being in the mail'. In other words, the delay of receipt to the next financial year was due to the postal service. The debtors had really paid in the financial year. Treating the first five working days of the next month (e.g. July) as belonging to the financial year (e.g. June) is typical. This approach results in reducing trade debtors and increasing cash at bank by the amount of cash received from debtors in those first five days of the next month.

The same idea is applied to creditors to make days creditors look better. This also results in cash at bank remaining about the same. Cheques are drawn on the last day of the financial year to 'pay' creditors. The cheques are stored in 'the drawer' and not sent to the creditor until later, e.g. the end of the first month of the new financial year. The cheques are processed as though paid in the current financial year thus reducing creditors and cash at bank by the same amount. Often this reduction in the bank account is a similar level to the increase caused by recognising the first five days of next month's cash receipts in the current financial year.

Usually we cannot tell whether or not 'window dressing' is occurring. Generally it is done each year which results in a similar effect on each year's trade debtors, cash at bank and trade creditors. This also means the distortion of the ratios is always similar and so the trend remains valid. A shift in days debtors or days creditors could be at least partly due to a change in 'window dressing'.

Days inventory

Formula is

$$\frac{\text{Year end inventories}}{\text{Sales}} \times 365 = \frac{511\,223}{3\,399\,504} \times 365 = \textbf{55 days}$$

Inventory is the amount before obsolescence provisions because the gross amount is what is to be sold. This figure is from note 8—inventories (current) being $508 723 plus the provision against raw materials of $2500. (Any non-current inventories could be included or excluded.)
Sales is from note 2—operating revenue.

Trend is

1993	1994	1995	1996	1997
69	72	72	53	55

This ratio shows how long on average it takes to sell inventory from the time raw materials are purchased. Management should aim to have as little inventory as possible because it costs money to hold it—interest paid on any borrowings used to purchase inventory and the cost of storing. There is an art to balancing the financial goal of little inventory with the need to have sufficient inventory to satisfy customers. If you cannot supply when customers want their goods, they will go elsewhere.

The ratio shows Alba has held less than two months' stock in 1996 and 1997, which is a significant improvement over previous years. This indicates that management reached a point where they thought they were holding too much inventory for the volume of sales and fixed the problem during 1996. Notice that this improvement coincides with the move to new premises. Perhaps the move provided an opportunity for overhaul of the inventory. The 1996 abnormal write-down of inventory might have been part of this review.

There is a shortcoming with this ratio as calculated. It is not strictly mathematically valid because the numerator and denominator are on different dollar bases. The denominator, sales, is valued at selling price (market) but the numerator, inventory, is valued at cost. (In days debtors, debtors are at selling price which gives consistency between numerator and denominator.)

Using cost of sales

The equation would be valid if cost of sales was used instead of sales. However, this is usually not shown in publicly available accounts. (A proposed amendment to AASB 1019, *Measurement and Presentation of Inventories* . . ., requires cost of sales disclosure. If approved, disclosure will be required from 30 June 1998.) Cost of sales information has been provided for Alba (at the end of chapter 4). This is the result when cost of sales is used.

Formula is

$$\frac{\text{Year end inventories}}{\text{Cost of sales}} \times 365 = \frac{511\,223}{2\,124\,601} \times 365 = \textbf{88 days}$$

Trend is

1993	1994	1995	1996	1997
116	121	120	86	88

The actual days taken to sell inventory are substantially greater than indicated when sales are used. This will always be the case because inventory is sold at substantial margins above cost so that an entity can make a profit. (See chapters 2, 4 and 5 under 'inventories' for information on how profit is calculated.)

The same trend is shown as for sales. Despite not really showing actual days inventories, using sales still shows trends on how well inventories are managed. Sales is used for all companies, which means comparisons between different companies are made on the same basis. There may be some distortion because the margin between sales and cost of sales varies between companies, however it is usually not a significant consideration.

Countries following the British system usually do not require the publication of cost of sales. Those following the USA, such as Indonesia and Thailand, do have this requirement.

Days finished goods

Formula is

$$\frac{\text{Year end finished goods}}{\text{Sales}} \times 365 = \frac{249\,617}{3\,399\,504} \times 365 = 27 \text{ days}$$

Finished goods is the amount before provision for obsolescence because the gross amount is what is to be sold. This figure is from note 8—inventories (current). (Non-current finished goods are unlikely as you would expect non-current inventories would be sold on completion.)
Sales is from note 2—operating revenue.

Trend is

1993	1994	1995	1996	1997
31	33	34	26	27

This ratio examines how long on average it takes to sell finished goods. Finished goods are ready for sale whereas raw materials and work in progress are not. The difference between days inventory and days finished goods is the average time it takes to manufacture goods from the time raw materials are acquired.

Retailers and wholesalers do not manufacture goods. They buy in and sell finished goods. For these entities, days inventory and days finished goods will be the same.

Alba's management of finished goods also improved greatly in 1996 but by a slightly lesser proportion than total inventory. (Days finished goods dropped by 23.5% [8/34 × 100]; days inventory dropped by 26.4%

[19/72 × 100].) This indicates that management aimed at improving control over total inventory.

Using cost of sales

Again we can use cost of sales with finished goods. This shows the same trends as the other inventory ratios.

Formula is

$$\frac{\text{Year end finished goods}}{\text{Cost of sales}} \times 365 = \frac{249\,617}{2\,124\,601} \times 365 = \textbf{43 days}$$

Trend is

1993	1994	1995	1996	1997
53	56	56	42	43

Inventory varies greatly between industries and even within industries. Some businesses which sell goods make money on selling large volumes at low margins while, at the other end of the spectrum, others make money through high margins and low volumes.

In the retail sector, Woolworths food and variety stores trade on volume whereas David Jones department stores trade more on service. In the manufacturing sector those making light-manufacturing goods tend to have a quicker production cycle than those making heavy industry goods. So in assessing inventory management we must consider the nature of the business.

Alba's inventory management

Alba is a manufacturer and seller of light industrial machinery (as stated in the directors' report). They are making machinery which is likely to be more complex than other light industry manufacture. The production cycle may, therefore, be quite reasonable. Perhaps there is scope to reduce the amount of finished goods held through tighter control of production lines. However there is a cost associated with setting up and running a production line. It may be cheaper to produce and hold greater volumes rather than reduce production lines and hold less inventory.

Days creditors

Formula is

$$\frac{\text{Year end trade creditors}}{\text{Sales}} \times 365 = \frac{382\,156}{3\,399\,504} \times 365 = \textbf{41 days}$$

> Creditors is from the balance sheet.
> Note 11 shows creditors consists of trade creditors, accrued expenses and other creditors. Many analysts only use trade creditors. I believe other creditors and accrued expenses should be included unless there is information which shows that one or the other is not creditors but something different in nature, like deposits received in advance from customers. (Any non-current trade creditors could be included or excluded.)
> Sales is from note 2—operating revenue.
>
> Trend is
>
> | 1993 | 1994 | 1995 | 1996 | 1997 |
> |------|------|------|------|------|
> | 50 | 45 | 45 | 41 | 41 |

This is the least accurate of the ratios we are using. Its only value is in showing a trend, which for Alba is a gradual reduction in the time taken to pay creditors. This is a good trend when considering liquidity improved over the same period. So liquidity improved even while paying creditors more promptly.

Creditors are the cost of buying items for the entity. For inventory, cost of sales is a better denominator. However, creditors are used for more than the purchase of items used in the production process. They are used to buy items allocated to distribution, selling, administration and other general overheads, and may be used to buy small items of plant and equipment. For creditors, purchases on credit is the appropriate denominator. This is not published and is usually not available in internal management accounts.

These shortcomings means the days creditors cannot be legitimately compared with days debtors to see if creditors are paid more slowly than debtors. This would be possible if the real days creditors could be calculated. The management of Alba would be able to check this, because they know their policy for payment of creditors and they know how long it takes to collect debtors.

Sometimes you may see the calculation of days working capital cycle being days inventory plus days debtors less days creditors. Because of the inaccuracy of two of these ratios, the ratio is indicative only. I prefer not to use it.

Despite the severe inaccuracy of the ratio there is one trend which provides a strong warning signal. Watch out for increasing days creditors combined with declining liquidity. Unless there is some other explanation it indicates increasing difficulty in paying creditors.

General comment on Alba's management efficiency

The three management efficiency ratios show an improvement in the turnover of inventory and stable collection of debtors. Debtors seem to be very well controlled and there may be scope for further reduction in the days inventory.

A very favourable trend is that the big improvements in management efficiency in 1996 did not affect the trend of improving liquidity. The more frequently occurring situation is that reduction in days debtors and inventory leads to reduced liquidity as the total debtors and inventories have dropped, which means excess of current assets over current liabilities is reduced. This may indicate that sales also increased substantially in 1996 over 1995, or that current liabilities dropped. Checking back to earlier accounts would allow us to isolate the reason.

FINANCING

Financing ratios measure the relationship of debt (liabilities) to equity and the comfort of the entity in meeting its debt. A term frequently used is 'gearing'. A highly geared entity has a high level of debt to equity whereas a low geared entity has a small level of debt to equity.

Interest cover

Formula is

$$\frac{\text{EBLIT}}{\text{Finance lease charges and interest}} = \frac{367\,361}{64\,859} = \textbf{5.7 times}$$

EBLIT means Earnings before finance lease charges interest and tax—see below for an explanation. Finance lease charges and interest are from note 3—operating profit before tax. Interest means interest expense.

Trend is

1993	1994	1995	1996	1997
4.6	4.4	4.2	5.3	5.7

Rule of thumb minimum is 2.0 and comfort level is 3.0.

The purpose of the interest cover ratio is to measure how comfortably profit covers the interest cost. The profit used is greater than operating profit (before income tax). This is because the profit used to pay interest cost is the profit before deduction of the interest expense. Interest expense is a tax deductible expense. Tax will vary depending on the amount of the expense. Therefore profit is considered before deduction of income tax expense.

Finance lease charges are included as they are the interest portion of finance lease payments made during the year. Some analysts vary this ratio by also including operating lease payments. They regard the operating lease payments more like a borrowing cost than a rental. If operating lease payments are included in the interest expense denominator of the equation, they must also be included in the EBLIT calculation to be consistent. Some analysts deduct interest received on the premise that it results from investment of excess cash held and is part of the financing strategy. If interest received is deducted in the denominator, it must also be deducted from EBLIT.

Alba has a very high interest cover which has risen from 4.6 to 5.7 over five years. Alba has more than five times the profit it needs to meet interest commitments and still have profit. This means Alba can borrow more and still cover the interest cost and rises in interest rates, while reducing profit will not cause the company to move into loss. Alba is able to meet its interest out of profits very comfortably.

The rule of thumb minimum level of 2 is considered to be the lowest acceptable level of cover. It means that interest rate rises will not result in losses and will still leave some scope for additional borrowings. The comfort level of 3 is considered the better minimum because it means interest is not an undue strain on potential profitability.

An interest cover level between zero and 1 means the interest expense takes the entity into an operating loss (before income tax). And negative interest cover means the entity is in loss even before interest expense is deducted.

Capitalised interest

Interest cost is not always treated as an expense. Sometimes it is added to the value of an asset (this is termed interest capitalised). You include interest capitalised only in the denominator of the formula if you want to measure the real interest cover. Interest is capitalised when borrowings are being used to finance the development of an asset, for instance by a property developer. The cost of the development includes the interest. Where interest is capitalised, it will be mentioned in the accounting policy note and the amount disclosed. The amount will probably be given in the operating profit note, but you may need to search elsewhere to find it.

EBLIT

EBLIT is Earnings before finance lease charges, interest and tax which is calculated as:

		$
	Operating profit before tax	329 316
less:	Abnormal item (gain on sale of investment)	26 814
	Operating profit before tax and abnormals	302 502
add:	Interest expense	36 457
	Finance lease charges	28 402
		64 859
gives:	EBLIT	367 361

Operating profit before tax is from the profit and loss statement. This gives us the 'EBT', that is Earnings before tax.

Abnormal items can be chosen to be removed or not. They tend to be removed on the basis that they are not 'normal' ongoing profit. They have been removed for this calculation. Abnormal revenues are removed by deducting them (because they are included in the operating profit figure), whereas abnormal expenses are added (because they have been subtracted to give operating profit). Operating profit before abnormal items (and tax) is also shown on Alba's profit and loss statement. This gives us 'EBT' independent of abnormal items. (When measuring profitability we will include and exclude them.)

Finance lease charges is from note 3—operating profit before tax

Interest expense is from note 3—operating profit before tax

EBLIT is

1993	1994	1995	1996	1997
$265 177	$286 698	$302 174	$355 255	$367 361

EBLIT rate of growth is

	8.1%	5.4%	17.6%	3.4%

Alba has increased EBLIT every year. This indicates Alba has a solid base of profits. How profitable it really is can be measured by its rate of profit, which is examined in the next group of ratios.

Why EBIT is used as a profit measurement

Earnings before finance lease charges, interest and income tax is a commonly used profit measurement. It measures the profit earned independently of how an entity is financed and so makes profit more comparable between entities with different financing structures. Different organisations use different mixes of equity and debt (borrowings) financing. The cost of equity is dividends and the cost of debt is interest. Only interest is included in the calculation of operating profit. So if profit before interest were not used and two entities were identical except for mix of equity and debt financing, the one with greater reliance on equity financing would look financially stronger.

Similarly, tax exposure can vary between entities. Entities with greater interest expense receive a greater tax deduction. So considering profit before income tax removes these possible distortions.

Analysts usually use the term EBIT (Earnings before interest and tax). We have used EBLIT to make it clear that finance lease charges are counted as interest expense. When reviewing ratios you should check whether or not finance lease charges (and operating lease payments) and/or interest received have been included.

EBIT using net interest

Analysts often use net interest in EBIT. Net interest is the interest expense less interest earned (received). This is on the basis that entities are usually net borrowers, so any interest earned is from temporary spare cash used to earn some interest income to offset some of the interest expense. However, some organisations might be very cash rich, deliberately holding cash rather than repaying debt. In fact some entities have cash rather than borrowings. For this kind of situation I think it is inappropriate and so I prefer not to use net interest.

Alba's net interest can be calculated from the information in notes 2 and 3 as:

Net interest is

		$
	Interest expense—note 3	36 457
	Finance lease charges—note 3	28 402
		64 859
less:	Interest earned (received)—note 2	12 671
gives:	Net interest	52 188

Should operating leases be included as 'interest'?

Another variation some analysts make is to treat operating lease expense as interest. Lenders are more likely to do this. It increases the perceived interest burden of the lender. The rationale for including operating lease payments is that the operating leases might really be finance leases disguised as operating leases. If they were finance leases there would be a finance lease charge. However it would not usually be the whole of the operating lease expense. As discussed in chapter 6, the finance lease results in depreciation and finance lease charge expenses which approximate the operating lease payments over time.

There are many valid operating leases which truly represent the rental of an asset and not its acquisition. The main example is property leases. To treat these kinds of situations as 'interest' misrepresents the real situation. Thus I do not favour automatically treating operating lease expense as interest. We should look at each situation. For instance, the airline, shipping and freighting industries typically lease their transportation. They are often termed operating leases. When you step on a Qantas, SIA or United Airlines plane, whose plane do you think it is? We might decide to treat such an operating lease expense as interest. We can always calculate the ratios using EBLIT including and excluding operating leases.

Debt to equity using total liabilities

Formula is

$$\frac{\text{Total debt (liabilities)}}{\text{Equity before outside interests}} = \frac{1\ 068\ 461}{1\ 339\ 393} = 0.8$$

Total liabilities is from the balance sheet. Financing formulas use the term debt to mean liabilities.
Equity is total of shareholders' equity before outside shareholders' interests and is from the balance sheet. (Alba does not have any subsidiaries or outside shareholders—see chapter 12 for information on consolidations.)

Trend is

1993	1994	1995	1996	1997
2.7	1.9	1.7	0.9	0.8

Rule of thumb for debt to equity (D/E) in Australia is 1:1 for most industries. Debt/equity ratios are often shown in percentage terms.

Debt to equity ratios show the dependence on debt (borrowings) finance compared with equity funding. The greater the reliance on debt financing, the greater the level of interest and the greater the risk from exposure to rising interest rates.

Companies listed on the stock exchange tend to follow a pattern of raising additional finance through borrowing for a number of years and then raise equity through issuing new shares. Equity will be used more when: the interest rate is too high; the share market perceives certain levels of debt funding to be bad; or market conditions favour a share issue, for example high or rising share prices.

Alba's D/E ratio was high in 1993. It was substantially reduced in 1994 and then again in 1996. We can only surmise as to the reason for the reduction in 1994, but we can see from the accounts for 1997 that the reduction was due to the 1996 issue of new shares at $200 000 and a large increase in equity from recognition of the profit on sale of property of $184 722. This was offset to a point by the new financing required for the new property which resulted in an overall increase in borrowings. The situation is now at a very comfortable level.

This brings up an interesting point. The profit on sale of the property is recognised fully in the 1996 accounts, but the gain is actually over a period of time. The real story is the gain in the value of the property over the period from the end of 1993 to its sale in 1996. The old property was revalued in 1993, which recognised the gain from time of purchase to that date. This means the debt to equity ratio was really lower than calculated for 1994 and 1995 (because the equity is understated).

Debt to equity using interest-bearing debt

Formula is

$$\frac{\text{Interest-bearing debt (liabilities)}}{\text{Equity before outside interests}} = \frac{415\,995}{1\,339\,393} = 0.3$$

Interest-bearing liabilities are from the balance sheet 'borrowings'—current plus non-current. (Under old Schedule 5 format the information was obtained by adding interest-bearing liabilities included within the current and non-current 'creditors and borrowings' notes.)
Equity is the total of shareholders' equity before outside shareholders' interests and is from the balance sheet.

Trend is

1993	1994	1995	1996	1997
1.3	0.9	0.7	0.4	0.3

A popular modification of this formula (and the total liabilities to equity formula) is to deduct cash from interest-bearing liabilities to recognise the additional financial strength of those entities which hold substantial cash funds.
Rule of thumb for interest-bearing debt is 0.5:1.

It is important to know what formula is used when you are reviewing ratios calculated by others. This formula considers only the borrowings. The argument is that these are the liabilities incurring interest and so place a financial strain on the entity.

The same trend is shown as for the first formula. The same comments on equity for 1994 and 1995 apply. Alba has reduced its dependence on borrowings to a very low level compared with equity.

Rule of thumb is half 'total debt to equity' because interest-bearing debt is expected to be half of the total liabilities for larger businesses.

Rules of thumb

The logical consideration is that, in the long run, borrowings should only be used to the extent that the rate of profit made on the assets funded by the borrowing exceeds the cost of borrowing (interest rate). The rule of thumb debt to equity level is much less important than this, but it tends to be treated as an absolute. The rule of thumb can vary in changing economic and market circumstances, e.g. prior to the 1987 Australian stock market crash 2:1 was okay. Why the change, other than that people became more aware of the extent of excessive borrowings at high interest rates used to buy assets that were giving little or no return?

During the 1980s the average D/E ratio increased from 0.5:1 to 1:1, reflecting the willingness of entities to borrow and lenders to lend in what were regarded as boom times. The rate of change may actually be greater, because during the late 1980s there was an increasing revaluation of non-current assets which caused the equity to be higher.

Always remember: rules of thumb probably apply in most but not all situations. For example, D/E ratios are much higher for financial institutions because they make their money by borrowing funds from the public and lending them out again. Their D/E ratios tend to be from 10:1 to 12:1.

Balancing debt, equity and assets

Consideration of D/E ratios brings us back to the section called 'Maintaining sustainable balance' in chapter 1. Short term borrowings are appropriate to fund current assets; for example, a professional firm uses a bank overdraft to finance its work in progress and debtors. Medium to long term borrowings are appropriate to fund non-current assets; for example, Alba used a $150 000 mortgage loan as part of the financing of its new property.

It is inappropriate to borrow short term to fund long term assets. Beware when you see this. It could mean lenders are concerned about viability and only prepared to offer short term financing.

Comparison of rate of profit with cost of borrowing

Formula is

If rate of return on assets (ROA) is greater than the calculated interest rate of borrowing, then borrowings have contributed to profit of shareholders. If less, then they have cost shareholders some profit.
ROA is explained under profitability below.
Interest cost is calculated as:

$$\frac{\text{Finance lease charge and interest}}{\text{Interest-bearing borrowings}} \times 100 = \frac{64\,859}{415\,995} \times 100 = 15.6\%$$

(See interest cover and debt to equity ratios above for places where these amounts are found or calculated.)

Trend is

	1993	1994	1995	1996	1997
ROA	20.4%	20.0%	19.9%	17.0%	15.3%
Interest rate	12.5%	15.3%	17.5%	16.1%	15.6%
Contribution?	yes	yes	yes	yes	no

As stated above, the only reason to borrow is if, in the long run, you make more money from the asset acquired through the borrowing than the cost of the borrowing. This can be measured by comparing the rate of profit earned on assets with the calculated cost of borrowing.

Return on assets is used to measure the rate of profit earned on assets. This is explained in the next section on profitability ratios.

Interest rate is determined by calculating that total interest cost (finance lease charges and interest expense) as a percentage of year end borrowings. This is only an approximation of the interest rates paid. A more accurate figure might be achieved by using the average borrowings for the year (opening borrowings plus year end borrowings divided by two—see days debtors above for limitation on measuring averages). The rates calculated for Alba appear high compared with interest rates available from 1995 to 1997. Averaging borrowings might help, but there may be additional borrowings at certain times of the year.

Alba made more from its assets than interest rate cost in every year except 1997. This is due to a declining return on assets since 1995. So the concern is not with apparently high interest rates cost but more with earnings on assets, which is discussed in the next section.

General comment on Alba's financing

Alba is comfortably financed, having liabilities being well within its capacity to service and repay. It could consider using the $150 000 cash on deposit to pay out the overdraft and reduce other debt. The only concerning feature is that the drop in profit generated on assets means that the interest rate cost on liabilities has just exceeded ROA in 1997, for the first time in at least four years. This may indicate the need to address the utilisation of assets. This is considered in the next section.

PROFITABILITY USING PROFITS

Gross margin

Formula is

$$\frac{\text{EBLIT}}{\text{Sales}} \times 100 \qquad \frac{\textit{excluding abnormals}}{} \qquad \frac{\textit{including abnormals}}{}$$

$$\frac{367\,361}{3\,399\,504} \times 100 \qquad \frac{394\,175}{3\,399\,504} \times 100$$

$$= 10.8\% \qquad\qquad = 11.6\%$$

EBLIT is explained under financial ratios. The difference between 'excluding' and 'including' abnormals is the abnormal item of profit on sale of investments of $26 814 in note 4—abnormal items. You must use the abnormal before income tax to be consistent with the way EBLIT is calculated. Sales is from note 2—operating revenue.

Trend is

	1993	1994	1995	1996	1997
no abnormals	12.1%	11.8%	11.6%	11.4%	10.8%
with abnormals	12.1%	10.8%	11.6%	16.5%	11.6%

This measures the level of profit being made on sales. Those businesses depending on high volume will have low gross margins (around 5%) and those depending on margin should have higher gross margins (around 15%–20%).

Alba's performance has declined slightly from just above 12 per cent to just under 11 per cent. If the pattern continues, it will be around 10 per cent in another three or four years. The continuing downward drift is of some concern.

The second aspect to consider is whether the level of 11 per cent is reasonable. This is a moderate rate of return, because interest and income tax expenses are still to be deducted. Perhaps Alba could aim to improve its rate of profit on sales.

A good result was to achieve 11.4 per cent in the year of the move to a new property. Moving manufacturing to new premises can be very disruptive.

Gross profit margin

Within a business they measure gross profit percentage. Gross profit is sales less cost of sales as discussed in chapters 2 and 3. Indeed, prudent businesses measure their gross profit at least by major products or product lines. However, cost of sales is not presently available as public information, meaning we cannot measure the ratio. The gross margin is the best approximation we have. (Alba's gross profit is given in chapter 3, so you can measure the gross profit return if you like by substituting gross profit for EBLIT.)

Which profit—before or after abnormal items?

As mentioned in the EBLIT calculation above, EBLIT provides a profit measurement independent of how the entity is financed or taxed. You may see variations of this formula where operating profit before tax or operating profit after tax is used.

Analysts tend to use the operating profit excluding abnormal items to measure profit performance. The aim is to use a 'normal' ongoing profit. Fluctuations from year to year are considered to distort the real profit potential. The aim of the profitability measures is to look at the real profitability potential. Now imagine you are part of company management. You know this too. So, it is in your interest to make the 'normal' profit as smooth and consistent as possible. It is in your interest to class fluctuating or loss items as abnormal or better still extraordinary items (they're never counted) or, if possible, to simply adjust retained profits. (These issues were discussed in chapter 8.)

Burns Philp example

Consider the situation of the Burns Philp group. From 1989 to 1991 it reported as follows:

	1989 $000	1990 $000	1991 $000
Operating profit before abnormal items and income tax	103 454	107 299	101 715
Income tax attributable to operating profit before abnormal items	(10 653)	(6 016)	(12 278)
Operating profit before abnormal items	92 801	101 283	89 437
Loss on abnormal items	(39 417)	(38 896)	(22 242)
Income tax attributable to abnormal items	2 125	1 425	1 642
Loss on abnormal items after income tax	(37 292)	(37 471)	(20 600)
Operating profit including abnormal items after income tax	55 509	63 812	68 837
The one abnormal item which occurred each year was			
Closure and rationalisation of businesses	(42 221)	(69 751)	(12 804)
Income tax attributable	4 019	822	234

The 1990 and 1991 costs related mainly to Fermtec (USA and Italian) operations and in 1989 the same plus Benchmark (New Zealand and Australian) operations.

Measuring Burns Philp's profitability when excluding abnormal items will be much more favourable than when including them. The recurring abnormal could be argued to reflect problematic past business decisions. If these losses are never included in the measurement of profit performance, an important part of the results of running the group will have been overlooked.

Those of you who have followed Burns Philp may have noticed a continuing trend of adverse and more sizeable abnormal items. In 1996 there were nine abnormal items totalling a loss before tax of $140.2 million. In 1995 there were four with a small gain before tax of $1.2 million. However, profit before tax on sales of business of $111.8 million was the only reason for not having a large loss.

Why not measure the profitability with and without abnormals? We have done this for Alba to let you see the difference. In Alba's case, each year's abnormal items are very different in nature. The 'normal' profit to use for Alba is *before* abnormals.

Return on assets (ROA)

Formula is   *excluding*   *including*
               abnormals   *abnormals*

$$\frac{\text{EBLIT}}{\text{Total assets}} \times 100 \qquad \frac{367\,361}{2\,407\,854} \times 100 \qquad \frac{394\,175}{2\,407\,854} \times 100$$

$$= 15.3\% \qquad\qquad = 16.4\%$$

EBLIT is as for gross margin.
Total assets is from the balance sheet.

Trend is

	1993	1994	1995	1996	1997
no abnormals	20.4%	20.0%	19.9%	17.0%	15.3%
with abnormals	20.4%	18.4%	19.9%	24.6%	16.4%

This measures how profitably the assets are being used. A rule of thumb comparison is to compare it with the rate of interest which could be earned if all the assets were converted into cash and placed on deposit. Alba is certainly running above this level.

Acceptable levels of ROA will vary between industries. Some industries require significant investment in assets to generate profit while others, such as a washing machine repair firm, probably do not need to acquire many assets. The reasonability of the ROA should be compared with industry averages.

As for gross margin, we will use operating profit excluding abnormals. The figures show that Alba was earning around 20 per cent (nice and high) from 1993 to 1995, and then it dropped sharply to 17 per cent in 1996 and fell again to 15 per cent in 1997. The fall between 1996 and 1997 is at a greater rate than gross margin.

Effect of valuation of assets

As with gross margin, this ratio is affected by what is included in EBLIT, such as abnormals. Another important issue is the basis of the valuation of assets. An entity which leaves its assets at cost is likely in the long run to have assets understated compared with one which revalues to market. If this was the only difference between two entities, the one with assets at cost would have a higher calculated ROA. It would appear to be more profitable than the other. The closer the asset values are to market, the more realistic the ROA. Let's consider this when we evaluate Alba's performance.

The value of assets in 1994 and 1995 did not recognise the rising value of the old property, which increased by \$184 722 since its 1993 revaluation as shown by the abnormal profit on its sale reported in the accounts for 1996. This means that total assets should have been increasingly higher in each of those years. If the property had been revalued each year, ROA would have reduced to about 19 per cent in 1994 and 18 per cent in 1995. This means a gradual dropping of ROA from 1993 to 1995 with a sharper drop in 1996 and another smaller fall in 1993.

In 1996 the significant change in assets was the sale of a property and purchase of a new one. The new property cost substantially more than the old one and (as discussed previously) was financed by the proceeds from the old property, new borrowings and the issue of new shares. There was surplus cash of \$80 000 which was placed on deposit. (This story was gleaned from the cash flows statement.)

Is new property too big?

The substantial drop in ROA in 1996 is probably a result of now having a bigger, more expensive property while revenue increase has continued at the historic rate. It needed to increase more significantly to give the same level of profitability on the new property. If this situation continues, it indicates that the property is bigger than Alba needs or, if fully used, more expensive than warranted for the profit the company can generate from it. The interest earned on the money on deposit would be lower than ROA. Unless Alba has some other need for cash, it should use the cash on deposit to reduce bank overdraft and loans.

In 1997 the property was revalued, which increased the asset base on which profitability is calculated. The amount on deposit almost doubled to \$150 000. This dampened ROA by another 1 per cent.

Return on equity (ROE)

Formula is

$$\frac{\text{Operating profit after tax and outside shareholders' interests}}{\text{Equity excluding outside shareholders' interests}} \times 100$$

excluding abnormals
$$\frac{184\,890}{1\,339\,393} \times 100 = \textbf{13.8\%}$$

including abnormals
$$\frac{211\,704}{1\,339\,393} \times 100 = \textbf{15.8\%}$$

Operating profit after outside shareholders' interests is calculated as:

		$
	Operating profit after income tax	211 704
less:	Outside shareholders' interest in profit	—
	Including abnormals	211 704
less:	Abnormal profits after tax (or add abnormal losses after tax)	(26 814)
	Excluding abnormals	184 890

Operating profit after income tax is from the profit and loss statement. Usually this figure is available after outside shareholders' interests in that profit. Outside shareholders' interests in profit is shown on the profit and loss statement. (Alba does not have any subsidiaries or outside shareholders—see chapter 12 for information on consolidations.)

Equity excluding outside shareholders' interests is from the balance sheet and for Alba is total equity.

Trend is

	1993	1994	1995	1996	1997
no abnormals	38.6%	29.5%	28.2%	16.1%	13.8%
with abnormals	37.0%	22.5%	28.8%	31.6%	15.8%

This ratio measures the rate of profit earned on shareholders' equity. It looks at the profit earned for all shareholders. It does not measure the profit earned in terms of what each ordinary shareholder gains or gets. This is measured by ratios used in the next section on market performance.

Alba's ROE follows virtually the same pattern as ROA except that the drop is greater. The same problems exist as for ROA with the accuracy of the ratio in 1994 and 1995. All the profit on the sale of the old property is recognised in 1996, which means the equity jumped by $184 722 in that one year. However the property gained value from 1993 to 1995.

If the property had been revalued, equity would have increased in each year, which would have reduced ROE to about 26 per cent in 1994 and 23 per cent in 1995. This shows a remarkably different picture. We now see a pattern of profitability from the shareholders' perspective dropping substantially each year from 1993 to 1997.

The remaining, sharper drop in 1996 is due to the $200 000 of issued shares (issued capital plus share premium).

The large ROE in 1993 might tie in with the high gearing of 2.7 (liabilities/equity). The greater use of liabilities combined with a strong ROA gave a fantastic ROE.

PROFITABILITY USING CASH FLOWS

Since writing the first edition I became aware of the value of the cash flows information. Working with one of my clients we developed 'profitability' ratios using cash flows. This gives an ability to compare the cash generation with the profit performance.

A simple way to look at business performance is a business should generate revenue with profit. If there is real profit there will be cash flow. If it is a creative accounting profit there will be a lack of cash flow.

Besides preparing fraudulent cash flows statements, the only way of manipulating cash flow is by arranging when receipts and payments will be made. However, this manipulation becomes difficult to continue in the one direction if we make comparisons over a number of years.

One risk that cash flows cannot cover is missing liabilities. Liabilities are unpaid items and as such do not appear in the cash flows statement. Unrecorded liabilities are not taken into account in the calculation of profit. A second risk is over-valued assets. These risks are discussed in chapter 9 under 'What cash flow does not show'.

As using cash flows performance ratios is not common, interpreting what they indicate is new. In my limited use of the following three ratios I have noticed an interesting indicator for any enterprises which trade primarily with inventories. The cash flows ratios trend changes the year before the profit ratios do. That is, an increase in cash flows ratios will occur one year before the profit ratios. Likewise for a decrease in cash flows ratios. I think this is due to cash outlays associated with inventory occurring before the impact of inventory is recognised in the profit and loss statement. The cash is paid when the inventory is acquired. Inventory is recognised in the profit and loss statement when sold. See if you find the same indication. What it means is that downward or upward trends for businesses trading in inventory are likely to be detected earlier using cash flows profitability ratios.

Gross cash margin

Formula is

$$\frac{\text{Gross operating cash flows}}{\text{Receipts from customers}} \times 100 = \frac{391\,550}{3\,851\,939} \times 100 = \mathbf{10.2\%}$$

All cash flows figures are obtained from the cash flows statement. Gross operating cash flows is:

		$
	Receipts from customers	3 851 939
less:	Payments to suppliers and employees	3 460 389
gives:	Gross operating cash flows	391 550

Trend is

1993	1994	1995	1996	1997
9.3%	10.5%	10.0%	12.7%	10.2%

The gross operating cash flows (GOCF) is similar to EBLIT, but excludes two more items than EBLIT does. GOCF excludes interest received and paid, dividends received and income tax paid. EBLIT excludes dividends and interest received.

The gross cash margin shows the rate of cash generation from trading, independent of tax, interest and dividends received. Its trend seems more constant than the gross margin. The 1996 figure is unusually high at 12.7 per cent. The analysis of Alba's cash flows in chapter 9 explained that cash flows were much higher in 1996 than 1997 due largely to inventory. The reduction of inventory from 1995 to 1996 contributed strongly to operating cash flow. The increase in inventory in 1997 reduced the operating cash flow. In fact this change meant that the gross operating cash flows declined from $451 101 to $391 550.

If we exclude 1996, the trend indicates constant gross cash margin of 10 per cent. If this trend is maintained, perhaps there might not be a continuing slight decline in the gross margin using profit.

Cash return on assets (CROA)

Formula is

$$\frac{\text{Gross operating cash flows}}{\text{Total assets}} \times 100 = \frac{391\,550}{2\,407\,854} \times 100 = \textbf{16.3\%}$$

Gross operating cash flows—see gross cash margin.
Total assets is from the balance sheet.

Trend is

1993	1994	1995	1996	1997
18.6%	20.8%	20.2%	21.6%	16.3%

The cash return on assets (CROA) shows the rate of cash generation from assets. It is constant or slightly increasing from 1993 to 1996 and then there is a dramatic drop in 1997. This is a very adverse change. Is it an isolated event or a proper indicator?

The shift in 1997 is explained by a decline in the gross operating cash flows (see above) combined with an increase in total assets of almost $400 000 to $2 407 854. We need to be careful when interpreting this shift. Remember that the level of gross cash flows was enhanced by the significant reduction in inventory in 1996. This was largely reversed in 1997. This means that 1996 gross cash flow was high compared with other years. The gross operating cash flows for the five years have been:

Gross operating cash flows is	1993	1994	1995	1996	1997
	$242 867	$299 172	$306 159	$451 101	$391 550

These figures show a gradually increasing gross operating cash flow from operating activities from 1993 to 1995 with a huge increase in 1996 and a drop in 1997. The 1997 figure is still easily the second highest. So overall there is an increasing gross operating cash flows from operating activities.

As for ROA, 1994 and 1995 CROA are understated due to property not being revalued annually. In 1996 the new property and $200 000 subscribed by shareholders increased the total assets significantly. Thus better interpretation of the trend in CROA is relatively constant from 1993 to 1995 with a relative decline in 1996 and 1997. This reflects a greater proportional increase in assets compared with the increase in cash flow.

Cash flows return on equity (CROE)

Formula is

$$\frac{\text{Cash flows from operating activities}}{\text{Equity before outside interests}} \times 100 = \frac{259\,948}{1\,339\,393} \times 100 = 19.4\%$$

Cash flows from operating activities is from the cash flows statement. Equity is total of shareholders' equity before outside shareholders' interests and is from the balance sheet.

Trend is

1993	1994	1995	1996	1997
39.0%	36.7%	30.9%	31.3%	19.4%

The cash return on equity (CROE) shows the rate of operating cash generation on equity. There is a general downward trend with a huge decline in 1997. The apparent improvement in 1996 is due to the significant reduction in inventory. As explained under the analysis of return on equity, due to recognising the property gain on sale in equity in 1996, equity is understated in 1994 and 1995. This means there is a greater downward trend in 1994 and 1995 than indicated by the ratio.

Overall the expansion to the new property and the issue of shares in 1996 has reduced the relative performance of operating cash flow in relation to equity. This reflects the lack of improved sales arising from the move to the new premises. This is the same pattern as seen in return on equity using profit. Percentages under both calculations are very similar.

General comment on Alba's profitability

Calculating the ratios using operating profit excluding abnormals shows that Alba has maintained gross margin, with ROA and ROE steady from 1993 to 1995 and then dropping significantly in 1996. The 1996 decline may indicate that selling the old property and buying a new one has provided more capacity than the company can use.

When allowance is made for the old property not being revalued in 1994 and 1995, we have a different situation. The ROA and ROE are declining each year with a more marked decline in 1996 on the acquisition of the new property. This is the truer assessment of the changing profitability of Alba.

The gross cash margin indicates a greater stability than the gross margin does. In fact the cash margin might be increasing rather than the decline evident in the gross margin. The CROA and CROE follow a very similar pattern to ROA and ROE reinforcing our analysis of the profitability performance using profit ratios.

Whichever way you look at it, Alba's profitability is in decline. Profit may be increasing in dollar terms, but it is not increasing rapidly enough to maintain a constant level of profit. Management should examine their revenue and expenses, and see if they can increase profit at a greater rate and so restore their former levels of profitability.

A final interesting point to consider is that revaluation gains and extraordinary items are not recognised in the profit calculation. In chapter 5 we considered how revaluation gains are not treated as profit. One of the ways Alba has grown over the five years is through acquiring and selling its premises. These properties were effective purchases in the sense that each time they were valued their value had increased; and the old property was sold at a profit on the 1993 revalued amount. So is this part of Alba's profit? Would we have more correct measurement of profitability if it was included? At present the prevailing view is that it should not be included. My view is that it should, provided revaluations are reliable, regular and at market value based on willing buyer, willing seller.

Market view of profitability

Analysts are concerned with more than the historical ratios. They consider the quality of management and the projected future profit. They meet with company executives and obtain other information to help them assess the impact of management quality on their analysis of the company.

Generally, profits projected one or two years ahead are regarded as more relevant than historical results. The risk with this approach is the reasonableness of the projections. The further into the future the projection, the greater the risk. The projections are based on the historical results, current market situation and knowledge of the company being assessed.

PROFITABILITY USING SEGMENT INFORMATION

Diverse enterprises generate profit from their different businesses. These businesses can be in different industries and/or countries. Segment information discussed in chapter 8 provides a view of this diverseness. The figures can, with discretion, be used to measure segment performance.

Alba Manufacturing operates in only one industry in Australia. So there is no segment performance to review.

James Hardie Industries Limited group segment information is included at the end of chapter 8. This shows a group operating in four industries and three main countries. We will use James Hardie's figures to calculate and compare the segment information and return to Alba for market performance.

Net segment margin

Formula is

$$\frac{\text{Segment results}}{\text{Segment sales}} \times 100 = \frac{94.2\,\text{m}}{686.9\,\text{m}} \times 100 = \mathbf{13.7\%}$$

This calculation uses building products 1996 figures as shown at the end of chapter 8.

Segment net margin is

	1995 %	1996 %
By industry		
Building products	16.9	13.7
Plumbing & pipelines	3.8	(0.6)
Building services	1.4	2.9
Irrigation	4.9	2.1
Investments	(22.9)	(12.4)
By geographic		
Australia	3.7	3.0
New Zealand	16.0	16.8
USA	6.2	10.1
Other	(20.4)	(19.1)

Segment return on assets

Formula is

$$\frac{\text{Segment results}}{\text{Segment assets}} \times 100 \; = \; \frac{94.2\,\text{m}}{609.8\,\text{m}} \times 100 \; = \; \textbf{15.4\%}$$

This calculation uses building products 1996 figures as shown at the end of chapter 8.

Segment ROA is

	1995 %	1996 %.
By industry		
Building products	17.1	15.4
Plumbing & pipelines	4.7	(0.7)
Building services	3.1	6.0
Irrigation	5.8	2.3
Investments	(4.7)	(3.1)
By geographic		
Australia	3.5	3.0
New Zealand	23.0	29.0
USA	4.6	7.6
Other	(10.4)	(11.4)

This segment analysis gives us an approximate assessment of profitability. The ratios are segment net margin (results/external sales) and segment ROA (segment results/segment assets). James Hardie have provided the results before tax. Sometimes the results will be after tax. James Hardie also show their abnormal items separately. So the calculated ratios are before abnormal items and tax.

Segment results should be interpreted with care. James Hardie's classification of businesses within segments has changed on two or more occasions from 1988 to 1996. This makes comparisons between segments difficult or unreliable over time. Segment results are affected by what are not allocated to a segment. In 1995 and 1996 there were large unallocated assets of $428.8 million and $363.1 million respectively. These are removed from the denominators for the industry segments and so make the performance look better.

Under industry segments building products is the best performer. Irrigation is shown as a separate segment. This business was sold during the 1997 financial year.

Under geographic segments New Zealand is the star performer with Australia providing very low levels of return on both sales and assets. Yet

Australia is by far the largest segment in absolute terms. Thus, assets seem poorly utilised in Australia and there is a low sales margin.

The breakdown into segments enables us to obtain some feel for which industries or countries are most profitable. What we see as the best performers for James Hardie in 1995 and 1996 are not necessarily the best over time. As with any ratios, we should look at this performance over time. However, when segments are changed during the period of comparison, it distorts the comparison.

MARKET PERFORMANCE

The four types of ratios discussed above (liquidity, management efficiency, financing and profitability) measured the performance of the entity, Alba. They did not measure the performance of the investment in terms of what individual shareholders are gaining. This section does, but even here remember that the shareholder really only gets the dividend paid and the selling price of any shares sold. The emphasis that analysts and the media place on earnings per share and price earnings ratios is questioned, because earnings per share is not what an investor physically receives.

Net tangible assets (NTA) per share

Formula is

$$\frac{\text{Net tangible assets}}{\text{Number of ordinary shares}} = \frac{1\,266\,143}{400\,000} = \mathbf{\$3.17}$$

Net tangible assets (NTA) is determined from the point of view of the interest in the business of the ordinary shareholders only, and so is calculated as:

		$
	Shareholders' equity excluding outside shareholders' interests	1 339 393
less:	Preference shares	—
		1 339 393
less:	Intangible assets and future income Tax benefits (FITB)	— 73 250
		73 250
gives:	NTA	1 266 143

Shareholders' equity excluding outside shareholders comes from the balance sheet. Any preference shares would be disclosed in the share capital note and they and any share

premium relating to them should be deducted.
Intangible assets would be from the balance sheet.
The FITB is from the balance sheet but would be from a note on other non-current assets under Schedule 5.
Number of ordinary shares is from note 15—share capital, and is the number of shares (not dollar value) issued to ordinary shareholders.

Trend is

1993	1994	1995	1996	1997
$1.00	$1.50	$1.71	$2.53	$3.17

This ratio shows the amount of tangible assets (after deduction of liabilities) for each share. It is calculated using book value of assets and so does not reflect the real asset value backing. Only tangible assets are included, because of the more indefinite nature and higher risk of loss of value on intangible assets.

The ratio is calculated from the point of view of ordinary shareholders. Preference shareholders are removed because, under the terms of their shares, they are usually only entitled to dividend and return of the amount invested at the time of redemption (if redeemable preference shares) or on the company being liquidated. The formula includes the deduction of share premium specifically related to preference shares.

Future income tax benefit is deducted because, as discussed under 'income tax' in chapter 8, there are severe limitations on ever attaining value for this asset in the event of sale or liquidation. It is much more like an intangible asset in nature than a non-current receivable. A variation of this formula is to offset any deferred tax liability (DTL) against the FITB. This will reduce the reduction effect of the FITB. It recognises that a DTL is often very unlikely to be paid in the near future.

This ratio reflects a current value to the extent the major assets are close to market value. On the other hand it does not suggest a liquidation value. The assets are not being considered on a 'forced sale' basis but on a 'going concern' basis. The underlying accounting assumption of the business being in a continuing situation (a 'going concern') is always assumed in financial statements, unless there is reason to prepare the statements on another basis.

Alba's NTA has steadily increased from 1993 to 1997. This is to be expected as the company has earned increasing profits over the period and always only distributed part of those profits. The greater increase in 1996 was due to the sale of the old property and purchase of a more expensive property. As we have noted above under 'profitability', the profit on sale was recognised entirely in 1996 whereas the gain in value of the old property occurred over the period from the last valuation in 1993.

The estimated NTA based on approximate 'retrospective' revaluations is $1.75 for 1994 and $2.25 in 1995. This changes the picture to one of larger increases in the earlier years with a slow down in 1996. This is probably more realistic for two reasons.

1   A hundred thousand new shares were issued in 1996 which means the NTA is calculated over a greater number of shares—a one-third increase actually. This is known as dilution—that is, the assets are spread over a larger number of shares so the value attributed to each share is diluted. This concept of dilution applies to all ratios which are measured on a per share basis.

2   A proportion of the increased assets in 1996 were funded by new borrowings as well as a share issue. The extent to which the increase in assets is funded by new borrowings reduces the net increase in asset backing of shares.

Given the increase in the number of shares in 1996, the fact that NTA still increased was quite an achievement. It often drops. A contributing factor to the result was that new shares were issued at a premium—shareholders had to buy in at a price closer to the real value of the shares. The additional shares cost $2.00, which was higher than calculated NTA for 1995 but lower than the recalculated NTA which allowed for asset revaluation.

Whichever way we look at Alba's NTA there is a pleasing increase in value and an indication of sound underlying asset backing of the shares. The NTA in 1996 and 1997 reflects assets valued close to market. The property, though at cost in 1996, was new and close to market value, and it was revalued in 1997 to what we think is closer to market value.

Dividend per share (DPS)

Formula is

$$\frac{\text{Ordinary dividend declared and paid}}{\text{Number of ordinary shares}} = \frac{60\,000}{400\,000} = \$0.15 \text{ per share}$$

Ordinary dividend declared and paid is from the profit and loss statement. Any preference dividends should be ignored as the ratio is from the ordinary shareholders' perspective. Number of ordinary shares is from note 15—share capital, and is the number of shares (not dollar value) issued to ordinary shareholders.

Normally you do not need to calculate DPS. The actual DPS is given in the accounts and/or the directors' report. You may need to add the interim and find DPS.

Trend is

1993	1994	1995	1996	1997
$0.15	$0.15	$0.15	$0.15	$0.15

Dividends are the income shareholders receive on their investment. Directors consider what they believe shareholders' dividend expectations are. Profit retained in the business is a cheap, simple and sensible strategy for funding expansion of the business. Thus, if the business needs to grow, it is best if most of the current year's profit can be retained and the level of dividend paid still meets shareholder expectations.

In the section on dividends in chapter 8, three listed company examples of dividend payments made out of all or other than current year's profits were given. This illustrates the importance attached to meeting shareholder expectations.

Alba has paid a consistent rate of dividend each year. Paying the same rate of dividend on a larger number of issued shares means the actual dividend payout increases. This is shown in Alba's profit and loss statement where dividend in 1997 is greater than in 1996.

Earnings per share (EPS)

Formula is

$$\frac{\text{Operating profit after tax, outside shareholders' and preference dividend}}{\text{Number of ordinary shares}}$$

excluding abnormals
$$\frac{184\,890}{400\,000} = \$0.462 \text{ per share}$$

including abnormals
$$\frac{211\,704}{400\,000} = \$0.529 \text{ per share}$$

The numerator is the same as ROE except that preference dividends are also deducted to give what is left for ordinary shareholders. Number of ordinary shares is from note 15—share capital, and is the number of shares (not dollar value) issued to ordinary shareholders.

Trend is

	1993	1994	1995	1996	1997
no abnormals	$0.450	$0.495	$0.538	$0.432	$0.462
with abnormals	$0.431	$0.377	$0.549	$0.851	$0.529

Earnings per share shows the amount of profit which can be attributed to ordinary shareholders. This is not simply the operating profit after income tax. In a group of companies, any profit which belongs to outside shareholders needs to be deducted (see chapter 12 for an explanation of outside shareholders). The company may have issued preference shares. The preference shareholders' dividend is a claim on profits which is payable before the ordinary shareholders have access to profits. So preference dividends are deducted.

The remaining profit is divided by the number of ordinary shares to give EPS. The formula uses the year end number of shares. Shares may have been issued during the year. Should EPS be calculated based on year end shares or should an average number of shares on issue during the year be calculated?

Alba's EPS rose steadily from 1993 to 1995 in proportion to the rise in operating profit after income tax. It dropped in 1996 on the issue of new shares and rose again in 1997.

Remember that shareholders receive dividend per share (DPS), not EPS.

EPS accounting standard

The overseas standards and the Australian standard AASB 1027, *Earnings Per Share*, (which applies to all listed companies) use the average number (with the average weighted to allow for partly issued shares, bonus shares and when shares were issued during the year). This can be difficult to calculate.

Another aspect is that *potential* ordinary shares may exist, e.g. likely conversion of convertible notes, a new rights issue announced or a bonus issue imminent. The Australian standard requires EPS to be calculated both excluding these potential shares (the 'basic' EPS) and including them (the 'diluted' EPS). Analysts do make adjustments for average and diluted shares.

The use of averages and dilution do not change the concept, but do change the ease of calculation. To help keep calculations easier, the number of year end ordinary shares (all assumed to be fully paid) has been used.

The view that year end rather than average should be used can be supported. At any point in time, it is the shareholders at that time who are entitled to the remaining profits left after liquidation of a company. Therefore, the year end number of ordinary shares is the relevant number, and the number of shares on issue at an earlier point during the year is irrelevant.

The issue of shares from time to time creates a situation where the profit is spread over more and more shares. Each new issue usually means a drop in EPS, as there is insufficient increase in profit to maintain or increase it. Listed companies can provide additional calculations. Earnings per share can be unadjusted or adjusted. Unadjusted means the EPS as calculated each year for the shares on issue during that year (as required by the accounting standard). Adjusted means the EPS has been recalculated using the shares on issue at the end of the current reporting year. This is done to eliminate the distortion created by the issue of shares.

Company management and directors are aware that the share market likes to see EPS maintained or gradually increasing. This is another subtle consideration in the calculation of profit. It may also be an issue in the calculation of EPS.

Accounting standard 1027 requires EPS to be calculated *after* abnormal items. Analysts prefer it to be calculated *before* abnormal items. The standard is not in line with analysts' requirements. It could require both. Many listed companies publish both.

Accounting standard 1027 disclosures required include providing explanation of any differences between reported profit and profit used for EPS and information on the average shares used.

As with the profitability ratios, EPS is affected by what is counted as profit. Alba's EPS is given excluding and including abnormal items. As reasoned under profitability ratios above, the operating profit before abnormals is the better representation of Alba's ongoing profitability.

Dividend cover

Formula is

$$\frac{\text{EPS}}{\text{DPS}} = \frac{0.462}{0.150} = 3.1\,\text{times}$$

DPS and EPS are calculated above. EPS excluding abnormals has been used. The same calculation using EPS including abnormals will give some variation but, other than in 1996, it is not significant to the trend shown.

Trend is

1993	1994	1995	1996	1997
3.0	3.3	3.6	2.9	3.1

Rule of thumb minimum for sensible growing of the company through retention of profits is 2:1; a very strong situation is 3:1.

This ratio shows the drain of profits in the payment of dividend. The more profit that can be retained the better for the growing of the company by self-funding.

Alba shows a strong ability to retain profits in the business. Shareholders are satisfied with a level of dividend that is not a strain on Alba's ability to self-fund future growth. The ratio has been around the very strong level of 3:1. The achievement for 1996 and 1997 is all the more creditable, because the amount of dividend paid increased in each year as dividend level was maintained on a larger number of shares.

As with all other ratios that include profit, this ratio is affected by what has been counted as profit. Earnings per share is determined on operating profit (and for Alba this is before abnormals). Extraordinary items are ignored. From what we know about Alba, its abnormal items have tended to be gains rather than losses or, if losses, have not been substantial. Where abnormal items and extraordinary items are really losses, the dividend cover is not what it seems to be. As shown in the examples under 'dividends' in chapter 8, it can really be paid out of profits of prior years or out of other reserves transferred to retained profits reserve to allow the legal payment of dividend.

Legally, dividends can only be paid out of profits—the current year's or retained profits from prior years, with some ability to use other reserves subject to legal requirements contained in the Corporations Law. The matter for financial statements users to monitor is the extent to which profits (from all sources) are drained from the company by dividend requirements.

Dividend yield

Formula is

$$\frac{\text{DPS}}{\text{Market price per share}} \times 100 \quad \frac{\$0.15}{\text{non-listed shares}} \times 100$$

To show how the calculation is done we will substitute NTA per share and assume it is a reasonable value of the shares.

$$\frac{\text{DPS}}{\text{NTA}} \times 100 = \frac{\$0.15}{\$3.17} \times 100 = \mathbf{4.7\%}$$

Comments on market price given under Price/earnings below apply here. DPS was calculated above.

Trend is

1993	1994	1995	1996	1997
15.0%	10.0%	8.8%	5.9%	4.7%

The ratio shows the shareholders' income earning rate on shares based on market value. Shareholders can calculate their own rate using the price paid for the shares. For instance, Alba shareholders who subscribed to the 1996 issue would use $2.00 and their dividend yield for 1997 would be 7.5 per cent ([0.15/2.00] × 100), which is a higher yield than normal for listed shares.

It is important to realise this ratio shows the return shareholders are actually achieving on their investment, using current market value for listed shares. The yield is usually around 3 per cent to 5 per cent. Why are shareholders willing to accept such low values?

- The yield is often an after-tax rate of return because of dividend imputation. Dividend imputation means that tax paid by the company is treated as if it were paid by the individual shareholder (see below). To the extent that the company has not been required to pay tax on its income, the amount of tax imputed to an individual is reduced. So where the company has not had to pay any tax on its profits, the yield is a before-tax rate.

- The yield is an after-tax rate of return for Australian companies receiving dividends from other Australian companies. They treat the dividend as income, then claim a tax rebate for the same amount. The tax treatment of dividend income received from overseas companies is more complex and beyond the scope of this book.

- Shareholders tend to regard their income from shares as being a mixture of dividend and the profit made on selling the shares. This is all very well if the share price rises and you do sell shares on occasion. In Australia, the share price has always risen in the long run.

- The emphasis on measurement of gain for shareholders focuses on EPS rather than dividend.

Alba's dividend yield has nose-dived over the five years. However, ours is a substitute rate because NTA has been used instead of market price. If the shares were valued in earlier years, they would probably have been at a higher value than NTA and the yield would be lower.

For listed companies the pattern is usually fairly consistent. In share market booms the yield may go down as the market responds more to feelings about future profits than it does to current profits. In slump times, it may be the opposite. These trends will be true to the extent that the company is able to maintain dividend payments. In recessionary times the company may have to reduce or eliminate dividends, which will certainly reduce or eliminate the dividend yield.

Dividend imputation

Dividend imputation means that the benefit of the tax paid by a company on its profit is passed on to a shareholder who is a person. A company pays tax at a rate of 36 per cent. Individual taxpayers' rates depend on their level of income.

Each person holding shares treats the dividend as income in their tax return, including not the actual amount received, but the notional amount before deduction of income tax paid by the company. As in calculating EBLIT, you add back the income tax expense.

For Alba in 1997, a person would show the dividend income on 100 shares as $23.44 ($15.00 × 100/64). The difference of $8.44

($23.44 – $15.00) is the tax counted as being paid by the company. The person then deducts $8.44 from their calculated income tax payable (on their total taxable income), to reduce their liability by that amount. The income tax paid by the company is treated as though it was paid by the person.

So people paying the top marginal rate of 47 per cent only have to pay tax on dividend income at an additional 13 per cent. (In addition, Medicare levy at the rate of 1.4 per cent is payable.)

Price/earnings (P/E)

Formula is

$$\frac{\text{Market price per share}}{\text{EPS}} \qquad \frac{\text{non-listed shares}}{0.462}$$

To show how the calculation is done we will sustitute NTA per share and assume it is a reasonable value of the shares.

$$\frac{\text{NTA}}{\text{EPS}} = \frac{3.17}{0.462} = \mathbf{6.9\,times}$$

Market price for listed companies is obtained from the Stock Exchange or financial press. The P/E ratio can vary depending on what date you select. The date should be after the balance sheet date to allow the market to react to the profit announcement, say one to three months after. EPS was calculated above.

Trend is

1993	1994	1995	1996	1997
2.2	3.0	3.2	5.9	6.9

This ratio shows how the market price is related to operating profit. It is often referred to as the universal indicator because it is used internationally. It does not measure amounts (share price and operating profit) but relationship, and so makes everything comparable.

Generally the higher the P/E the better the market perceives the quality of the share. The price is based on perceived increasing profitability—a good future. The lower the ratio the worse the market perceives the quality of the share. Where there is doubt about future profitability, the share market may be valuing the share more on the NTA backing. You will notice I use the term 'perceived'. I do this because perceptions swing considerably with booms and slumps of the stock market. The market frequently seems to react emotionally to changes in the economy, governments, government policy— you name it!

What does a P/E ratio mean? Alba's P/E ratio is 6.9 in 1997. Net tangible assets is used as a substitute for market price. In Alba's case it means it will take seven years of profit at the same rate to cover the asset backing of the shares. To put it another way it shows profit is being earned at the rate of 14.5 per cent (100/6.9 to convert into percentages).

If the NTA were the market price of the share, it would mean that if the shares were acquired at that price it would take seven years of profit to recover the share price, which is the same as an interest rate of 14.5 per cent. This seems a reasonable rate of return. But wait! What do shareholders actually earn? They earn the dividend.

Alba's dividend is $0.15 per share. If we substitute DPS in the equation for EPS we get 21.1 times ($3.17/$0.15). This means it takes twenty-and-a-half years for the dividend to cover the cost of shares. Or, expressed as interest rate, a return of 4.7 per cent—a very low rate for the risk taken. (This is the dividend yield.)

Should we use P/D (price/dividend) instead of P/E? We cannot really do this because the dividend may be greater than the year's profits, in which case it is artificially high. Secondly, if it was measured on this base, the level of dividend would be determined on the basis of what it will do for improving the share price.

Perhaps an answer is to keep both in mind. In the long run, for a growing company, less than half the profits should be paid out as dividend. In the long run the company should be profitable, which may mean some lean years along the way. In the long run the share price should not move too high above a 'fundamentals' P/E multiple of 8 or 10:1 if it is to be really related to the profit-generating capability of the company. (Many analysts suggest that if shares are being valued by the market on the fundamentals, i.e. the ability to generate profit, rather than on speculation or anticipation of a rising share price, then P/E is usually around 8 to 12:1.)

So, a P/E of 20 means it takes twenty years of profit to cover the cost of the investment. Goodness knows how long it would take for the dividend to cover the cost!

Performance measurement

With performance measured in relationship to yearly profit, there is great pressure on maintaining short term performance. The more management performance is monitored and measured on the basis of share price and market perception, the more concerned management will be with good, growing operating profits, the 'right news' hitting the market, and quickly pouring oil on troubled waters.

In this situation what happens when long term forecasts and planning show there is a need to change direction, and that this change of direction will take some years to achieve and will reduce short term profits? There is a significant risk of not beginning the change early enough. The change comes when there is a slump or the company can no longer resist the change, i.e. it's change or perish. When this happens the cost of the change is much greater in terms of time, problems to rectify, stress placed on management and staff, and turning in a new direction. Western society's preoccupation with short term performance costs us dearly—but will we change to a more balanced approach?

P/E measurement and the market

Our calculations have used historical profit. Investment analysts frequently substitute prospective profits. When these prospective profits are higher than the historical (as in the case of moving out of a recession), the P/E using prospective will be much lower and closer to the more fundamental 8 to 12:1.

I believe share prices tend to be too high when you consider the real profitability of companies. We have seen several examples in this book of how items not classed as part of normal operating profit are often losses rather than gains. This means total profit is frequently less than operating profit before abnormals—our usual figure plugged in to all the equations.

I hope you agree with me that there is an important issue here as to the real value of shares traded on Stock Exchanges around the world. How can it really be surprising if there are crashes after booms—booms which are based on ever-increasing P/E multiples?

And what about the basis of reward in the industry? Rewards for executives based on share price? Reward for brokers is based on commission. Commission is quoted as a percentage of the value of the shares traded. The higher the share price, the higher the commission. Is this a subtle underlying influence on the boom–bust cycle?

General comment on Alba's market performance

In this section I have made some comments on what I see as weaknesses in the way market performance is measured. I have suggested that too little attention is given to income earning on shares in the form of dividend. Because dividend yields are so low, the hope is for increasing share prices. In the long run the share prices must be influenced by the real profit of the company.

Alba's market performance shows increasing and solid underlying asset backing, which in 1996 and 1997 is based on assets valued at close to market value. The EPS has increased in each year except 1996, when 100 000 new shares were issued. The EPS has followed the pattern of growth in operating profit. The DPS has been maintained at a constant $0.15 per share which meant an increase in the total dividend in 1996 when 100 000 new shares were issued. Dividend cover is very strong at about 3:1, which means that most of the profit is retained in the business and so helps to fund future growth. Dividend yield and P/E ratios could only be based on NTA because the shares are not listed on a Stock Exchange, nor were there any share valuations.

All market ratios using profit are affected by how profit is measured. The common approach is to use operating profit before abnormals. This was used for Alba, but Alba's abnormal profits tend to be gains or, if losses, not too substantial. Further, there have been gains from holding property, some of which have been accounted for as revaluations. They are a positive element not reflected in profit measurement. Thus elements of profit not included in profit performance measurement would enhance, rather than detract from, Alba's market performance assessment.

There remains the niggling under-utilisation of increased capacity. If prospects for growth are limited perhaps increased dividends and return of capital would be better for shareholders.

HOW DID ALBA FARE?

We have examined Alba's performance over the five years to 1997 by looking at the company's liquidity, management efficiency, financing, profitability and market performance. In summary what this assessment shows is:

■ Alba's liquidity has improved to a position where it is now at a comfortable level even though the current ratio is just above the 1.5 rule of thumb minimum.

■ Management efficiency has reinforced the reasonableness of the liquidity situation, with debtors being collected in a reasonable 47 days and with significant improvement in days inventory ratio in 1996 which was maintained in 1997. Inventory levels should be further reduced if there is scope to do so without affecting the ability to supply customers.

■ Financing is in a healthy state, with Alba easily able to pay its interest out of profits. Further, its dependence on liabilities including borrowings has been reduced significantly over the five years, to now be at very comfortable levels compared with equity of 0.8:1 and 0.3:1 respectively. The one adverse feature is that the cost of borrowings exceeded the rate of profit for the first time in 1997. The issue seems to be the level of profitability, not interest rates.

■ Profitability is the area Alba needs to improve. All three measures using profit being gross margin, ROA and ROE have declined over the five years, with the last two being the strongest downward trends. The gross cash margin showed a steadier trend. The CROA and CROE showed a similar trend to ROA and ROE. It seems that Alba has had a struggle with the new property acquired in 1996 to generate more revenue and profits to justify the additional cost of this property, compared with the amount which had been invested in the old one.

■ Market performance has been strong with NTA rising steadily over the five years, after allowing for the issue of 100 000 new shares in 1996.

Dividend per share has been constant at $0.15, and two-thirds of the profit has been retained in the business as shown by dividend cover of around 3:1 from 1993 to 1997. The EPS has risen steadily (following increases in operating profit after tax), except for a fall in 1996 with the issue of new shares. Dividend yield and P/E ratios could not be based on market price of shares as Alba is not a listed company, nor had shares been valued at any stage during the five years reviewed.

In short, Alba is a healthy company with solid and usually improving performance from 1993 to 1997, except for profitability. Management should aim at improving profit performance through better utilisation of assets and some improved margin on sales.

POINTS TO REMEMBER

✔ Financial statements present assets, liabilities, equity, profit and cash flows, but *performance* needs to be interpreted. Ratios measure the relationships between balance sheet, profit and loss and cash flows items. They reduce absolute amounts to proportional relationships which can be compared over time in the one entity, between entities, with industry averages and with rules of thumb.

✔ Industry information is available from various sources such as industry bodies and commercial providers.

✔ Ratios can be used to assess: the ability of an entity to pay debts; how well working capital is managed; the reasonableness of the balance between debt and equity financing of the business and the level of comfort in handling the debt financing; the level of profitability; and the profitability and security for the investor.

✔ Analysts favour different ratios and vary formulae to suit their needs and preferences. Valid comparison is only possible when the same formulae are used for each of the entities being compared. Check what formulae have been used. The importance of a rule of thumb for a ratio can vary between industries.

✔ Ratios must be applied and calculated with care. The right figures must be obtained from the accounts. You may want to adjust the figures presented in the accounts if you hold a different view on their accounting policies or other accounting issues. The financial statements as provided are a starting point for intelligent analysis.

✔ The most problematic issue is what is profit. Profit used in ratio analysis is usually operating profit excluding abnormal items (whether before or after tax). However, ignoring abnormal items, extraordinary items, revaluation gains added direct to reserves, and mere adjustments to retained profits may mean the real profitability of the entity is not being assessed.

✔ Cash flows statements provide additional information. This enables compilation of cash flows profitability ratios which can be compared with profit ratios. Very few analysts seem to have created cash flows ratios. Using cash flows enhances your interpretation.

✔ Ratios are very useful in the understanding and interpretation of financial performance when applied knowledgeably, systematically and thoughtfully.

11 Analysing micro businesses

Ratios and ratio rules of thumb are geared to larger businesses. Much of business is conducted by 'Mum and Dad' sole traders, partnerships, companies or trusts. These Mum and Dad businesses are typically very small in comparison with other small businesses. The term 'micro businesses' has been used to describe them.

In this chapter I suggest an alternative way of analysing micro and smaller businesses. Using standard ratios often provides results which suggest the business is not viable. But we have to consider how these Mum and Dad small business owners actually run their businesses; how they get their money out. Good analysis should always consider the nature of an enterprise and how it is run. I believe the application of ratios to analysing micro businesses for the purpose of assessment is usually useless.

This chapter covers setting up decent accounts, the over dominance of tax, measuring performance by considering what the owners are getting out of the business and how to calculate cash flows from balance sheets and a profit and loss statement.

DEMAND DECENT ACCOUNTS

The accounting information of many micro businesses might not be worth the paper it is written on. Is it produced months after the event? Is it just tax driven? Is it just cash driven? Do the tax return and accounts prepared by the accountant at the end of the year dramatically change the story from what the owner thought it was? If your answer is 'yes' to any of these questions you should demand timely decent accounts.

Typical micro business operators only keep cash records during the year. They present a 'shoe-box' of records to their accountants at year end. They only use their accountant to generate a tax return and set of accounts. These might be received six months after the year end. They are already halfway through the next year. Thus, any useful information for running the business is delayed. The business situation might have changed and the information might be useless.

If you run a micro business, be sensible; demand or arrange appropriate regular accounting reports. A good accountant will help you with business oriented accounting advice. A good accountant is more than a tax adviser or preparer of tax returns. According to lenders attending seminars I conduct, good accountants can be hard to find.

As the minimum recording requirement, each business should maintain a cashbook which is updated monthly. This shows the cash received and payments made. It is agreed (reconciled) with the bank statement monthly. The information from the reconciliation is used to correct and update the cashbook.

There are good accounting packages available which can be used by those of us who want to have more control over our financial destiny. These packages range from computerised cashbooks to quite sophisticated accounting packages—some for under $500. Your accountant can advise you.

A business survives on cash. Cash comes from customers. If yours is a cash sale business how do your systems ensure you always collect cash at the time of sale? If you have credit sales, how do your systems ensure you invoice all sales? Do you know if you are really making a profit?

Do you know which products or services contribute to profit and which don't? Liquidators often find the accounting systems of failed businesses were inadequate, not providing accurate information on product profitability. Could your decisions be based on poor information?

As discussed in this book, profit is more than cash. There are non-cash expenses such as depreciation, increases in employee entitlements, provisions for doubtful debts, write-down of obsolete stock. When you rely only on cashbook accounting during the year, these effects are only recognised at year end. They can be sizeable and are generally negative.

On the other hand we do not want to get too complex. So here are some suggestions based on how I have established my accounting records to help me run my business.

Sales

Typical accounts prepared by accountants for small business only show one figure for sales. This does not identify the kinds of sales. Three examples are set out below.

1 TV sales and repair business—it would be useful to at least show separately the television and parts sales from repairs' income. It could also be useful to separate television and parts sales. If some televisions are rented, then rental income should be shown separately.

2 Retailer—useful to at least show separately the broad categories of goods such as white goods, entertainment equipment, furnishings. These could be sub-divided, e.g. white goods as refrigerators, washing machines, dryers, dishwashers.

3 Professional services such as a law firm—useful to separate kinds of work, e.g. separate conveyancing, mortgage/lending, family law, wills.

This is simply achieved in a cashbook by creating more cash received columns. In a computerised system you achieve it by creating separate general ledger sales accounts.

If you break down your sales you can compare them month to month and year to year. You can see whether your mix of sales changes over time. This assists in forecasting sales.

Cost of sales and gross profit

As discussed in chapter 1, accountants typically split expenses into 'cost of sales' and 'expenses'. Cost of sales is deducted from sales to give gross profit. For micro and small businesses the cost of sales is usually limited to stock.

For the TV sales and repair business we could end up with a distorted view of gross profit. This is because the cost of sales only relates to goods sold, not labour sold. Instead of looking at:

	1997 $	1996 $
Sales	297 275	167 814
less: Cost of goods sold being		
Opening stock	13 377	13 635
add: Purchases	151 674	62 567
	165 051	76 202
less: Closing stock	17 000	13 377
Total cost of goods sold	148 051	62 825
Gross profit	149 224	104 989
Gross profit % of sales	50.2%	62.6%

We would be better off looking at:

	1997 $	1996 $
Television sales	217 105	85 437
Cost of goods sold	132 433	48 450
Gross profit on televisions	84 672	36 987
Gross profit % of sales	39.0%	43.3%
Spare parts sales and parts used in servicing	19 678	17 250
Cost of goods sold	15 618	14 375
Gross profit on spare parts	4 060	2 875
Gross profit % of sales	20.6%	16.7%
Servicing labour sales	60 492	65 127
Trading profit	149 224	104 989
Total gross profit % of total sales	50.2%	62.6%

This breakdown shows us much more of the story. We now see the increase in sales is all due to increased sales of televisions. Spare parts sales increased slightly while service labour sales declined.

Additionally we can see that the gross profit percentage on television sales has reduced by over 4 percentage points. The increased sales were achieved with a drop in margin. The drop is not too large.

Thus the apparently large drop in gross profit does not really identify the issues. This drop is caused by the shift in mix of sales; television sales have become the dominant means of generating revenue.

The calculation of cost of goods sold has not been shown to keep the information simpler.

In chapter 4, Alba's cost of sales included labour and manufacturing overheads. Alba is a manufacturer whereas the television and repair business is not. In a micro business which manufactures, labour and manufacturing overheads might not be included in cost of sales. They might simply be listed in expenses.

Those of us with service businesses can have costs of sale. For example, in running seminars these can include commissions paid to those who find you work, outside contractors to conduct the whole or part of the seminar, course materials purchased from a third party, royalties and so on. If you have staged a public seminar it can include costs such as—advertising, venue hire, catering etc. There still needs to be a gross profit after all of these kinds of costs to contribute to the other costs of the business (see 'expenses' below) and to provide profit.

Expenses

Expenses are typically listed in alphabetical order. A more useful approach is to cluster them in meaningful groups. In my business I have clustered them as:

- marketing—advertising, brochures, mailing promotional material, entertainment;
- general administration—accounting and statutory fees, bank charges, dues and subscriptions, general, fringe benefits tax;
- equipment—depreciation, repairs and maintenance, lease costs, insurance;
- communication—postage, courier, telephone, stationery;
- office accommodation—rates or rent, utilities, repairs and maintenance;
- travel and accommodation;
- finance—interest and borrowing costs;
- employees—workers compensation insurance, training and development, wages, superannuation.

Profit, tax, dividend

The expenses are deducted from the gross profit to give the profit (or loss) figure. There might be some other income such as interest earned. Income tax is paid if the business structure is a company. Dividend can be declared and paid if it is a company.

A sole trader pays tax on all income including the profit of the business. A tax return is completed for a partnership and a trust but these legal entities do not pay the tax. Instead the individual partners and the trust beneficiaries must include their share of partnership profits or distribution (respectively) in their individual tax returns. Similarly, shareholders include dividends in their tax returns.

The calculation of income tax is discussed in chapter 8. Tax-effect accounting would not be used for a micro business. Instead, the income tax expense for a micro business is the amount of tax payable for the year.

TOO MUCH EMPHASIS ON TAX

Is Australian small business too concerned with minimising tax? Too often, the answer is yes, it is. Much advice sought from and given by accountants is to do with income tax. However, we are better off concentrating on improving the performance of the business.

The more profit we make the more tax we will have to pay but after tax the better off we will be. The government takes tax at the tax rate. It does not take the whole profit.

In financial terms the purpose of a business is to generate revenue with profit which in turn generates cash flow. The profit is subject to tax. If the focus is on minimising tax, then revenue and business growth opportunities might not to be pursued. One furniture manufacturer tells the story of how his accountant always advised him on ways of minimising tax. This business-man felt he had missed opportunities over the twenty years he had followed that advice. Do you have an accountant who is interested in helping you succeed in your business? You will probably be paying higher fees if you do. However, you will be receiving much more useful information and probably have a more successful business.

On the other side there are the business people who are making a lot of money but not declaring their earnings. These people are not contributing their fair share to their fellow citizens. Those of us who are employees on the PAYE (Pay as You Earn) system or are employers who declare our income are having to pay more than our fair share.

People who choose not to declare their income might be disadvantaged when applying for a loan. Under legislation, credit providers can only use income and profits shown in accounts, tax returns and other relevant documentation. They cannot rely on assertions that there is additional undeclared income.

Income tax, capital gains tax and other tax planning is sensible. I believe it should be in the context of succeeding in your business. Business success comes first. Tax planning, as with any other cost, should be in the context of the business need and success. It should not be the dominant consideration.

Finally, micro business profit and loss statements tend to be tax driven. There is a tendency to only record items which are tax deductible now. Ones which will be tax deductible in the future are not included. Thus, expenses (and related liabilities or reductions from assets) which tend not to be recorded are provisions for annual leave, long service leave and doubtful debts. The employee entitlements could be significant liabilities.

So, are the accounts of small businesses worth the paper they are written on?

PERFORMANCE—WHAT DO THE OWNERS GET?

In micro business traditional ratios often look unsatisfactory. Ratios are typically not the best measure. The better question to ask and answer is: 'How do the owners get money out of the business?'.

Micro business people use their businesses to generate income but often invest their wealth through other vehicles. Thus, the income generated by the business is taken to meet personal needs and to invest. Typically, profits are not left in the business unless required for self-generation. More likely the micro business people will tend to borrow rather than use much of their own money to fund the business.

Therefore, we should assess how the micro business people get money from their business. If they take out so much money that they are 'bleeding the business', then that is bad. But if they take out all the profits that is okay. The owners can take money in the form of wages, superannuation, directors' fees and distribution of profits. In a company, profits are distributed by dividend. In a trust, trustees distribute in accordance with the trust deed. Owners might derive benefits in other ways such as the company car. Many of these means attract fringe benefits tax. If private expenses, such as school fees, are paid by the business then that is really a distribution of profit.

A bad sign is when owners are bleeding the business by taking more than it is generating. For example, the partners draw out more than the profits which means they draw on their contribution. In a partnership excessive drawings can lead to the liabilities exceeding the assets. In any legal structure loans to the owners can be used. This might reflect excessive transfer of cash to the owners. The Australian Taxation Office tends to treat such loans to owners or directors as a distribution of profit or wages. They can be subject to income tax and/or fringe benefits tax. Is your accountant advising you on ticklish issues like these?

Therefore, lenders should assess the capacity of the business to reward owners and the extent to which owners are drawing cash and other benefits out of the business. The owners should be drawing on the business within its capacity.

Conceptually, the business should be rewarding the owners for what they put into it.

■ If they work for the business, they should be able to derive a wage (which might include superannuation, car and other allowances) which reflects a commercial value commensurate with their knowledge, skills and experience.

■ There should also be a reward for risk. They should be earning more than just a wage. If they invested substantial funds, the reward, conceptually, should be even greater.

■ If a property is owned and used in the business, there should be an element of landlord return.

In the real world there are many businesses which, when assessed in this manner, are not very successful. Perhaps the owners are not thinking enough about the appropriate reward level and how to achieve it. Perhaps it is a very competitive environment, the economy is down, or there is some other external adverse factor. Perhaps the business was really the acquisition of a job.

The owners should be realistic in their appraisal of their reward. The lender can use this approach to think about the real capacity of the business to handle the borrowings. Lenders tend to provide most of the financing for a micro business with the owners providing as little as possible. In reality the lenders are risking the money. So it is not surprising lenders seek security. Security means the owners are then accepting some of the risk. I think it is very reasonable that lenders require security if they are providing most of the cash. Although, it is unreasonable if they demand excessive security or guarantees.

Micro business example

Figure 11.1, Television sales and services partnership, consists of a summary balance sheet and profit and loss statement for the partnership together with some ratios. The ratios are calculated in accordance with the formulae in the preceding chapter.

Ratios

We have established at least two reasons why ratios will not apply as effectively with a micro business. The first is because owners tend to take all the profits out of the business. They use other legal structures to build their wealth. Thus, profitability ratios will often look poor. Secondly, micro business people tend to finance their businesses through borrowings and minimise the amount they have to invest in the business. This means liquidity ratios and financing ratios often appear poor.

Figure 11.1

**Television
sales and
services
partnership**

Summary balance sheet	1997 $	1996 $
Current assets		
Cash at bank, deposit and on hand	1 346	175
Trade debtors	4 369	2 719
Inventories at cost	17 000	13 377
	22 715	16 271
Non-current assets		
Land—at cost	32 743	32 743
Buildings—at cost	46 217	46 217
Provision for depreciation	(11 511)	(10 356)
WDV (written-down value)	34 706	135 861
Plant and equipment—at cost	74 362	70 869
Provision for depreciation	(47 230)	(39 383)
WDV	27 132	31 486
Goodwill	100	100
	94 681	100 190
Total assets	117 396	116 461
less: Liabilities		
Current liabilities		
Trade creditors	—	2 763
Bank overdraft—secured	—	7 117
Other loans	24 812	10 315
	24 812	20 195
Non-current liabilities		
Bank loan—secured	59 263	61 579
Total liabilities	84 075	81 774
Net assets	33 321	34 687
Partners' equity		
Partner 1	15 427	16 108
Partner 2	17 894	18 579
	33 321	34 687

Summary profit and loss statement		
Sales	297 275	167 814
Cost of goods sold	(148 051)	(62 825)
Gross profit	149 224	104 989
Other income (TV rental and rent received)	28 203	21 383
Gross profit and other income	177 427	126 372
Expenses:		
Depreciation—building	(1 155)	(1 155)
Depreciation—plant and equipment	(7 847)	(8 360)
Wages and employee costs	(92 412)	(58 260)
Other expenses	(38 122)	(30 147)
Total expenses	(139 536)	(97 922)
EBIT (Earnings Before Interest and Tax)	37 891	28 450
Interest expense	(6 044)	(8 592)
Profit	31 847	19 858

Figure 11.1

continued

Ratios		1997	1996
Liquidity	Current ratio	0.9	0.8
	Acid test	1.1	0.8
Management Efficiency			
	Days debtors	5	6
	Days inventory	42	78
	Days creditors	—	6
Financing	Interest cover	6.3	3.3
	Debt to equity	2.5	2.4
	Interest bearing debt to equity	2.5	2.3
Profitability	Gross profit margin	50.2%	62.6%
	Gross margin	12.7%	17.0%
	Return on assets	32.3%	24.4%
	Return on equity	95.6%	57.2%

The following provides a commentary on what my experience indicates can be typical results for ratios calculated on micro businesses. The situation for the partnership example is included. (See previous chapter for general commentary on ratios.)

■ Liquidity ratios—both the current ratio and the acid test tend to be about 1.0:1 or lower compared with the rules of thumb being 1.5:1 and 0.8:1 respectively. An overdraft is often a major source of finance. It causes current liabilities to be about the same or even higher than current assets. Overdrafts are usually relatively small for medium to large businesses. When overdrafts are substantial the acid test tends to be about the same as or higher than the current ratio (overdrafts cause a large reduction of the denominator). We see this occurring in the example.

■ Management efficiency ratios are only relevant to the extent an entity sells for credit, trades inventory or has creditors. In this example only days inventory, which has significantly reduced, is of interest. The reduction is because televisions were a much higher portion of the increased sales in 1997, but inventory level did not rise much. Proportionally more of the sales are of stock which results in the apparently better performance. For a more accurate and meaningful figure we have used inventory cost of sales (which is available) in the formula. Many micro businesses do not have creditors because of the tendency not to accrue liabilities. In our example there are no creditors at 30 June 1997.

■ Financing—interest cover will only be meaningful if the business reports a profit, i.e. the owners have not paid all the profit out in the form of wages, directors' fees and superannuation. Our example reports a profit. With interest added back to give EBIT there is a good interest cover.

If there are significant borrowings, debt to equity ratios always look high compared with the rule of thumb comfort level of 1:1. This is because the owners tend to minimise their funding and rely on borrowings. Additionally there is generally minimal difference when using interest-bearing debt to equity (its rule of thumb comfort is 0.5:1). This is because most of the liabilities are borrowings and other liabilities such as employee entitlements tend not to be recorded. Debt to equity ratios of 2.5 to 3:1 seem to be common for micro businesses.

In this example the owners have $33 321 tied up in the business as at 30 June 1997. As it is a partnership, they could withdraw it through drawings. Perhaps a lender would want the borrowers to undertake to keep a certain amount of partner funding. A letter of understanding might be signed between the parties. This letter cannot be legally enforced but might provide moral suasion.

■ Profitability ratios have meaning to the extent a profit is made and the balance sheet contains assets or equity. The gross profit ratio can often be helpful. In this example it looks to have declined very seriously. However, remember when we considered the sales and costs of sales separately for televisions, spare parts and servicing there was a much more reasonable and reassuring picture. Can micro business people really monitor their performance if there is no dissection of sales?

The gross margin can be helpful when some profit is measured in the business. If the owner takes 'profit' as wages, superannuation and so forth, leaving nil profit and there is no interest expense, EBIT will be zero. The ratio will look horrible. Meanwhile the owner might be making a very nice living from a successful business. In our example the gross margin is of some value. It has declined because expenses increased more quickly than EBIT. Our limited listing of expenses shows that the increase is primarily due to wages.

Return on assets seems to have improved substantially. This is due to a significant increase in EBIT while total assets have remained steady.

Return on equity has almost doubled to an astounding 95.6 per cent. However this is spurious. It is caused because profit increased substantially. You will notice that equity slightly reduced. This means the partners' drawings took all the profits and a bit more.

I think this discussion shows that ratios need to be interpreted even more carefully for micro businesses than for larger businesses. Divergence from rules of thumb are common. Profitability ratios can be meaningless and not a valid basis for assessment. The assessment is the consideration of how much the owners get out of the business without draining the business.

The financial statements themselves

Now let's consider what the actual financial information shows. We know the sales have increased, but the gross profit and gross margin have dropped.

The breakdown of sales shows gross profit dropped due to the sales increase being entirely due to television sales. This translated to gross profit increasing by over $50 000 to $177 427. However EBIT only increased by about $9000 to $37 891.

The summary profit and loss statement shows the main increase in expenses was 'wages and employee costs' which increased from $58 260 to $92 412. When interviewing the owners they told us an additional person was employed as a salesperson. This person was successful. However, can the person generate even more sales? If (s)he can't the extra sales have been gained at a lower gross margin.

The owners also told us they only receive profits from the business, not wages. They do work about ten hours a week each without pay. Their tax returns show they have no other source of income except the profit.

On the basis of assessing a business by how much the owners get out of the business do you think $31 847 is very successful? The borrowings of the business constitute all the liabilities of $84 075. The business is covering the interest cost. But how can the owners repay the principal when they claim to be living on just $31 847 profit? Unfortunately there are many small businesses which really don't do that well.

What is the cash flow?

So far we have been limited to the 'two-legged stool': the balance sheet and profit and loss. We have not looked at a cash flows statement. Unfortunately laws and accounting standards do not require most enterprises to produce cash flows statements. In my opinion this is a great disadvantage to the owners, lenders and others interested in the business. But do not despair, we can derive a 1997 cash flows statement from the 1997 and prior year's balance sheets and the 1997 profit and loss statement.

HOW TO CALCULATE CASH FLOWS

Lenders often use a very simple formula for determining the cash flows of an enterprise being—profit, add back depreciation, and interest expense. From our example it is:

		1997 $	1996 $
	Profit	31 847	19 858
add:	Depreciation	9 002	9 515
gives:	Supposed operating cash flows	40 849	29 373
add:	Interest paid	6 044	8 592
gives:	Supposed capacity to meet replacement interest on loans and principal	46 893	37 965

A very important item affecting cash flows has been omitted; namely the change in working capital. Working capital is the difference between current assets and current liabilities. Increasing working capital drains cash flow. In an expanding business working capital typically increases. Our example is an expanding business.

We can calculate the working capital effect from the differences between the assets and liabilities between the years. For instance, an increase in debtors or inventory reduces cash. An increase in debtors means we are waiting for more cash to come in. An increase in inventory means we have spent more money on building up stock than we have received from selling it during the year. The opposite helps cash flow. Reduced stock means we have received more cash out of the inventory than we put into it during the year. Likewise, lower debtors means we have collected more cash from customers than we have made credit sales to them.

The exact opposite is true for liabilities. An increase in trade creditors assists cash flows because it means we owe more to the creditors than before. Thus we have bought more on credit during the year than we have paid. This saves cash going out. However, we still owe the money at the end of the year. The liability will have to be paid. Conversely, a decrease in creditors means we have paid more to the trade creditors than we bought on credit during the year.

So for our example we can calculate the change in working capital as:

	1997 $	1996 $	Difference $
Trade debtors	4 369	2 719	(1 650)
Inventories at cost	17 000	13 377	(3 623)
Trade creditors	—	2 763	(2 763)
Drain caused by increased working capital			(8 036)

All three items were a drain on cash flows: trade debtors and inventories increased, tying up more cash; and trade creditors reduced, paid down to zero. Usually with an expanding business creditors increase. Perhaps the zero value indicates creditors are understated. The lack of recognition of liabilities in a micro business is a big risk.

Thus, the increasing working capital has drained cash flows by $8 036. A better picture of the cash flows generated from operating activities is:

		1997 $
	Profit	31 847
add:	Depreciation	9 002
less:	Increase in working capital	(8 036)
gives:	Estimated cash flows from operating activities	32 813

This calculation shows cash flows from operating activities are just slightly higher than profit. Ignoring working capital when it is increasing means we overestimate the real cash flows from operating activities. We should always include the working capital effect as well as depreciation prior to adding back interest to look at capacity.

I do not think it is necessary to add back interest if a lender is simply replacing existing borrowings. The interest will still be there, perhaps reduced. The calculated cash flows are after the interest has been paid and show what is available to meet investing and financing cash flows requirements. (See chapter 9 for commentary on cash flows.) In this instance we know that all the profit was taken by the partners. Therefore no cash was left available to cover investing activities. Thus, the increased plant and equipment (cost increased by $3 493 to $74 362) must have been funded from financing or running down the cash.

The balance sheet shows that cash has increased. Therefore, the acquisition of plant and equipment must have been funded from borrowings. Figure 11.2 presents a worksheet which can be used to calculate a full cash flows statement from two balance sheets and a profit and loss statement. (You are welcome to copy and use this worksheet. If you reproduce it, please acknowledge the source.) It is in the same format as the accounting standard except that:

- financing is split between lender and owner; and
- we do not readily have the information to determine 'receipts from customers' or 'payments to suppliers and employees'.

Figure 11.3 shows the worksheet completed for the example. You can check how this was compiled by tracing from the balance sheets and the profit and loss statement to the worksheet.

An Excel spreadsheet analysing micro businesses is available from the author (see p. xiv). You enter profit and loss and balance sheet information. The spreadsheet provides the profit and loss, balance sheet, calculates a full cash flows statement in the accounting standard format and provides the ratios listed above plus the three cash flows profitability ratios. Workings for deriving some of the cash flows figures are shown. Summary and detailed calculations of the ratios are shown.

Figure 11.2

Cash flows worksheet

Worksheet for calculating a cash flows statement (Write negative numbers in brackets)			Calculated cash flows $
Operating activities			
Profit/(loss) after tax (from profit and loss statement)			
Add back non-cash item of depreciation (from P & L)			
Change in working capital (take 'Total Z' from end of worksheet)			
Subtotal			
Other (should be nil or small—calculated as ['Total A' less subtotal])			
Total A (calculated as totals D − B − C)			
Investing activities (Take figures from non-current assets in balance sheet excluding provision for depreciation—i.e. usually cost)	Prior year $ X	Current year $ Y	Calculate as X − Y
Land			
Buildings			
Plant and equipment			
Investments			
Goodwill			
Intangibles			
Total B (sum of above)			
Financing activities	$ X	$ Y	Calculate as Y − X
Provided by lender *Change in interest-bearing liabilities:*			
Bank overdraft			
Bank loan—current			
Other loans—current			
Bank loan—non-current			
Other loans—non-current			
Total provided/(repaid) to lender			

Provided by owner			$
Issued capital/units/contributions (taken from balance sheet for company or trust; taken from changes in partnership accounts for a partnership)			
Dividend/drawings/distribution (taken from P & L appropriation for company or trust; taken from changes in partnership accounts for a partnership)			
Total contrib/(distributed) to owner			
Total C (sum of total lender and owner)			
Total D—Net change in cash (difference of current year minus prior year cash)			
Change in working capital	Prior year $	Current year $	$
Current assets	X	Y	Calculate as X – Y
Trade debtors			
Other debtors			
Inventory			
Prepayments			
Other—current			
Other—non-current			
Current liabilities			Calculate as Y – X
Creditors and accruals			
Employee provisions—current			
Income tax provision			
Other provisions—current			
Employee provisions—non-current			
Other provisions—non-current			
Other			
Total Z—Net change in working capital			

Figure 11.2

continued

Figure 11.3

Completed cash flows worksheet

Worksheet for calculating a cash flows statement (Write negative numbers in brackets)			Calculated cash flows $
Operating activities			
Profit/(loss) after tax (from profit and loss statement)			31 847
Add back non-cash item of depreciation (from P & L)			9 002
Change in working capital (take 'Total Z' from end of worksheet)			(8 036)
Subtotal			32 813
Other (should be nil or small—calculated as ['Total A' less subtotal])			(1)
Total A (calculated as totals D – B – C)			32 812
Investing activities (Take figures from non-current assets in balance sheet excluding provision for depreciation—i.e. usually cost)	Prior year $ X	Current year $ Y	Calculate as X – Y
Land	32 743	32 743	0
Buildings	46 217	46 217	0
Plant and equipment	70 869	74 362	(3 493)
Investments			
Goodwill	100	100	0
Intangibles			
Total B (sum of above)			(3 493)
Financing activities	$ X	$ Y	Calculate as Y – X
Provided by lender *Change in interest-bearing liabilities:*			
Bank overdraft	7 117	0	(7 117)
Bank loan—current			
Other loans—current	10 315	24 812	14 497
Bank loan—non-current	61 579	59 263	(2 316)
Other loans—non-current			
Total provided/(repaid) to lender			5 064

Provided by owner			$
Issued capital/units/contributions (taken from balance sheet for company or trust; taken from changes in partnership accounts for a partnership)			
Dividend/drawings/distribution (taken from P & L appropriation for company or trust; taken from changes in partnership accounts for a partnership)			(33 212)
Total contrib/(distributed) to owner			(33 212)
Total C (sum of total lender and owner)			(28 148)
Total D—Net change in cash (difference of current year minus prior year cash)	100	1 271	1 171

Change in working capital	Prior year $	Current year $	$
Current assets	X	Y	Calculate as X – Y
Trade debtors	2 719	4 369	(1 650)
Other debtors			
Inventory	13 377	17 000	(3 623)
Prepayments			
Other—current			
Other—non-current			
Current liabilities			Calculate as Y – X
Creditors and accruals	2 763	0	(2 763)
Employee provisions—current			
Income tax provision			
Other provisions—current			
Employee provisions—non-current			
Other provisions—non-current			
Other			
Total Z—Net change in working capital			(8 036)

Figure 11.3

continued

POINTS TO REMEMBER

✔ Internal accounts are more useful when sales and related cost of sales are separated into clusters by kind or groupings of products or services rather than shown as one sales figure, e.g. a television sales and repair business could split sales into televisions, spare parts and servicing.

✔ Accounts of micro and small business operators are often only produced annually for tax return purposes up to six months after year end. Such delay makes accounts useless for monitoring and planning purposes. Owners should either increase their internal record keeping or extend their accountant's services to include useful management accounts, at least quarterly.

✔ Focusing excessively on minimising tax can debilitate your business success. Aim to generate more revenue with more profit and real cash generation. Control your expenses and engage in tax planning in the broader context of business success.

✔ When analysing micro or small businesses the key is to know how much the owners get out of the business without bleeding the business. Thus it is useful to separate the expenses that owners receive from the list of expenses.

✔ Owners of micro and small businesses generally want to extract income from their businesses and develop wealth through other vehicles. Thus, profit is not retained in the business and borrowings tend to be the main or only source of financing. This reduces or negates the usefulness of ratios, particularly the profitability ones. It is better to interpret by considering how much the owners get out of the business (wages, directors' fees, superannuation, dividends etc.) without draining the business.

✔ Most businesses and enterprises produce balance sheets and profit and loss statements but not cash flows statements. Thus we are sitting on a 'two-legged stool'. If we want cash flow information we have to calculate it ourselves. At a minimum 'cash flows from operating activities' should be calculated as profit (after tax) then add back depreciation and allow for changes in working capital (subtract if an increase, add if a decrease).

✔ You can calculate a full cash flows statement provided you have the current and prior periods balance sheet and the current profit and loss statement. The result can be fairly to very realistic. A worksheet has been provided for your use. Note that the 'cash flows from operating activities' has been limited to what is the 'reconciliation' note 19 in Alba, chapter 4.

12 Groups of companies

So far we have concentrated on understanding and interpreting a single entity. However, businesses of any size usually operate using a number of different legal structures, in particular owning all or parts of many companies. All that has been considered so far does apply to groups, but we need to consider some additional issues.

Recognising interests in other entities can be approached in four different ways:

1 investments;
2 consolidation;
3 equity accounting;
4 joint ventures.

At its simplest, in appropriate cases, recognition is made by including the interest in another entity as an investment under non-current assets. Investments were considered under that heading in chapter 5.

Recognition of the interest in another entity as other than an investment means we are recognising a closer relationship than simply 'savings for a rainy day'. The closer relationship is recognised by accounting for it as part of the owning entity. Consolidation is the closest relationship, where everything is added together as though the group were one entity. Equity accounting and joint ventures lie between consolidation and investments.

Before launching into the detailed information, it is worth noting that the approach to recognising consolidations in Australia changed enormously in 1991/92. In many ways the Australian approach is quite radical and leads the world. What is included in Australian consolidated accounts for financial years ending 31 December 1991 onward can be quite different from before. We will consider the new approach and the old approach, which is still used in other countries.

CONSOLIDATION

Terminology

The consolidation accounting standard is AASB 1024, *Consolidated Accounts*. Prior to this standard, guidance for consolidation was available from recognised texts and precedents—there was no predecessor Australian accounting standard.

The terms used are set out below.

■ *Entity*, which is any legal form of existence that is able to use scarce resources. This ranges from individuals through partnerships, trusts, superannuation funds, joint ventures to companies. This book has used the term entity as well as or in place of 'company'.

■ *Economic entity* is a group of entities which consists of the parent entity and its subsidiaries. The old term is 'group', which is a very familiar term throughout the world and has been used in this book in preference to 'economic entity'. So wherever the word group is used in the book, the term economic entity is understood to be the technical and legal equivalent.

■ *Parent entity* is the vehicle that is at the top of a group and is frequently a company. This is obvious when you are reading listed company financial statements. Other terms used which mean the same are holding company and parent company. In consolidated financial statements, figures are given for the group and the parent entity. A typical user is interested in the group figures with, perhaps, an occasional interest in the parent entity.

■ *Subsidiary* refers to an entity controlled by a parent entity. These are often companies but can be any other legal form of corporate existence (such as trusts and partnerships). In the past in Australia (and still in most other countries) consolidated accounts were limited to the parent entity and subsidiary companies, not other kinds of subsidiary entities.

■ *Control*—the key concept in the accounting standard. An entity is consolidated if it is controlled. The standard (in paragraph 9) defines control to mean:

> . . . the capacity of an entity to dominate decision-making, directly or indirectly, in relation to the financial and operating policies of another entity so as to enable that other entity to operate with it in pursuing the objectives of the controlling entity.

The previous criterion for consolidation was based on ownership. If a company was owned more than 50 per cent directly or indirectly then it was usually consolidated. 'Directly' means that one entity owns the interest in the other entity itself, whereas 'indirectly' means it owns the interest through one or more other entities in which it owns interests.

■ *Outside equity interest* means any equity held in any part of the group by someone other than the parent entity. This will be explained below. Other terms used are minority interests, outside shareholders' interest and variations on these.

Recognition

Consolidation is a method of recognising the reality that organisations frequently function through more than one legal form. At law each entity is a separate legal structure and, unless there is some legally binding obligation, the collapse of one does not necessaily mean the other will also collapse. But when viewed as to the substance of the situation, the separate legal entities are part of one big enterprise. Consolidation enables this to be recognised.

Basically consolidation is the aggregation of all of the assets, liabilities, profits and cash flows of the whole group. It means presenting the financial statements as one group. In simple terms, you add each kind of asset (e.g. trade debtors) and each kind of liability (e.g. bank overdraft) to determine the total of that kind of asset or liability for the group.

Consolidated accounts aim to represent the relationship of the group with its external world. So any internal relationships are eliminated, that is, cancelled or offset against each other. One internal relationship is that the parent entity owns subsidiaries. The parent entity's accounts include these subsidiaries under investments in non-current assets. The subsidiaries' issued shares all belong to the parent entity. On consolidation the investment asset is offset against the equity. There often are some additional things that must be allowed for when doing the calculation, but the essence of the elimination is as described.

Another very common internal relationship is that one subsidiary sells goods to another subsidiary. So one subsidiary has a trade debtor and the

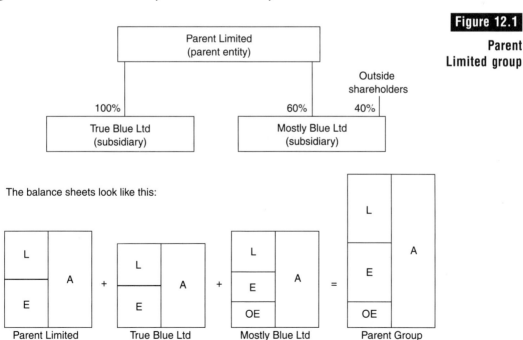

Figure 12.1

Parent Limited group

other a trade creditor. The trade debtors are offset against the trade creditors so that the trade debtors of the consolidated accounts are only external trade debtors and likewise for trade creditors.

Figure 12.1 shows the consolidation of three companies.

The consolidated balance sheet for Parent Group is not simply the addition of the assets and liabilities, because of relationships between the companies. The equity of Parent Group is more than that of Parent Limited because the retained profits and other reserves earned by each subsidiary, since becoming a part of Parent Group, belong to the whole group.

Parent Limited only owns 60 per cent of Mostly Blue Ltd. So, it only has an interest in 60 per cent of the net assets of this subsidiary. It is

Figure 12.2

Consolidated shareholders' equity

Following the accounting standard	1997 $	1996 $
Shareholders' equity		
Parent entity interest		
Issued capital	200 000	200 000
Reserves	345 963	327 442
Retained profits	558 219	479 003
	1 104 182	1 006 445
Outside equity interest		
Issued capital	15 000	15 000
Reserves	34 587	34 587
Retained profits	59 618	47 392
	109 205	96 979
	1 213 387	1 103 424

The more common disclosure throughout the world

This approach can be used in Australia provided there is a supporting note showing the components of the outside equity.

Shareholders' equity		
Issued capital	200 000	200 000
Reserves	345 963	327 442
Retained profits	558 219	479 003
Shareholders' equity attributable to members of Parent Limited	1 104 182	1 006 445
Outside equity interest in subsidiaries	109 205	96 979
	1 213 387	1 103 424

entitled to only 60 per cent of the profits each year. This is recognised on the balance sheet by splitting the equity into two parts. The 40 per cent of the equity in Mostly Blue Ltd which is owned by outside shareholders is shown separately after Parent Limited's equity and is called outside equity interest. The components, being issued capital, reserves and retained profits, are shown. (Prior to the standard only a total outside shareholders' figure was given.) This is shown in the consolidated accounts of Parent Limited group in figures 12.2 and 12.3. The outside equity interest can be shown as one line on the consolidated balance sheet with a note showing the components.

The profit and loss statement of Parent Group will include the outside shareholders' interest in operating profit and extraordinary items, which is deducted from total profit to give the profit attributable to the shareholders of Parent Limited as shown in figure 12.3.

Figure 12.3 is incomplete as in real life it would include retained profits at beginning of year, transfers to and from reserves, and dividends paid. Prior to the standard, the outside equity interest would have been shown as one total and not split between operating profit and extraordinary items. Outside equity would have been described as outside shareholders' interest or minority shareholders' interest.

The notes to the accounts must include:

■ the name of the parent entity and, if the group is part of one or more larger groups, the name of the ultimate parent entity in Australia and,

Figure 12.3 **Consolidated profit and loss**

Following the accounting standard	1997 $	1996 $
Operating profit	187 384	169 349
Income tax expense attributable to operating profit	82 361	73 045
Operating profit after income tax	105 023	96 304
Profit on extraordinary items	23 841	—
Income tax expense attributable to profit on extraordinary items	2 772	—
Profit on extraordinary items after income tax	21 069	—
Operating profit and extraordinary items after income tax	126 092	96 304
Outside equity interest in operating profit after income tax	10 990	6 415
Outside equity interest in extraordinary items after income tax	1 236	—
Outside equity interest in operating profit and extraordinary items after income tax	12 226	6 415
Operating profit and extraordinary items after income tax attributable to members of Parent Limited	113 866	89 889

if part of an overseas group, the name of the ultimate (highest level) parent entity;

■ the name and country of incorporation of each subsidiary, showing which ones have become subsidiaries during the year;

■ the name and details of entities which ceased to be controlled during the year;

■ identification of those subsidiaries in which ownership and/or voting rights are less than 50 per cent, with an explanation of how control exists;

■ identification of any entity where, although ownership and/or voting rights are greater than 50 per cent, it is not included as a subsidiary, with an explanation of why control does not exist;

■ details of any gains or losses made by the parent entity and by any outside equity interest on new issues of shares by subsidiaries.

What must be consolidated?

Under the accounting standard all entities which are controlled (whether directly or indirectly) must be consolidated. The general meaning of control was given under 'terminology' above. 'All entities' means any kind of legal structure, e.g. trust, partnership and company.

Prior to the accounting standard and corresponding amendments to the Corporations Law only companies which were classed as subsidiaries could be consolidated. The Corporations Law included a definition of subsidiary, but the major determinant was that, if a company (either directly or indirectly) owned more than 50 per cent of the voting share capital of another company, the latter was classed as a subsidiary. This ownership approach is followed by many countries.

As we have considered elsewhere in this book, there can be a real desire to keep liabilities off the balance sheet to make the balance of debt to equity look acceptable, and to keep the total assets lower so that ROA looks better. Prior to the accounting standard the effort was to make a company not a subsidiary; now it is to make an entity not 'controlled'.

Under AASB 1024, control is thought to exist where direct and indirect ownership is greater than 50 per cent, and is less likely to exist if ownership is 50 per cent or less. This is not an absolute but a guiding consideration. Control (though this is unlikely) may not exist when ownership is greater than 50 per cent and it may exist (this can be much more likely) when ownership is 50 per cent or less. The standard provides much guidance on what constitutes control.

Prior to the standard the view was often taken that subsidiary companies which operated a business dissimilar to the rest of the group should not be consolidated, as this distorted the financial situation of the group. This was often the case where companies trading in goods had a finance subsidiary that financed customers' purchases of the goods. The subsidiary would have a high debt equity ratio because it borrowed funds from depositors to lend to customers, and could have a dramatic effect on the group's debt to equity ratio when consolidated. The standard nevertheless requires such subsidiaries to be consolidated.

Prior to the standard it was possible not to prepare consolidated group accounts by arguing that they were inappropriate for the group. This is not allowed under the standard.

When subsidiaries come and go

Goodwill is explained in chapter 5 under 'intangibles' as existing when an entity acquires a business or a subsidiary. The assets are revalued to fair value (usually market price). The goodwill is the difference between the purchase price and the fair value of the net assets. Sometimes the purchase price consists partly or wholly of other than cash, such as when shares are issued in exchange for other shares. This can complicate the determination of the purchase price and is a matter beyond the scope of this book. (The relevant accounting standard is AASB 1015, *Accounting for the Acquisition of Assets*.)

The following matters are considered when accounting for subsidiaries in consolidated accounts.

■ All the operating profits and other gains and losses earned by the entity up to the date of acquisition were earned by the previous shareholders. The purchase price allows for this. These profits are referred to as pre-acquisition and are not recognised as part of the equity of the group, because they have not been earned by the group. Pre-acquisition profits and reserves are eliminated in the consolidation process—they are part of the removing of the investment in subsidiaries and equity of subsidiaries.

■ All the profits and changes in reserves that occur after acquisition are recognised as belonging to the group and, so, are added to the group accounts' equity. These are called post-acquisition profits and reserves. Any portion belonging to outside equity interests is added to the outside equity interests with the rest going to the parent equity interests.

■ Sometimes subsidiaries are gradually acquired. This complicates the recognition of what is pre-acquisition and post-acquisition profits and reserves. There is a point when the entity becomes a subsidiary with recognition being as just described. From the date of becoming a subsidiary the post-acquisition profits and reserves are recognised and allocated between parent equity and outside equity interests. As the parent percentage of ownership increases so does its portion of post-acquisition profits and reserves. As the outside equity decreases, what was their proportion of post-acquisition profits and reserves becomes part of pre-acquisition profits and reserves, when considered from the point of view of the shareholders of the parent entity—which is the prime view of consolidated accounts.

■ A subsidiary ceases to be a subsidiary because it is sold or because the parent entity loses control—for example, another independent entity buys all the other shares and effectively gains control, or the parent entity sells shares to the extent that it no longer has control.

■ In the group accounts, the gain or loss on disposal of shares sold (which causes the entity to no longer be a subsidiary) is the difference between the selling price and the original purchase price plus the post-acquisition profits and reserves. These too must be removed as the entity is no longer a subsidiary and as such cannot be a part of the equity of the group accounts.

		$
	Selling price	3 465
less:	Current book value of investment in parent entity's accounts (which could be original purchase price or revalued amount)*	1 783
	Post-acquisition gains in profits and reserves (including the changes in profits and reserves during the current financial year up to the date of sale)	915
		2 698
gives:	Gain or (loss) on disposal	767

* This will be the proportion of the subsidiary sold. A book value remains for the part of the investment still retained.

■ Another disposal situation occurs when the parent entity reduces its interest in a subsidiary but still retains control. This means it is still a subsidiary at the end of the year. It is similar to the above except that only the proportion of post-acquisition profits and reserves sold will be deducted, so that the consolidated accounts will then have post-acquisition profits and reserves reflecting the new percentage of the subsidiary held. The post-acquisition profits and reserves sold become part of outside equity interest.

You may find this difficult to understand. Don't be concerned if you do. The consolidation requirements are the responsibility of management to handle correctly. You should aim to have an appreciation that preparing consolidated accounts includes the need to recognise goodwill, post-acquisition profits and reserves, and gains or losses on disposal of parts of or all of subsidiaries.

When control does not exist but influence is very strong

It is likely that, when ownership or voting rights are 50 per cent or less, control does not exist. However, much influence may be exerted. One method of recognising this is equity accounting (which is discussed in the next section). Another method is partial consolidation (which is used for joint ventures—see below).

The consolidation standard does not cover the idea of partial consolidation. This allows scope to keep significant assets and liabilities off balance sheet. An interesting example to consider where partial consolidation would have changed the accounts was TNT Limited. TNT, the former Australian-owned multinational transport group, had three significant ventures in which it held 50 per cent. These were Ansett Transport Industries Ltd (an Australian domestic and partly international carrier [TNT sold its interest to Air New Zealand in 1996]), Ansett Worldwide Aviation Services (AWAS—an aeroplane leasing company) and GD Express Worldwide (TNT's European parcel service arrangement with the Canadian and some European Post Offices).

These ventures were recognised by including the amount invested in them as investments and recognising 50 per cent of the profits or losses in the profit and loss statement. TNT used equity accounting for the investments which were held as shares and the recognition of the amount of the investment and proportion of profit for the AWAS partnership. This is a normal approach to recognition, but the consequences of it for the balance sheet were significant.

The balance sheet did not include the proportionate interest in the assets and liabilities of these ventures. During the 1992 financial year the European joint venture was established by selling TNT's European parcel business into the joint venture. The assets and liabilities of the European parcel operation were removed from the balance sheet—this amounted to over $500 million-worth of liabilities taken off balance sheet.

TNT's 1992 annual report disclosed the following information about the assets and equity of these investments:

	GD Express Worldwide NV $000	Ansett Transport Industries Ltd $000	AWAS $000
Total assets	1 171 708	3 854 258	1 657 086
Total shareholders' equity and subordinated shareholders' loans	365 616	506 763	566 228
Thus liabilities are	806 092	3 347 495	1 090 858

None of these liabilities were included as liabilities of TNT.

Partial consolidation would mean that half the liabilities of these investments would be included on the balance sheet of TNT, together with the same amount of assets (because E + L = A). Instead of a net asset figure of investments, there would have been the aggregation of 50 per cent of all the debtors, fixed assets, creditors, loans etc. of each of the entities added to the corresponding items already in the balance sheet.

An estimate of the liabilities and assets which would have been added to the balance sheet based on this information is half of the above liabilities which was \$2 622 223 000 (being GD Net \$403 046 000, AWAS \$545 429 000 and Ansett \$1 673 748 000). The effect can be illustrated using the 1992 annual accounts. A high gearing becomes a much higher gearing!

	As reported 1992 $000	As adjusted 1992 $000
Total assets	3 050 340	5 672 563
Total liabilities	2 386 108	5 008 331
Shareholders' equity	664 232	664 232
Debt to equity is	**3.6:1**	**7.5:1**

Full consolidation must be used where there is control. Perhaps this example is an indication that partial consolidation should be used where there is not control, but still a very significant influence—much greater than that for which equity accounting is appropriate. What do you think?

EQUITY ACCOUNTING

Equity accounting is a way to recognise a situation where an investment is not a subsidiary, but is more than just owning some shares in another entity. Equity accounting bridges the gap between control and little or no influence by recognising there can be significant influence.

A new accounting standard, *Accounting for Investments in Associates by the Equity Method*, was issued in May 1997. It will replace AASB 1016, *Disclosure of Information about Investments in Associated Companies*, when a date from which it becomes operative is determined; the Corporation Law has to be amended first. The ASC has issued a class order allowing the provisions of the standard to be applied from financial years ended 30 June 1997, even though it is contrary to the current law. The new standard requires equity accounting to be recognised in the financial statements. These notes have been prepared on the basis of the existing standard and the new accounting standard.

Certain sections of the Corporations Law have meant that equity accounting could not be legally applied in the main body of the financial statements. Equity accounting information has been supplied as supplementary information. Equity accounting is a commonly applied concept throughout the rest of the world. Therefore, on the removal of the legal impediment, equity accounting will be applied in the consolidated accounts again in Australia. (It was applied in the 1970s.)

Accounting standard AASB 1016 only applies to investments in 'associate' companies. The new standard applies to all 'associate' entities. This will then be the same as the consolidation concept.

Consolidation recognises the assets and liabilities of all the entities in the group on the balance sheet, and the post-acquisition profits and reserves of all the entities in the group in the profit and loss and accumulated in the equity on the balance sheet. Owned entities which are consolidated are called subsidiaries. Plain old investments are recognised as a non-current asset and can be at cost, directors' or independent valuation; the income is the dividend received.

Equity accounting is an in-between recognition applied when there is significant influence. The profit or loss of the entity in which the investment is held is recognised in proportion to the percentage of ownership. It also recognises proportionate changes in other reserves, e.g. revaluation gains. The investment asset is initially recognised at cost and then adjusted to recognise the proportionate gains and losses year by year. The entity invested in and accounted for using equity accounting is called an associated entity or investee. The entity holding the investment is called an investor.

The issues to consider in equity accounting are:

- significant influence and the risk of recognising equity-accounted profits;
- how equity-accounted profits are recognised;
- disclosure of the information in the consolidated accounts or those of the investor entity.

Associated Ltd (see figure 12.4) earned a profit during the year of $260 000 and declared a dividend for the year of $100 000. Parent Limited has received a dividend of $35 000 which, if Associated Ltd is treated simply as an investment, is what will be recorded as income in Parent Limited's own and group accounts. If Parent Limited has significant influence over Associated Ltd, then equity accounting should be applied. This means Parent Limited's group accounts, once the new standard is issued, would show the share of operating profit from Associated Ltd of $91 000. Currently the group accounts include the information as a note or supplementary accounts.

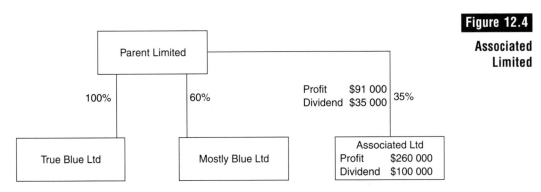

Figure 12.4

Associated Limited

There is a risk in recognising $91 000 as income. Will Parent Limited really ever receive it or have influence over it? The dividend received is definite. So the key issue is significant influence.

Significant influence

The accounting standard provides guidance for what constitutes significant influence. The starting point is the level of ownership. Significant influence is said to be likely to exist where voting ownership is between 20 per cent and 50 per cent, and is likely not to exist where ownership is less than 20 per cent. So if ownership is 20 per cent or more, evidence showing there is no significant influence is required for equity accounting not to be used. If ownership is less than 20 per cent, strong evidence is required to show there is significant influence.

Other matters to consider in determining whether or not there is significant influence include, but are not limited to:

■ the level of representation on the board;
■ participation in deciding on distribution and retention of profits;
■ participation in policy-making decisions;
■ the other shareholders in the associated company—for example, if it is largely owned by one other entity, influence is more likely to be limited than if there is a widespread shareholding; if there are one or two other similar size shareholders, influence is more likely to be significant if the major shareholders are cooperating in, rather than competing for, influence over the associated company.

Each situation has to be considered on the facts of the case. Sometimes the decision can be difficult. However, the temptation for entities such as our fictitious Parent Limited is to use equity accounting because it boosts reported profit. Users of financial statements need to form their own opinion on whether or not significant influence exists in the light of information provided in the financial statements and other knowledge of the situation.

The risk involved is that equity accounting may be used so that additional profits can be shown—when the degree of influence as well as prudent commonsense dictate that recognition should be limited to dividend income.

Accounting for associated companies

At the time of writing the standard requires equity accounting information to be reported only in the notes to the accounts (paragraph 22). This limitation exists because the Corporations Law (and the former Companies Code) recognised only separate legal entities, and restricted accounting beyond separate legal entities to consolidated accounts.

The new standard will require equity accounted consolidated profit and loss and balance sheets. Meanwhile, some companies still provided equity

Figure 12.5 Equity accounts

Parent Limited group accounts	1997 Equity accounted $	1997 Consolidated $
Operating profit		
Economic entity	152 384	187 384
Associated company	129 731	—
	282 115	187 384
Income tax expense attributable to operating profit		
Economic entity	82 361	82 361
Associated company	38 467	—
	120 828	82 361
Operating profit after income tax		
Economic entity	70 023	105 023
Associated company	91 264	—
	161 287	105 023
Profit on extraordinary items—economic entity*	23 841	23 841
Income tax expense attributable to profit on extraordinary items	2 772	2 772
Profit on extraordinary items after income tax	21 069	21 069
Operating profit and extraordinary items after income tax		
Economic entity	91 092	126 092
Associated company	91 264	—
	182 356	126 092
Outside equity interest in operating profit after income tax	10 990	10 990
Outside equity interest in extraordinary items after income tax	1 236	1 236
Outside equity interest in operating profit and extraordinary items after income tax	12 226	12 226
Operating profit and extraordinary items after income tax attributable to members of Parent Limited		
Economic entity	78 866	113 866
Associated company	91 264	—
	170 130	113 866

The accounts would include as one of the investments:
Investments in associated company — 1 493 264 — 1 437 000

* 'Associated company' is not mentioned which means the associated company did not have any extraordinary items.

consolidated accounts side by side with consolidated accounts (which have not included equity accounting). The standard requires a clear distinction between equity accounted profit and other profit.

Equity accounting information includes the ownership interest in operating profit before income tax, income tax, extraordinary items net of income tax, dividends received, movements in reserves, the cumulative portion of retained profits and reserves attributable to associated companies and movements in the value of the investment on the balance sheet. The separation of retained profits and other reserves is frequently handled by creating a separate associated companies reserve, which is used for all accumulated proportions of associated companies' reserves.

We will consider how the consolidated accounts of the Parent Limited group might show this information. To do this we will assume the 35 per cent interest in Associated Ltd was acquired on 1 July 1996, the beginning of the financial year. The amount paid for the shares was $1 437 000. The additional information in the accounts is shown in figure 12.5.

Under AASB 1016 the information in figure 12.5 is disclosed as supplementary information in the accounts. Typically this is as a note but it can be disclosed as two sets of columns on their balance sheet and profit and loss statement. Under the new accounting standard the equity accounted column is shown as the 'consolidated profit and loss'. The column in figure 12.5 labelled 'consolidated' would not be shown.

The differences between the consolidated accounts and the equity-accounted consolidated accounts profit and loss is:

		$
	Consolidated operating profit after income tax	105 023
less:	Dividend received from Associated Ltd	35 000
		70 023
add:	35% share of profit of Associated Ltd	91 264
gives:	Equity-accounted consolidated operating profit after tax	161 287

The reason the income tax expense for the economic entity is the same under consolidated and equity columns is that the dividend income is free of income tax. The reconciliation of operating profit before tax is the same as after tax except that operating profit before tax is used.

Associated Ltd did not have any extraordinary items.

There were no movements in the reserves of Associated Ltd during the year. If there had been, the information would have to be included in the reserves note of Parent Limited group accounts.

Under the new accounting standard a note to the accounts is required to explain the change in the value of the investment since last balance sheet date:

		$
	Purchase of shares in associated company	1 437 000
add:	35% share of profit of Associated Ltd	91 264
		1 528 264
less:	Dividend received from Associated Ltd	35 000
gives:	Equity accounted investments in associated company	1 493 264

The proportion of the associated company's operating profit and extraordinary items after income tax are added to the value of investments (which keeps in balance E + L = A). The dividend received from Associated Ltd is treated like a rebate on the amount paid for the investment. It is not recognised as income in the equity-accounted profit.

Parent Limited group's proportion of any increases or decreases in Associated Ltd's reserves would be added to or subtracted from the value of the investment too.

In this example there was no opening balance in the shares in associated company because they were purchased on 1 July 1996.

In chapter 5, Assets, you were advised that assets are stated at cost, directors' or independent valuation. Here is a fourth—cost plus. The equity accounted investment is first recognised at the cost value and then adjusted for profits and reserves attributable to the investor. This does not reflect market value which for a listed associated company is the quoted share price, and for an unlisted one would be determined by a valuation. The equity-accounted investment value is meaningless in terms of what the shares cost or are worth.

You will recall from chapter 5 that non-current assets are not allowed to be valued on the balance sheet above their recoverable amount. Under the existing and new accounting standard the investment in the associated company is valued at cost unless revalued to directors' or independent valuation. The recoverable amount test must be applied.

The new standard makes it clear that the asset cannot be revalued upwards in accordance with AASB 1010, *Accounting for the Revaluation of Non-Current Assets*. (See chapter 5 for discussion of AASB 1010.)

Other disclosures for associated companies

Besides the information regarding the accounting for associated companies which has to be reported, other useful pieces of information are required:

- the name and main activities of each associated company;
- the percentage owned in the associate company and the percentage of voting shares;
- any significant events occurring after the associate's balance date;

■ information on any difference from the accounting policies of the investor which could not be adjusted for in recognising the equity profit.

Ceasing to equity account

There are advantages in equity accounting while the associate is profitable, but it can be painful when it is not. This happens from time to time and equity-accounting quite often ceases soon after this occurs. How can the requirement to equity-account be removed? Simple—reduce ownership in the associated entity to remove the significant influence. Then the accounting reverts to merely recognising it as an investment with, if a company, dividend income.

The directors still must consider the value of the investments, which cannot be valued at more than their recoverable amount.

The minimum amount that the equity accounted for investment or ordinarily accounted for investment can be reduced to is nil. An exception occurs if the investor company has given some guarantee over the associated company which has become enforceable. In this unhappy circumstance the investment moves from being an asset to becoming a liability.

JOINT VENTURES

Accounting standard AASB 1006, *Accounting for Interests in Joint Ventures*, specifies what a joint venture is and how to account for it. A joint venture is limited to unincorporated business projects between two or more entities. Companies are excluded as they are incorporated, but the standard also excludes partnerships and trusts. The method of accounting is partial consolidation, which was discussed under 'consolidation' above.

The most common large joint ventures have been for the development and exploitation of natural resources. The Tomago aluminium smelter in the Hunter Valley of New South Wales is an example.

The entities in the joint venture are called 'joint venturers'. The joint venture is established under a legal document which specifies the proportional interest of each venturer. It prescribes when contributions are required and specifies the entity which will manage the joint venture. The management entity may be one of the venturers or an entity established for the purpose. Usually the main venturer or the venturer with the natural resource expertise is the manager or controls the management entity.

The output received by the joint venturers is not a dividend or proportion of profit, but is their proportion of the product produced. In the case of a coal mining project the product split between the venturers is the washed coal ready for sale. The agreement may specify that the manager is responsible for selling the output or that each joint venturer is responsible. Similarly, the collection of the debt can be the manager's responsibility or that of each venturer.

The revenue from the sale of each venturer's proportion of product is its income. The project manager will request funding for new equipment and for expenses of the project such as wages and its management fee.

The venture commences with each venturer making its contribution as specified in the joint venture agreement. This might be cash, equipment or certain expertise—there are many possible ways to contribute.

While investment in a company is generally limited to the extent of the unpaid issued shares, this is not the case with a joint venture. There is no protection through limited liability. A venturer is at least fully liable for its proportion of all liabilities and may even be liable for the other venturers' proportion of liabilities in the event that they default. These requirements will be specified in the agreement. There needs to be provision in the agreement about what should happen in the event of a venturer becoming insolvent. The agreement also needs to specify procedures in the event of one of the venturers wanting to sell—for example, the other venturers have first right to buy and can veto a proposed purchaser.

Accounting for the joint venture

The joint venture is partially or 'proportionately' consolidated. At the beginning of the venture the value of each contribution is determined. It may be cash. It may be equipment for which a value has to be determined. The cash or equipment contributed to the project remains the asset of the venturer. True, the asset may need to be depreciated, or the cash is spent and becomes an expense or is used to acquire another type of asset.

At each balance date the accounts of the parent entity venturer and its group accounts must include under assets and liabilities the venturer's proportional interest in the joint venture. The share of expenses of the project and sales of its share of product are included in the calculation of the venturer's profit.

Thus the group account assets could include, in the fixed assets, some of the venture's fixed assets, and the group's trade creditors could include some of the venture's creditors.

How do we know what the extent of the investment and commitment to a joint venture is? There must be a note in the parent entity or group accounts which shows for each material interest in a joint venture:

■ the name of the joint venture and its main activities;
■ the percentage interest in the output of the joint venture during the year.

And in total of all the joint ventures:

■ the amount classified under each class of asset and liability;
■ contingent liabilities and capital commitments—contingent liabilities can be to the extent of the other joint venturers' liabilities if the agreement provides for a joint venturer to meet any liabilities defaulted by another joint venturer.

CSR's 1996 annual report note 30 discloses joint ventures as shown in figure 12.6.

Figure 12.6
CSR's interests in joint ventures

Interests in joint ventures are included in the accounts in the following categories:

	Consolidated	
	1996	1995
Current assets	**$mil**	$mil
Cash	**0.4**	0.5
Receivables	**3.2**	3.2
Inventories	**41.4**	29.0
Other	**1.0**	0.9
	46.0	33.6
Non-current assets		
Receivables	**1.1**	1.2
Inventories	**3.6**	3.8
Property, plant and equipment	**431.3**	420.2
Other	**10.6**	10.5
	446.6	435.7
Total assets employed in joint ventures	**492.6**	469.3
Total liabilities	**36.6**	31.7
Net assets	**456.0**	437.6
Contracted capital expenditure	**0.8**	0.9

Details of interests in joint ventures

Joint venture	Principal activities	Share of production [A$ million] **1996**	1995	% Interest **1996**	1995	Consolidated **1996**	1995
Tomago	aluminium	**111.4**	99.4	**36.1**	35.0	**368.9**	364.9
Gove	bauxite, alumina	**86.5**	81.9	**30.0**	30.0	**87.1**	72.7
Total interests in joint ventures						**456.0**	437.6

Revised standard

A draft revision of the standard was issued in June 1997. The proposed revision extends the concept of 'joint venture' to be more compatible with the international accounting standard IAS 31, *Financial Reporting of Interests in Joint Ventures*. Reporting of unincorporated joint ventures remains the same. The term 'joint venture operation' is used to describe them.

The term 'joint venture' is extended to include all forms of joint arrangements including partnerships and incorporated entities. These other kinds of joint ventures are to be accounted for using equity accounting, which was discussed in the previous section.

Once a revised AASB 1006 is issued, it will take effect only when the new equity accounting standard AASB 1016 does. Accounting standard AASB 1016 will take effect only with a change in the Corporations Law (see previous section).

POINTS TO REMEMBER

✔ Consolidation is a method of showing a group of entities in one set of financial statements. The assets and liabilities, the revenue and expenses, and the cash flows of all entities are added together. The shareholders' equity consists of the issued shares of the parent entity, together with its interest in the profits and reserves retained in the group plus the interest of outside shareholders. All internal relationships within the group are eliminated so that the set of accounts represents the relationship of the equity with the outside world.

✔ Consolidated accounts look the same as for an individual entity except that they now represent a group of entities. Additional information is provided, such as information on subsidiaries, to enable a user to understand the group.

✔ All controlled entities are consolidated under the Australian accounting standard. Prior to this only companies were usually consolidated which is still the situation in most countries. The 'controlled entity' approach makes it more difficult not to consolidate a subsidiary. Non-consolidation can improve the look of the balance sheet.

✔ The standard does not allow partial consolidation. This means that entities which are not controlled but which are very significantly influenced can only be accounted for by using the equity accounting method. Partial consolidation would require the proportion of liabilities and assets of the entity to be included on the group balance sheet, whereas equity accounting does not.

✔ Equity accounting recognises that some investments fall between simple share investments and subsidiaries. Where an investor has significant influence over another company, equity accounting should be applied. Equity accounting recognises the ownership percentage of profits and changes in reserves in the investor's own accounts or group accounts.

✔ The risk of the equity accounting method of recognition is that the investor may never really have access to these profits but only the dividend. Where this is the case, equity accounting overstates the profit of the investor.

✔ Until introduction of a new accounting standard equity accounting information is supposed to be disclosed in the notes to the accounts or as supplementary accounts, and must not be shown as the main accounts.

In addition to recognising equity accounted profit and investment, information is provided about the ownership interest in and activities of the associated companies.

✔ Joint venture accounting is partial consolidation limited to the situation of unincorporated joint ventures. An unincorporated joint venture is not a company, partnership or trust. The amounts of joint venture assets and liabilities included in the group accounts are disclosed in a note, together with information on the joint venture activities and ownership percentage.

13 Disclosures and themes

The purposes of this chapter are to suggest additional or changed disclosures which would be beneficial for users of financial statements, and to review this book's main themes.

Accounting is an evolving professional field of study which has developed from the creation of bookkeeping by Pacioli in the late fifteenth century. The growth of the company legal form over the last few centuries has had a significant effect on the development of accounting. In the latter half of this century the demand for useful information has increased.

Accounting development owes more to the needs and perceptions of the preparers of financial information than it does to the users, who generally have not been very involved. Accounting tends to look backwards with concepts such as historical cost. The increased use of revaluation is one indication of the need to provide more current information.

My thoughts on what accounting should be have changed during my years of showing users how to read and interpret financial statements. I have always been persuaded that market value is more relevant than historical cost (which stems from studying accounting at Sydney University in the early 1970s during the professorship of Ray Chambers—a world renowned accountant and active proponent of the cause of market value accounting). Users tend to support this view.

My thinking has shifted to seeing accounting as pragmatic rather than a perfectly whole theory. Accounting does not represent any absolute—it is not a natural law of the universe. Accounting is a device to represent the events and transactions engaged in by a business, a government, a school or some other entity, using currency as the means of communication. Any measurement in money terms can only be a representation of the real thing. It is not the real thing. It should be a usable and practical view.

I suggest that financial statements should present realistic, pragmatic and relevant financial information. Realistic, by looking at the substance of what has occurred and what the situation is at the date of the financial statements. Pragmatic, by adopting the KISS principle, Keep It Simple Stupid—a close representation in an uncomplicated manner that is fairly cheap to do. Relevant, by measuring assets primarily at current market value. Unfortunately the current trend is to increase the complexity of preparation, measurement and disclosure.

I believe the key accounting principle is substance over form. Most creative accounting is forcing form to override substance.

WANTED—ADDITIONAL DISCLOSURES

My suggestions for additional or changed disclosures are:

1   All significant non-current assets to be revalued to market value at least every three years. With some assets, such as listed shares, this can be done annually through the share market price at the balance sheet date. Market value is based on a likely agreed value between a willing seller and a willing and informed buyer in the normal course of business. Thus assets should be valued at market values which reflect a risk factor when discounting future profit or cash flows into current dollars.

2   The name and qualifications of the valuer, the approach adopted to the valuation and the capitalisation rates or discount rates used to be shown.

3   Revalued assets which would be subject to capital gains tax should be shown net of the estimated tax, because this is what would be received for the benefit of the owners. The notes to the accounts would show the valuation amount and the capital gains tax applicable.

4   The address and nature of ownership of all land held freehold or on long term lease to be shown.

5   Liabilities should continue to be valued at the amount which is estimated to be payable if the liability were paid out at balance sheet date. For loans this is usually the principal outstanding. For provisions the estimate can be more fuzzy. The simple approach for annual leave is to determine the untaken leave at balance date and value it at the wage rates at year end. It is a mistake to have moved in the direction of predicted future payments discounted back to current day terms as has been done for non-current long service leave. This adds too many uncertainties and complicates calculation.

6   Creditors, borrowings, provisions, and deferred or unearned income should always be shown as separate classes of liabilities on the balance sheet.

7   Repayment schedules of non-current borrowings—the repayments should be allocated at least as they are for lease commitments, that is: due within one year (which is current); one to two years; two to five years; and five years and over. This last category could be divided: five to ten years and ten years and over. At present companies classed as

borrowing corporations must, and some other companies voluntarily, provide this.

8 Estimated schedules of payment of non-current provisions could also be provided on the same basis.

9 The profit and loss statement should at least include cost of goods sold, gross profit and other overhead expenses by categories such as selling and administration. Concerns about disclosing information advantageous to competitors will be a debating point. Accounting standard AASB 1034 allows these disclosures.

10 All revenues and expenses, gains and losses should be included in calculating profit, including revaluations upwards and exchange fluctuations from translating overseas financial statements into local currency for the purpose of consolidation. The profit or loss effect on prior year's profits on the introduction of a new accounting standard should still be treated as an adjustment of retained profits and clearly labelled.

11 On changing an accounting policy, the comparative profit and loss figures should be changed to reflect the new accounting policy. A note to the accounts should make it clear that the comparatives have been adjusted and state what the reported amounts were in the prior year.

12 All changes in accounting policy should continue to be clearly stated in the accounting policy note. If there have been no changes in accounting policies, a statement to that effect should be made at the beginning of the accounting policy note.

13 Income tax should be recognised on an 'income tax payable' basis instead of tax-effect accounting. This means the estimated tax payable for the year is shown as the income tax expense. Future income tax benefits and deferred tax liabilities are not created. Information about tax losses can continue to be disclosed in a note.

14 Partial consolidation should be used for significant investments where these entities are not controlled but are very significantly influenced. Indeed, perhaps equity accounting should be discontinued, with very significantly influenced associated entities accounted for using partial consolidation and the others treated as simple investments.

15 The creation of intangible assets should be discouraged. Limit the life of all intangible assets to a maximum of five years, except those such as patents which have a legally longer life. Readily allow the immediate expensing of goodwill. Intangible assets can be described and assigned a 'market' value in the notes to the accounts.

16 All financial information should be presented in tabular format.

Financial statements require time and effort to develop the skills to understand and interpret them meaningfully. Though desirable that they should be easily read by any user, this is unlikely to be really achievable. Financial statements should be capable of being read and understood by a literate person with reasonable numeracy skills, who is prepared to learn what they are and mean.

Let's keep the KISS principle as much as possible. Let's use plain English in all parts of the financial statements. There is too much use of expressions used in the Corporations Law or accounting standards.

REVIEW OF UNDERLYING THEMES

I have tried to cover all the significant aspects of financial statements. This has meant considering what is currently done, criticising some current approaches and introducing likely trends for the future. The important themes I have addressed are:

1   There is no short road to gaining the skill to be a competent user of financial statements. You need to apply yourself to develop these skills. This book required committed reading to maximise your gain.

2   Accounting is a way of preparing and presenting the story of an entity in dollar terms. Thus it is a language of communication used to represent reality.

3   Accounting is not a scientific study of natural phenomena, but is an art form to describe what has occurred. As an art form it should be realistic, pragmatic and relevant.

4   Preparers are motivated by self-interest and will present the best possible view of their organisation. Financial statements are a picture painted within the framework of the existing rules and regulations. Preparers choose (as far as the framework allows) accounting policies which help their cause.

5   Rules and regulations need to stress substance over form and encourage compliance with the spirit of painting the real picture. To do this there is a need to specify certain requirements. Much is specified or being specified in accounting concepts statements, accounting standards and the Corporations Law. I have suggested changed or additional items in the first section of this chapter. However, too much specification results in regulation overload and concentration on avoiding the rules.

6   The balance sheet is the financial statement which should record all assets primarily at market value and all liabilities at the estimated amount payable (to pay out the liabilities at balance sheet date). This approach means the equity shows the net worth of the owners' interest. Users can use this to make their own judgement of the added value due to matters such as profitability.

7   Care needs to be taken when considering intangible assets because of their lack of concreteness. The spectacular corporate collapses in Australia in the late 1980s and the early 1990s often reflected the overpayment for, and overvaluation of, these items. Overpayment for intangibles continues.

8   Profit comes from all revenues and expenses whether realised or unrealised. Naturally, disclosure of the amount of significant unrealised items is desirable. Abnormal items and the trend in abnormal items should be considered carefully.

9   Taxable income is related to but different from accounting profit because income tax is governed by a specific set of laws used to raise government revenue.

10   The cash flows statement shows where cash has come from and where it has been used. It is not the same as profit; for example, sales are recorded as revenue but the cash comes when the debtor pays. Further, cash is used for balance sheet items such as the purchase of plant and equipment by paying cash, obtaining finance or leasing. Over time an entity needs profit and positive cash flow to survive and grow.

11   Ratios are used to measure performance. Valid comparisons can only be obtained by applying ratios consistently over time and between entities, and by carefully reviewing the financial statements to decide what figures should be used in the ratio numerators and denominators. Ratios have limitations. For small (micro) businesses looking at how the owners get money out of the business is more helpful than ratios are.

I hope that this book has met many readers' needs in effectively understanding and interpreting financial statements. Those of you who would like to pursue this subject further are referred to the references at the end of the book. There are also several kinds of courses available from universities, TAFE, commercial providers and training consultants such as the author.

The final chapter, Warning signals, lists items to beware of. It is not exhaustive. You might find more.

May you have many years of enjoyable reading of financial statements!

14 Warning signals

Throughout the book many issues have been canvassed; warning signals have been mentioned. This short chapter provides a non-exhaustive list of what I consider to be warning signals. Any one of these signals could show problems with the financial situation of the entity. The more warning signals that exist, the likelier that there is a problem.

I first developed these warning signals during a project I undertook for the Australian Commonwealth Department of Finance in 1994. I acknowledge and appreciate the help received in refining them, in particular from Geoff McDonald.

Each warning signal is referred to the relevant part of this text.

Page
reference

1.00 Directors' report and statement, auditors' report

1.01 Is there anything in the statutory directors' report indicating serious financial or other difficulties? 47, 50, 51

1.02 Have the directors stated any part of the accounts are not true and fair or the entity cannot pay its debts as and when they fall due? 47, 53

1.03 Is the auditors' report qualified? What is the nature of the qualification(s)? Do any of the qualifications indicate serious financial or other difficulties? 47, 52

2.00 Balance sheet

2.01 Are other debtors large in comparison with trade debtors? (This is not necessarily relevant if trade debtors are nil or relatively small.) What are these other debtors? (We expect the main current receivable to be trade debtors.) 91

Page
reference

2.02   Is there evidence that a significant portion of inventory is   94, 95,
        valued at net realisable value? (This can be determined when   98
        inventory at cost and NRV are separately disclosed.) [This
        situation indicates problems with quality and/or saleability
        of inventory.]

2.03   Is there evidence of deferral of expenses (other than prepay-   115,
        ments)? Is the level of deferral increasing over time? [Can   116
        be a very strong indicator of accounting generated profit.]

2.04   Is there evidence of 'capitalisation' of expenses as part of   116
        other assets such as property, plant and equipment? (This is
        a kind of deferred expenses. An example is where interest
        on borrowings used to acquire major non-current assets is
        added to the cost of that asset. This is a legitimate account-
        ing approach, but the cost value of the asset could become
        excessive compared with its worth.)

2.05   Is the useful life of fixed assets being extended? [Extending   103,
        useful life reduces the depreciation expense and increases   105
        reported profit. This technique is often combined with
        deferring expenses to increase reported profit.]

2.06   Are there changes in the values of property which might   83
        indicate difficulty with the quality of the property portfolio?
        (For example, properties are being devalued against the asset
        revaluation reserve and/or through the profit and loss state-
        ment.)

2.07   Are there large future income tax benefits arising from tax   172,
        losses? Have these existed for two or more years with little   173
        or no reduction in the amount achieved? (Tax losses are only
        allowed to be included in the future income tax benefit asset
        if there is virtual certainty of recovery.) [Possible overstate-
        ment of assets and retained profits in equity.]

2.08   Are there large increases or decreases in provisions which   137
        are changing at a greater rate than sales, EBIT and/or profit
        or the particular item to which the provision relates? (For
        example, provision for doubtful debts relates to trade debt-
        ors.) [This may indicate deliberate manipulation of profit.]

2.09   Has profit been achieved largely due to the change in one 129–37
        provision? (Some industries have key provisions which
        greatly influence profit. For example, doubtful debts for the
        finance industry, claims for the general insurance industry.)

Page
reference

3.00 Profit and loss statement

3.01 Is operating profit, excluding abnormal items, low or a loss?

3.02 Is the pattern of operating profit volatile rather than steady?

3.03 Has a change in accounting policy been a significant reason for improving reported profit or minimising reported loss? [Considering if profit is generated by an accounting principle rather than revenue.]   41, 42

3.04 Do abnormal items tend to recur? Is there a pattern of abnormal items? [A recurring pattern probably indicates the abnormal items should be considered part of the regular profit performance.]   154, 155

3.05 Does profit exist in some years because of favourable abnormal items (i.e. there would be losses otherwise)?   154, 155

3.06 Are operating profits regularly reported while abnormal items are generally losses which result in low net profits or net losses?   154, 155

3.07 Are significant abnormal items reduced by one or more abnormal gains? [These gains might indicate that good assets are being sold to reduce the extent of the abnormal losses, perhaps weakening the long term viability of the organisation.]   154, 155

3.08 Are there adjustments to retained profits brought forward from the prior year? Do these adjustments reduce the retained profits? Do these loss adjustments enable significant losses never to be reported as part of the profit or loss of the entity? [New accounting standards often require retrospective adjustments. Voluntary changes in accounting policy which enable retrospective adjustments are more likely to be of concern.]   151, 152

4.00 Statement of cash flows

One or more of the first three warning signals occurring fairly regularly could indicate very serious problems.

4.01 Are the receipts from customers lower than the payments to suppliers and employees? Or is the excess of receipts from customers over these payments very small?   188

Page
reference

7.00   Ratios

7.01   Are the current and acid test ratios declining while the days   207
creditors ratio is increasing? [Could indicate real liquidity
difficulties.]

7.02   Are the current and acid test ratios low? Does the statement   187,
of cash flows show a lack of cash generation from operating   200
activities?

7.03   Are days debtors rising significantly? [Could indicate lack   201,
of control of credit and possible bad debts.]   202

7.04   Are days inventory ratios rising significantly especially when   203
profitability ratios are declining? [Might indicate overvalued,
obsolete or unsaleable inventory.]

7.05   Do one or more of the financing ratios show a strain from 208–15
the reliance on debt funding?

7.06   Is debt funding not linked to the assets being financed?   224
(Watch especially for current borrowings used to finance
non-current assets.)

7.07   Is more than one of the profitability ratios declining? Is the 215–20
decline over a number of years? [Might indicate seriously
and permanently declining profitability requiring remedial
action.]

7.08   Are the cash flows profitability ratios declining? Is the 221–4
decline over a number of years? [Might indicate seriously
and permanently declining profitability requiring remedial
action.]

7.09   Do the profitability ratios appear satisfactory but the cash
flows profitability ratios don't? (Cash flows profitability
ratios are generally higher than profit because of non-cash
expenses such as depreciation. For entities with inventory
the cash flows ratios often show a downturn the year before
the profitability ratios do. This is due to cash spent on
increasing inventory while the higher inventory results in
reported higher profits.)

▮ Appendix

ACCOUNTING STANDARDS

This is a listing of Australian accounting concepts statements, approved accounting standards and international accounting standards in existence at 30 June 1997.

Accounting concepts

These are introduced in chapter 3 and SAC4 is considered in chapters 5 to 8. They provide guidance on accounting principles and treatments and are non-mandatory.

SAC Statement of Accounting Concepts
1   Definition of a Reporting Entity
2   Objective of General Purpose Financial Reporting
3   Qualitative Characteristics of Financial Information
4   Definition and Recognition of the Elements of Financial Statements

AASB ACCOUNTING STANDARDS

These standards have the force of law for companies. If a company is a reporting entity in terms of AASB 1025, all relevant standards must be applied. See chapter 3.

AAS ACCOUNTING STANDARDS

This is a list of accounting standards adopted by the professional accounting bodies which have not been approved by the Australian Accounting Standards Board. Other AAS standards are noted against AASB standards above.

Members of these bodies are required to encourage compliance. This covers all kinds of entities.

INTERNATIONAL ACCOUNTING STANDARDS

IAS	Accounting Standard	AASB Ref.
1	Disclosure of Accounting Policies	1001
2	Inventories	1019
4	Depreciation Accounting	1021
5	Information to be Disclosed in Financial Statements	1034
7	Cash Flows Statements	1007
8	Net Profit or Loss for the Period, Fundamental Errors	1018
	and Changes in Accounting Policies	1001
9	Research and Development Costs	1011
10	Contingencies and Events Occurring After the Balance Sheet Date	1002
		1034
11	Construction Contracts	1009
12	Accounting for Taxes on Income	1020
13	Presentation of Current Assets and Liabilities	1034
14	Reporting Financial Information by Segment	1005
15	Information Reflecting the Effects of Changing Prices	—
16	Property, Plant and Equipment	1010
17	Accounting for Leases	1008
18	Revenue	1004
19	Retirement Benefit Costs	1028
20	Accounting for Government Grants and Disclosure of Government	
	Assistance	—
21	The Effects of Changes in Foreign Exchange Rates	1012
22	Business Combinations	1015
23	Borrowing Costs	—
24	Related Party Transactions	1017
25	Accounting for Investments	1010
26	Accounting and Reporting by Retirement Benefits Funds	AAS 25
27	Consolidated Financial Statements and Accounting for Investments in	
	Subsidiaries	1024
28	Accounting for Investments in Associates	1016
29	Financial Reporting in Hyperinflationary Economies	—
30	Disclosures in the Financial Statements of Banks and Similar Financial	
	Institutions	1032
31	Financial Reporting of Interests in Joint Ventures	1006
32	Financial Instruments: Disclosure and Presentation	1033
33	Earnings Per Share	1027

■ References and suggested reading

CCH Tax Editors 1997, *1997 Australian Master Tax Guide*, CCH Australia Limited, Sydney

Curtis, Donald A. 1990, *Management Rediscovered—How Companies Can Escape the Numbers Trap*, Dow Jones Irwin, Homewood, Illinois

Flavel, Ron 1991, *How to Value a Small Business*, Small Business Corporation of South Australia, Adelaide

Fridson, Martin S. 1991, *Financial Statement Analysis—A Practitioner's Guide*, John Wiley & Sons, New York

Hey-Cunningham, David 1997, *Understanding Company Reports*, The Securities Institute of Australia, Sydney (Subject 24C of the Certificate in Financial Markets course)

Kenley, W. John 1989, *Using Financial Statements*, CCH Australia Limited, Sydney

Popoff, B. and Cowan, T. K. 1989, *Analysis of Financial Statements*, 3rd edn, Butterworths Pty Limited, Sydney

Reynolds, Wal, Savage, Warwick and Williams, Alan 1994, *Your Own Business—a practical guide to success,* Thomas Nelson Australia, Melbourne

Roth, Martin 1995, *Analysing Company Accounts*, Wrightbooks Pty Ltd, North Brighton, Victoria

Shaw, J. C., Arnold, J. A., Cooper, M., (eds) 1990, *Financial Reporting—the Way Forward*, The Institute of Chartered Accountants in England and Wales, London and The Institute of Chartered Accountants of Scotland, Edinburgh

Simini, Joseph Peter 1990, *Balance Sheet Basics for Non Financial Managers*, John Wiley & Sons, New York

Smith, Malcolm 1994, *New Tools for Management Accountants*, Longman Professional, Melbourne

Smith, Terry 1996, *Accounting for Growth—Stripping the Camouflage from Company Accounts*, 2nd edn, Century Press, London

Stanley, Philip 1985, *How to Understand and Use a Balance Sheet*, Rydge Publications (Aust.) Pty Ltd, Sydney

Tracey, John A. 1989, *How to Read a Financial Report*, 3rd edn, John Wiley & Sons, New York

Warren, Roy 1988, *How to Understand and Use Company Accounts*, 2nd edn, Hutchinson Business, London

Index

AUSTRALIAN STOCKMARKET INVESTOR

John English

Do you want to begin investing in the stockmarket but you're not sure where to start? Do you want to know more about your current investments? From speculative shares to blue chips, futures to options, private portfolios to unit trusts, *Australian Stockmarket Investor* is packed with all the practical information you need to manage your own investment program.

This accessible guide takes the mystery out of investing by offering clear and accurate information for a range of investors. *Australian Stockmarket Investor* is the first book to provide both clear guidance for the new investor and sophisticated advice for the seasoned investor.

1 86448 614 7

HOW TO ORGANISE AND OPERATE A SMALL BUSINESS IN AUSTRALIA

Sixth edition

JOHN ENGLISH

This is the most comprehensive small business handbook in Australia. For over a decade, it has been used by tens of thousands of Australians to become self-employed. *How to Organise and Operate a Small Business in Australia* is designed for the individual who wants a practical commonsense explanation about how to organise a small business and operate it successfully. It describes information, skills and techniques which are easy to understand and simple to operate.

In the sixth edition, John English focuses on the modern changes in small business management that are vital for survival and prosperity during the 1990s and into the 21st century.

1 86373 820 7

MONEY AND CAPITAL MARKETS

Second edition

MICHAEL SHERRIS

Money and Capital Markets provides up-to-date, practical coverage of the pricing and analysis of financial instruments and transactions available for Australian and international capital markets.

It covers the underlying tools and techniques for the valuation and risk management of short-term money market and capital market securities and their derivatives. In a clear and direct way, Michael Sherris outlines fixed interest securities, forwards, futures, swaps, options and interest rate derivatives (new in the second edition). Everything—from yield calculations to tax and horizon effects to interest rate risk measures—is lucidly explained and extensively illustrated with examples.

An invaluable reference for money market professionals, *Money and Capital Markets* is essential reading for tertiary students of finance, accounting and actuarial studies.

1 86448 159 5